Teach Me to Be Generous

Teach Me to Be Generous

The First Century of Regis High School in New York City

Anthony D. Andreassi, C.O.

Empire State Editions
An imprint of Fordham University Press
New York 2014

Fordham University Press also publishes its books in a variety of electronic formats. Some content that appears in print may not be available in electronic books.

Library of Congress Cataloging-in-Publication Data is available from the publisher.

Printed in the United States of America
16 15 14 5 4 3 2 1
First edition

To my parents,
from whom I first learned what it means to be generous

Contents

Foreword

When St. Ignatius Loyola founded the Jesuits, the purpose of the order was to "strive especially for the progress of souls in Christian life and doctrine and for the propagation of the faith by ministry of the word, by spiritual exercises and works of charity, and specifically by the education of children and unlettered persons in Christianity" (*Regimini militantis Ecclesiae*, Pope Paul III, 1540). No one could have foreseen the vast network of schools that grew rapidly in Europe and throughout the world over the next almost five centuries. Where the Church carried out missionary work, there the Jesuits were, and their schools soon followed. Their high schools and colleges have contributed mightily to the growth of the Church in the United States, many on the East Coast, from the early days of the Republic. The dream of this network was that education could be provided for all who wished, without cost. Economic reality almost equally quickly made that a distant reality.

What a surprise it was when the *Catholic News* in New York, in June 1913, announced the imminent opening of a free Jesuit high school for boys in Manhattan, dedicated to the Jesuit saint John Francis Regis. Established as the first freestanding Jesuit high school in the country (earlier schools were the lower divisions of colleges), Regis High School was built by an extraordinary history of anonymous generosity that kept it operating for a century without charge to its students and their families. In the story of Regis High School lies a singular history of Catholic philanthropy to rise out of the Gilded Age. That story deserves to be told. And now, at the school's centennial anniversary and after its founding family has passed away, Father Anthony Andreassi, C.O., weaves the tale of how extraordinary charity built a landmark edifice where the brightest and most talented young men have been awarded scholarships for a century now. Their success has been a vanguard of immigrant Catholics coming of age in the United States—building society, strengthening the Church, and serving as leaders in every imaginable field.

The history of Regis High School also coincides with the rise of New York as the world capital, as well as with the development of independent secondary education. The metropolitan area has provided no lack of talented young men, many of whom would never have been able to afford a private education, let alone one for gifted students. The legacy of generosity that built and funded the school for the first half of its history continued, after the founding family passed from the scene, in the ranks of alumni and friends who continue to ensure that deserving young men have the opportunity for a free Catholic education in the Jesuit tradition. The Church in New York is richer because of the opportunities Regis High School provides.

A historic institution deserves a first-rate history. As a historian of the Church in America myself, I can attest that Regis High School now has one! Father Andreassi is a good storyteller! Watch how the spark of an idea for something great grew in one pious woman aided by an imaginative Jesuit. One hundred years later, the results speak for themselves. Now we hope for a second century of greatness and generosity in providing the only all-scholarship Catholic education in the United States.

TIMOTHY MICHAEL CARDINAL DOLAN
Archbishop of New York
July 2013

Illustrations

Acknowledgments

When Father Philip G. Judge, S.J., '80, became president of Regis High School in the fall of 2005, he very quickly began thinking ahead to the school's upcoming centennial in 2014. In consideration of this, Father Judge began work toward the establishment and cataloging of the school's archives (much of which he did himself) as well as explorations toward the commissioning of a scholarly history of the school. After reaching out to some graduate programs in history in the hopes of finding an interested master's or doctoral student did not yield any results, Father Judge asked me if I would like to take up the task. I accepted his gracious invitation almost immediately. With graduate training in U.S. history and a long interest in the story of American Catholicism as well as experience in teaching in three different Jesuit high schools, including Regis, once I began the project my efforts quickly became a labor of love. Throughout all my research and writing, Phil has been both encouraging and helpful, offering me complete editorial freedom. From the outset he wanted a serious and intellectually honest history of the school and not just a coffee table book with pretty pictures. For this, he should be commended; I hope this final product lives up to his expectations.

As I began work in the archives, I soon realized that some Regis students might find it interesting to help with this research and possibly even do a little writing of their own using these sources. As it turns out, I was ably assisted by several seniors who elected to take a tutorial using the Regis archives. Although still high school students, these young men did outstanding historical research, and I was able to use a good bit of what they uncovered. These young men to whom I owe a great deal of thanks include Shane Ulbrich, '07, Brian Varian, '07, Nick Domino, '08, Kevin Neylan, '08, Louis Masi, '09, James R. Simmons, '09, Thomas White, '10, James Elliott, '12, Travis Guzzardo, '12, Ryan Phillips, '12, Chris Siemer, '12, and Leland Chan, '13. Some others who volunteered their time to do some research include James Elustondo, '12, and Joe Pollicino, '12. Finally, concerning my debt of thanks to Regians, I would be remiss if I did not acknowledge the several who were assigned to me as "jug" workers. These indentured servants performed some of the thankless grunt work involved in historical research. Since their names are lost to mists of time (and to my memory), their labors will be remembered by God alone.

One of the particular strengths of Regis is its fine and dedicated faculty, and over the past decade I have had the blessing to call many of them not only colleagues but friends, too. Several of them have helped me in the preparation of this book in ways ranging from fact-checking and Latin translations to reviewing whole chapters. For all this, I am very much indebted to Father Arthur Bender, S.J., '67, Mr. Brian B. Pinter, Mr. Brian FitzGerald, '94, Mrs. Mary Henninger, Mr. James Phillips, Dr. Ralph Nofi, Mr. Christian Talbot, Ms. Kristin Ross, and Dr. Gary Tocchet. I am grateful to Mrs. Pat Peelen of the principal's office, who never tired of lending me keys to the file cabinets containing student records. I am especially indebted to Mr. John Connelly, '56, Dr. John Tricamo, and Mr. Frank Walsh. Since among them their time at Regis adds up to more than a century, they represent a living memory of the life of the school going back to 1952 when John Connelly arrived as a freshman. They were always most gracious in answering my countless questions. I would also like to thank John Balletta, 2010, and my good friend Kevin Rooney for helping me with the proofreading.

I also owe a large debt of gratitude to persons outside of Regis. These include Father Joseph T. Lienhard, S.J., '58, who reviewed several chapters with an eagle eye only editors have; Father John W. O'Malley, S.J., who was very gracious to meet with me at his office at Georgetown and answer my questions regarding the first Jesuit schools; Father Peter Schineller, S.J., '57, archivist of the New York Province of the Society of Jesus, who was always most generous and helpful; Mr. Ken Bailie, '60, who volunteered to serve as a research assistant as well as reviewing several chapters; Ms. Ellen S. Palmer of the Jesuit Secondary Education Association for her help in obtaining decades-old tuitions at other Jesuit high schools; Professor Robert Emmett Curran, my thesis mentor at Georgetown, who continued to advise me on this work, which was most helpful given his almost encyclopedic knowledge of American Jesuit history; and Mrs. Anita P. Golinski, Mr. Brendan Kolbay, and Father Joseph McLafferty, whose longtime and strong friendship helped me many a time when my spirits were flagging and needed some boosting. I am also greatly indebted to the fine people at Fordham University Press, most especially Fred Nachbaur, Eric Newman, and Nicholas Taylor, who never lacked patience and generosity in guiding me through the publication process. An important note of thanks is owed to Msgr. Thomas J. Shelley. Tom is responsible for getting me started on the study of church history and has never waned in his encouragement of my scholarly writing. His mentorship and friendship has shaped so much of who I am both as a priest and as a teacher, and I have relied on him again for this book.

Finally, I would be remiss if I did not offer my sincere appreciation to my Oratorian brothers in Brooklyn. Welcoming me into your "nido" almost a decade ago has brought me countless blessings, including the support and the confidence needed to bring this work to birth. I hope this study of a Jesuit high school brings honor to both St. Philip Neri and St. Ignatius Loyola, under whose patronage I have tried to work each day.

Lord, teach me to be generous.
to serve you as you deserve,
to give and not to count the cost,
to fight and not to heed the wounds,
to toil and not to seek for rest,
to labor and not to ask for reward,
save that of knowing that I do your will.

ST. IGNATIUS LOYOLA

Introduction

When Frank Miller arrived for the first day of classes on September 14, 1914, he was still a few weeks shy of his twelfth birthday. At the time of his registration earlier that summer, Frank had been assigned to the "F" section of the first class of the newly established Regis High School. The Jesuit administrators had decided to separate the first students of the new high school by height, which was an old Jesuit tradition. Since Frank was so young, it is not surprising that he was placed in the last section with all the other smaller ones. Almost 250 boys had registered for Regis's first class, but since a few had gotten jobs over the summer, not all of them showed up. On this first day, the new students gathered for an assembly on the second floor in the area that would eventually become the library. A graduate of the St. John the Evangelist parochial school on East 55th Street, Frank was soon separated from his classmates, and each section met with its assigned instructor. Four of the school's first teachers were Jesuit scholastics (seminarians) and the other two were laymen. At their first meeting with their teacher, the students received a list of books they would need to purchase, which cost a little less than five dollars. A few students were unable to afford this, so the school absorbed the cost. After these practical details were attended to, *schola brevis* was declared and the students were dismissed at ten thirty.[1]

When the brand-new Regis High School opened its doors that September, it was widely admired for its state of the art facilities, including what one account in the press described as the "uncommon dignity" of the 84th Street facade in the style of Italian Renaissance. In addition to the noteworthiness of its architecture, the school represented a new and unique chapter in the history of Jesuit education in the United States. An important step forward in the Americanization of Jesuit schools, Regis was designed to be a freestanding, four-year high school with no connection to any of the Society of Jesus's colleges or universities. In addition, thanks to the incredible generosity of the Grant family, who not only founded the school but also remained its most important single benefactor for almost a century, Regis became the only successful attempt by the Jesuits in the United States at operating a tuition-free school. Almost a century later, the school continues to hold to this remarkable distinction. (The Cristo Rey Network of schools, some of which are sponsored by the Jesuits, approximates this in some ways, though a relatively small tuition is charged to most students.) Regis's founding as tuition-free actually connected the new school strongly with the first schools the Society of Jesus had opened in the sixteenth century, which also did not require students to pay to attend.[2]

While it is doubtful that Frank Miller or any of his classmates knew the significance of Regis in the history of Jesuit education in America, it would be safe to assume that most of these boys came to their new school that day filled with awe and apprehension, as do most freshmen on their first day of high school. Surely some of them had older brothers who had gone to one of the other four Jesuit high schools in New York City, so perhaps they had some idea of what to expect in an institution run by the Society of Jesus.[3] However, it is unclear if any of these first Regians had any appreciation of the venerable tradition of education the Jesuits had started three and a half centuries earlier. Like the schools that were founded before it, at its birth Regis became part of an educational tradition that stretched back centuries to the opening of the first Jesuit school in Messina, Sicily, in 1548. In addition, Regis was also heir to a local tradition of Jesuit schools in New York City that could trace its roots to the 1680s.

As early as February 1683, John Warner, the provincial superior for all Jesuits in England, predicted that a Jesuit school would thrive in New York. In a letter to Charles de Noyelle, the superior general in Rome, Warner wrote, "In that colony [New York] is a respectable city fit for the foundation of a college, if faculties are given, to which college those who are now scattered throughout Maryland may betake themselves."[4] Of all the possible apostolic or charitable works the Jesuits could have started in New York, it is not at all surprising that the English provincial set his sights on a school. Not long after the Society's foundation, the education and spiritual formation of youth became a primary focus of this new religious order, and Jesuits would carry out this formation primarily in secondary schools known as "colleges," which educated students ranging in age from about twelve to nineteen.

Jesuits and Education

In the very early years after the founding of the Society of Jesus in 1540, St. Ignatius Loyola and the other first Jesuits saw themselves primarily as "pilgrims" or itinerant preachers as they moved about to "help souls." And given the nature of this ministry on the move, schools were not considered a possible future work because of their need for stability. However, less than a decade after the order's official foundation, this emphasis on a peripatetic ministry was amended. Once these early Jesuits recognized the particular advantages that schools offered to their overall goal of the salvation of souls, they no longer hesitated to establish and maintain permanent institutions such as these. Soon the Society considered the education of youth to be not simply one ministry among many but in a category by itself.[5] This recognition of the privileged place education would take among all the works of the Society led to the point that by the suppression of the Jesuit order in 1773, it was conducting more than eight hundred educational institutions around the world, most of which were institutions of secondary education (though this number also included universities and seminaries).[6]

This Jesuit emphasis on education had consequences far beyond the spiritual impact their schools made on their students. Their network of colleges actually changed the way Europeans viewed education as a whole. According to Professor Olwen Hufton, the Jesuits represented "the first systematized and urgent protagonists of the principle that an entire civil society is the product of its educational system."[7] In view of this background, it is not surprising that the English provincial started hatching plans to open a school in New York.

The Jesuits got their first real chance for this venture during the governorship of Thomas Dongan, a member of the Irish Catholic gentry from Country Kildare. Dongan was appointed governor of the colony of New York in 1682 by the Duke of York (later King James II), who was also a Roman Catholic. Arriving the next year, Dongan brought with him the Jesuit priest Thomas Harvey, who offered the first Mass ever celebrated in New York on November 30, 1683. Two other Jesuits made the voyage from England not long after. The evidence suggests that by 1685 these three Jesuits had opened a school at the corner of Broadway and Wall Street on King's Farm, roughly where Trinity Episcopal Church is now located. Having good relations with their Protestant neighbors, the Jesuits used the bell of the Dutch Reformed Church in the nearby fort to call the students to class each day. During its brief existence, the small Jesuit school earned a reputation for academic excellence with a fair number of sons of the leading Protestant families in attendance.[8]

However, this first attempt at a Jesuit school in Manhattan proved to be short-lived. The Glorious Revolution in 1688 in England toppled James II from his throne, and with this came an end to this brief period of toleration of Catholics in the colony. After learning of the king's overthrow, revolutionaries led by Jacob Leisler seized control of the city. The school was closed, the chapel (which the Jesuits also administered) was shuttered, and the priests fled. Riding a wave of anti-Catholic fury, in 1700 colonial officials passed the "Act Against Jesuits and Popish Priests," which threatened any priest entering the colony of New York with life imprisonment. The law further stipulated that if a priest imprisoned for this were to escape and then return to the colony, he would then be executed.[9] With such a law in place, Catholics had to wait until the American Revolution, almost a century later, for another chance to open a school.

In 1785, New York Catholics established their first parish in New York with the opening of St. Peter's on Barclay Street, and in 1800, the parish established the first Catholic school, which was staffed not by nuns but instead entirely by laypeople. The Jesuits returned to the scene in 1808 with the arrival of Father Anthony Kohlmann, a native of Alsace, who was appointed the vicar general of the newly established diocese in the absence of the first bishop, Richard Luke Concanen, O.P. Kohlmann not only served as vicar general of the diocese from 1808 to 1814, but he also set about planning to open a new Jesuit school.

Industrious and multilingual, the Alsatian-born Jesuit began the new school in a rented building on Mulberry Street, in close proximity to the first cathedral, which was then still under construction. Named the "New York Literary Institution," the college was given over to the daily administration of Father Benedict Fenwick, but with scholastics and later two other priests doing the bulk of the instruction. Since the school soon began to take in boarders, larger quarters were quickly needed, so Kohlmann bought property in much more bucolic surroundings a few miles north of the city limits. It was here on what is now the site of the present-day St. Patrick's Cathedral at Fifth Avenue and East 51st Street that the second Jesuit school in New York made its eventual home. By 1813, the school boasted almost forty boarding students, including the sons of several prominent Protestant families. The curriculum heavily stressed instruction in languages including Latin, Greek, and French, as well as offering courses in English literature and, of course, catechism.[10]

Despite the school's fairly sustained growth, this next attempt by the Jesuits to establish a school in New York, like the first, proved to be short-lived. However, this time the school's demise would come not from the hands of a Protestant mob but from the Jesuit superiors themselves. In August 1813, Father John Grassi, the superior of the Jesuits in the United

States, ordered the New York Literary Institution be closed. Citing the fact that the Society's manpower was too thinly spread, he instructed the Jesuit instructors at the Literary Institution to relocate to Georgetown College. In making this decision, Grassi disagreed with Kohlmann's assertion that New York would be a better place to conduct a school since the region in which the nation's capital was located would "always be a poor, beggarly place." The Jesuit superior also had other realities to keep in mind when considering which college to close. Since Georgetown had been founded by John Carroll, a former Jesuit and now the archbishop of Baltimore (who was also the first American bishop), the new school in New York did not have a prayer. Despite Kohlmann's continued attempt to persuade Grassi to change his mind, the school was closed for good in April 1814. Thus, the next chapter in the history of Jesuit schools in New York came to an inglorious end with this second attempt at a school having a life only briefly longer than the first.[11]

The first successful attempt at starting and keeping alive a Jesuit college in New York City came when Father John Larkin, S.J., opened the College of St. Francis Xavier in 1847. Originally founded as the "College of the Holy Name of Jesus," in 1850 it moved to West 16th Street, where it has remained ever since. Xavier College's founding was closely related to the arrival of the Jesuits at St. John's College in the Fordham area of southern Westchester County. In 1846, the Society agreed to staff the college, which had been founded five years earlier by Bishop John Hughes. As part of this agreement, Hughes allowed the Jesuits to open a school and a parish in New York City.[12] While these two institutions provided similar courses of studies, in other ways they were quite different. While St. John's was founded principally for boarding students and charged a hefty $200 per year for tuition and fees, Xavier charged only $60 per annum and took in no boarders. Due to its far lower cost and thus its accessibility to the sons of the Catholic lower middle class, by the end of the nineteenth century the Jesuits' school in the city had become the premier Jesuit college in the United States, counting among its alumni some of the city's leading Catholic businessmen, lawyers, and politicians as well as a large number of diocesan priests.[13] And by the end of the century it had become the largest Jesuit college in the United States.[14]

An Old-Fashioned Jesuit College

At the time of the opening of Xavier and St. John's, Jesuit colleges in the United States were radically different from what most institutions of higher learning would come to look like by the early twentieth century.

With a curriculum based on the Jesuit *Ratio Studiorum* (plan of studies) of 1599, these institutions offered a combination of secondary education and some college-level academic training.[15] Rooted in the experience of education Ignatius had at the University of Paris in the 1530s, the *Ratio* consisted of a strictly sequential order of studies: Faculty of Letters, Faculty of Arts, and Faculty of Theology.[16] The Faculty of Letters included the study of the humanities and rhetoric. The Faculty of Arts offered courses in philosophy and mathematics. And finally, the Faculty of Theology focused only on theology and represented the highpoint of the course of studies. Theology faculties were only to be found in universities, which were still few and far between in Europe even as late as the early nineteenth century. Jesuit colleges founded in the sixteenth century onward typically only offered courses in the faculty of letters and possibly a part of the faculty of arts. While few students would make it all the way to a university to study theology, a larger number would move on to study law or medicine to enter one of the professions.[17]

While the actual number of years a boy spent in a Jesuit college varied over place and time, by the middle of the nineteenth century the program of study typically lasted about seven years. These schools took in boys as young as the age of twelve, and if the young man completed the entire course he probably graduated between the ages of seventeen and nineteen. Since some of the upper-level courses were taken by older boys and were part of the faculty of arts, Jesuit educators considered this latter work to be university-level.[18] This fluid relationship between what is now called high school and the first years of college was also to be found not just at Jesuit colleges but also at most Catholic colleges in the United States, including places such as the Christian Brother–run Manhattan College in New York (founded in 1853) or the Benedictine-run St. Vincent's College in Pennsylvania (1846).

By the time of the American Civil War, the Jesuits had founded more than a dozen of these colleges around the country, ranging from College of the Holy Cross in Massachusetts (1843) to Santa Clara College in California (1851). Many of these schools eventually earned state charters as well as respect from even non-Catholics because of their strong academic reputation. For example, Gonzaga College in Washington, D.C., which offered a course of study similar to the ones in place at the Jesuit schools in New York, had the honor of President Zachary Taylor presiding at its commencement in 1849. And in 1858 the school won a charter from the U.S. Congress signed by President James Buchanan. After the school amended the course of study and dropped the college division, the name was eventually changed to Gonzaga College High School.[19]

Challenges to the Jesuit Educational Model

By the late nineteenth century more and more non-Catholic institutions of higher learning had come to demand a strict separation of secondary-level academic work from a university education. For various reasons, private (non-Catholic) and state institutions had moved firmly to the "four-four" model of four years of secondary school followed by four years of undergraduate training. However, most Catholic institutions, including those operated by the Jesuits, came to adapt themselves to this changed landscape only slowly and begrudgingly. For example, beginning in 1889 the New York State Department of Education began to demand that private schools adhere to the same curriculum and standards that it had demanded of public schools since the late 1860s. After 1873, state monies were no longer given to church-sponsored schools, so the Jesuit administrators felt a great deal of independence on academic matters. Since these purse strings had been cut, administrators initially resisted any attempt by state authorities to dictate their curriculum. However, other pressures began to bear down on Jesuit schools, forcing them to change their model of education.[20]

In the 1890s, a Georgetown College student who had completed his fourth year of studies (out of seven) was denied admission to Columbia Medical School. When he contested this, he was told that he had not covered enough of the material that students in public high schools normally do.[21] Since graduates of Jesuit colleges might not be able to gain admission to nonsectarian professional schools, the Jesuit administrators reluctantly accepted the fact that their course of studies would have to be conformed to the prevailing secular model. Criticism of the Jesuit model of education was even coming from the highest levels in secular institutions. In 1899, Charles Eliot, president of Harvard, lambasted Jesuit schools in the influential *Atlantic Monthly,* calling their system of education "impossible and absurd" because of their refusal to adapt the course of studies to the prevailing American model.[22] And eventually the American Association of Universities refused to admit into its ranks any college or university that had a high school department.[23] If Jesuit administrators wanted to continue to attract students to their schools, they would have to adapt their curriculums.[24]

As a result of this outside pressure, by the early twentieth century many of these Jesuit colleges (which by 1900 numbered over two dozen) began to Americanize themselves and separate the high school from the college divisions or eliminate one part from the other. However, not all did it in the same way. Some remained as one institution but with strictly separate divisions, each granting its own degree. For example, in 1927 the high school (preparatory) division of Georgetown University legally separated itself from the college of which at that point it was still a subdivision. This break was preceded in 1919 by the removal of the prep from the main campus of the university to its current location in Garrett Park near Rockville, Maryland. Because of other constraints, some Jesuit colleges were more radical in their response to the changed educational landscape. Rather than separating the two sections (college and preparatory), both of which had existed since its foundation in 1843, the College of the Holy Cross in Worcester simply closed its high school department in 1914. In contrast, in 1912 Xavier College in Manhattan closed its college division and renamed itself "Xavier High School."[25]

Despite this general trend of separating high schools and colleges, the movement was not universal. As late as 1908 the Jesuits established Brooklyn College in the Crown Heights section of the borough with both high school and college departments, though with strictly separate courses of studies.[26] Xavier originally purchased the property in Brooklyn with the expectation that its college division could be relocated there. It was hoped that with more physical space, the college could expand and remain competitive against Fordham and other area Catholic colleges. However, this attempt lasted barely five years. By 1913 the school was renamed the Brooklyn Academy (though most often called Brooklyn Prep) and remained as a four-year high school until its closing in 1972.[27] Even in 1900, when the Loyola School was opened on Park Avenue in Manhattan, it was not founded as a strictly freestanding, four-year high school. In addition to its planned high school division, the new school was also to admit students in their last three years of grammar school. As it turned out, because initial enrollment was low, the school was opened with students only in the upper grades of grammar school, and high school grades were added only over time.[28] Thus, with its opening in 1914, Regis holds the distinction of being the first freestanding Jesuit high school founded in the United States.

Despite all these changes to Jesuit schools, one thing remained the same for all of them, and that was their heavy reliance on tuition to make ends meet. However, the charging of tuition by Jesuits to support their schools was not originally part of the first schools back in the sixteenth century. Only the exigencies of the times forced this.

"Per tutti quanti, poveri et ricchi": Tuition and Jesuit Schools

At the time of the founding of the first Jesuit school in Messina, Sicily in the 1540s, the officials of the city promised that they would pay for everything so that the Jesuits could run the school without charging tuition. Not long after, the city fathers in Palermo petitioned Ignatius for a school for their city, and to seal the deal, the wife of the viceroy pledged to endow the school so that finances would not be a concern. The Jesuit constitutions prescribed that all Jesuit ministries be done gratis, so a way had to be devised to fund their schools since education then, as now, can be quite expensive. Soon this practice of offering a free education became standard practice as Jesuit colleges spread throughout Europe. For example, in 1551, the sign announcing the opening of the Roman College (now the Gregorian University) clearly stated, "Classes in Grammar, the Humanities, and Christian Doctrine. No Tuition." And the next year Ignatius reminded his men in Perugia that their school here must be "per tutti quanti, poveri et ricchi" (for everybody, rich and poor). By the time of the promulgation of the *Ratio* in 1599, no tuition would become a hallmark of a Jesuit education.[29] This practice continued as long as the nobility and the rich were willing and able to endow Jesuit colleges around Europe, though even then it was still a struggle.[30]

The suppression of the Society of Jesus in 1773 and the coming of the French Revolution not long after changed all of this. Since most of its schools were now gone or confiscated, after the Society was restored in 1814 it found it next to impossible to reestablish and then support its schools at no charge. If the Jesuits were going to run schools, they were going to have to find new sources of support rather than relying on the generosity of Catholic nobles. A similar situation was true across the Atlantic in the United States, where there had never been the tradition of Catholic gentry underwriting Catholic schools. However, despite this new financial landscape, the Jesuit rules and customs concerning charging tuition had not changed. Conflict was inevitable.

In 1827, Jesuits at the Washington Seminary, which admitted some lay students in addition to the Jesuit scholastics studying theology, ran afoul of their superiors in Rome by charging tuition. Because of the violation of this ancient custom of the Society, the Jesuit authorities in Rome demanded that the school be closed. A similar situation also occurred in the Midwest. In 1827, the Jesuits took over administration of St. Louis College in St. Louis, which had previously been founded by the diocese in 1818. In order to meet expenses, the Jesuits charged students a tuition of five dollars per year. When the Roman authorities challenged this, the Jesuit rector, Father Peter Verhaegen, argued that the funds were needed to provide for basic support of the Jesuits teaching there. In addition, he explained that in the United States charging tuition would actually attract more students, especially from the "better class," whose parents seemed suspicious that something free was of lower quality. The Jesuit superior general at the time, Luigi Fortis, would have none of this and demanded strict adherence to the prohibition against charging tuition, since operating free schools was very much associated with providing education for the poor. Fearing the loss of the school his predecessor had founded, Bishop Joseph Rosati of St. Louis petitioned Rome for a relaxation of the rule on this point. In January 1833, Pope Gregory XVI granted this dispensation. Technically no Jesuit could petition for this since their vows prohibit them from ever seeking any relaxation of the vow of poverty. However, the new general, Father Jan Roothaan, drew up terms for the application of this relaxation of the rule on the question of tuition for schools in the United States. These provisions stipulated that tuition must be similar to comparable schools in the area; poor boys were never to be turned away; and Jesuit schools would never have recourse to civil courts to recover unpaid tuition.[31]

Now that the charging of tuition was possible at Jesuit colleges in the United States, the model of a free education for students in Jesuit schools seemed like a distant memory. Many of the Jesuit colleges in the nineteenth century attempted to offer scholarships to as many students as possible, but no Jesuit college in America had figured out how to remain true to St. Ignatius's ideal of a free education. By the time of the Great Depression, tuitions at Jesuit high schools ranged widely, with boarding schools like Georgetown Prep charging $1,200 for tuition, room, and board, and day schools such as Creighton University High School (now Creighton Prep) charging $50.[32] However, even a tuition of $50 might have been too much for families like Frank Miller's, let alone the $300 charged by the Loyola School.[33] Even as late as the end of the Second World War, two-thirds of American Catholics were still rated as being part of the "lower class."[34] From a neighborhood in Midtown filled with tenements, first- and second-generation Irish Americans like the Millers might have found any fee for high school beyond their reach. Only a free Jesuit school along the model of the first schools founded by the Society would work for parents like the Millers and many of the other parents of the boys in Regis's first class.

The Uniqueness of Regis High School

Over much of its existence, most especially during its first half century, Regis has been able to offer an outstanding education to generations of Catholic boys from the New York City area (like Frank Miller), many of whom would not have been able to afford such an opportunity had their parents been required to pay the tuitions charged by the other area Jesuit high schools. While these other schools have continued to offer some scholarships as they had in the nineteenth century, this financial aid was minimal at best and could help only a few students in each class. (In the 1930s, one Jesuit estimated that at the Society's schools, one full scholarship was awarded for every thirty to forty tuition-paying students.)[35] Without the establishment of Regis, many bright Catholic boys in the New York City area would not have had access to the superior education and future opportunities that a Jesuit training has traditionally afforded its students. Because of Regis, thousands of young men were able to attend college and university, many of them with the help of generous scholarships, which came as a result of both their good grades as well as having been a graduate of Regis. Eventually, with their college degrees, these Regis alumni were able to enter the professional and middle classes and forge lives that might not have been possible otherwise.

In addition to this singular contribution of Regis to needy boys in the New York area, the school is unique also in its ongoing relationship with and reliance on the Grant family, who founded the school and supported it for almost a century. (As of this writing, Regis was poised to receive about $10 million as part of the final disbursement of the family fortune.) The story of the family's original gift to build and start the school is of course central to the story of Regis's early years. However, at several points in the school's history, especially in the 1970s when it experienced severe economic challenges, the Grants came to its rescue with several large gifts. If the family had not done this, it is not clear if Regis could have kept its doors open without charging tuition to even just some students (a proposal that was raised but ultimately rejected in the mid-1950s). With the death of the last Grant in 2007 came also the family's last gift. Now the school must rely entirely on alumni financial support ($5.1 million in 2012) as well as parents to bridge the gap between the school's endowment and its annual budget. If not, then maybe the only successful model of a free Jesuit education for all, poor and rich alike, is the one the Society's first schools utilized in having one rich family underwrite the costs of the school, and while their money lasted, the Grants' support of Regis remains as the only modern example of this approach. Only time will tell.

Although founded for Catholic boys who otherwise would not be able to attend a Catholic high school, Regis has never employed the use of a strict "means test" to determine a whether a student would be accepted at Regis. Even in the first few decades of the school's history, there were at least a few students who were accepted who came from wealthy backgrounds. Nevertheless, through the Depression and the Second World War, the vast majority of the students at Regis were the sons of the working poor, and there is a good deal of evidence (detailed in Chapter 2) that if a free Regis education had not been given to them, it is highly unlikely that they would have gone to another Catholic high school, including those run by the Jesuits. For example, when Brooklyn Prep was opened in 1909 its tuition was already $100 per annum, and by the mid-1930s the Loyola School was charging $500 per year.[36] After the war, when both the Brooklyn and New York dioceses began building a network of high schools, the families of a growing number of boys who applied to and attended Regis could have afforded the relatively modest tuitions of these new schools—Cardinal Hayes High School, for example, which opened in 1941 with a tuition of $5 per month, whereas tuitions were rising at Hayes and other diocesan schools like it to between $100 and $150 per annum by the 1950s.[37] As important as these schools were in providing a Catholic secondary school education to a very large number of girls and boys at an affordable cost, in no way could they match the educational experience of a classical Jesuit education in a school composed of only very bright students.

As expanding prosperity came to the United States in the 1950s and 1960s, a growing number of American Catholics moved up the social ladder and into the middle class. The student body at Regis slowly began to reflect this demographic development with a greater number of students coming from middle- and upper-middle-class homes. With the white flight that took place in New York after World War II, many of the new groups that had taken the places of the working-class Irish, German, and Italians as they had moved to the suburbs were not Catholic in as large a percentage. This was especially for the African American population of New York City, which historically has never had a large Catholic percentage.[38] After the war Puerto Ricans were the one new immigrant group to the city that was predominantly Catholic, with their population in the city rising from 61,000 in 1940 to 431,000 twenty years later.[39] Unfortunately Puerto Ricans and other Hispanic immigrants who began settling in New York in large numbers after them were arriving at time of a general weakening of public education. As early as 1961, per capita spending on education in most U.S. cities was half of that in the neighboring suburbs, and this, as well as other factors, was greatly affecting pupil performance. In this same year, on average more than 80 percent of suburban high school students went to college, while about half of their urban counterparts did not even graduate from high school.[40] In addition, the arrival of Hispanic immigrants to New York City was also coinciding with a huge decline in Catholic elementary schools. For earlier generations, the city's parochial schools had offered a basic but strong education to poor and immigrant children to ensure a steady pipeline of well-prepared eighth-grade boys to sit for the Regis entrance exam.[41] (The stories are legion of eighth-grade nuns choosing and coaching their best and brightest for this test.) But that all began to change starting in the late 1960s, about the same time that the public schools were experiencing tremendous stress. For example, in the Diocese of Brooklyn (which also includes Queens), the number of students in Catholic schools declined from 217,103 in 1968 to 85,383 in 1990.[42] Thus, unfortunately, Hispanics, the one growing and still largely poor Catholic immigrant group in New York City that could have replaced at Regis the other groups that had moved up the economic ladder, were not able to do so in large numbers due to these changes in the educational landscape.

By the late 1960s, with the Jesuits' new emphasis on social justice, the leaders of New York province began to question whether this unique characteristic of Regis—as a school that historically had offered a large numbers of boys from disadvantaged backgrounds a superior education—might be slowly slipping away. With this new sensitivity, the school no longer determined admission based solely on an applicant's previous academic performance, and for the first time began taking into account financial need when deciding admission (though by no means was this an absolute necessity for acceptance). However, even with this new consideration of economic need, by the 1990s the school's Board of Trustees, which since 1975 included laypeople, was still raising concerns about the loss of the school's central identity of offering a Jesuit education to Catholic boys in financial need. With continuing problems in urban public education and the ongoing closure of Catholic elementary schools, the pipeline of smart but needy Catholic boys seemed to be slowing to a trickle. After several years of discussions and studies, in 2001 the board decided to establish an enrichment program for more academically talented but financially needy Catholic middle-school boys. Christened "REACH" (Recruiting Excellence in Academics for Catholic High Schools), the new program was founded to "grow" a few dozen boys who would be able to sit for the entrance exam and be equally prepared as their counterparts who had attended better-supported (public, private, or Catholic) schools. Now ten years into its existence, REACH has offered enrichment education to more than two hundred boys, with sixty-eight winning admission to Regis. Despite the many successes of REACH, the board and the administration of the school remain concerned that Regis remain faithful to its mission in educating Catholic boys who otherwise could not afford a Catholic education, while also not lowering the school's well-known and very high admissions' standards, which have helped to make a Regis education such an impressive achievement now for a century.

These changes in the demographics of the Catholic community, the decline of public education, the closing of parochial schools, and developments in Regis's admission policies were still decades in the future when Frank Miller and his classmates piled into their new school as high school freshmen in the fall of 1914. It is here, of course, where the history of Regis should begin. But actually the story of the nation's only completely free Jesuit high school goes back further than this, back to the Gilded Age, Tammany Hall politics, and a devout and generous Catholic widow.

1 Mrs. Grant's Gift

The Death of a Former Mayor

By the time the priest got to his bedside to offer the sacraments of the dying, the man was already dead. Father David W. Hearn, the Jesuit pastor of St. Ignatius of Loyola Church on Park Avenue, had been called late on the evening of November 3, 1910, to the home of one of his parishioners, Hugh J. Grant. When he arrived at his residence at 20 East 72nd Street, the Jesuit found Grant's wife, Julia, his two daughters, Edna and Julie, and his only son and namesake, Hugh, Jr., gathered around the body.[1] It was said that Mr. Grant had been out that evening to play poker with some friends but wound up returning home early after feeling ill. Upon arrival he had become dizzy on the staircase and had to be carried to his bed. His personal physician was immediately called, but before he or Father Hearn could arrive, the poor man had expired.[2]

The coroner determined that Grant had died of Bright's disease (acute nephritis). His health had been poor since an attack of influenza the previous winter had left him in a generally weakened state. He had only recently returned from an extended stay in Hot Springs, Virginia, where his physicians hoped the curative waters, brisk air, and long horseback rides would restore his strength. Grant's friends and family all said that his health had been fair since his return to the city. In fact, he had spent much of that day at his office on Wall Street and had not complained of feeling unwell. Many of these same friends who had pronounced him looking hale in recent days rushed to his residence when they heard he had suddenly died. Among them was Alfred J. Johnson, who had served as Grant's personal secretary since Grant's time as mayor of New York from 1889 to 1892.

The Young Hugh J. Grant

At the time of his election as mayor in 1888, Hugh Grant was already a very rich man.[3] And it was much of this wealth that his widow, Julia, would use to found and support Regis High School. Unlike most other

Mrs. Julia M. Grant and her three children: Hugh, Edna, and Julia.

children of Irish immigrants to New York in the mid-nineteenth century, Hugh Grant had the good fortune to have parents who were members of the rising middle class. He was born on September 10, 1858, on West 27th Street, and it seems that his mother died when he was still very young. (Unfortunately there is no record of her name or background.)[4] However, more is known about his Irish-born father, John Grant. A prosperous saloonkeeper and liquor merchant, the older Grant made a small fortune through real estate speculation in Greenwich Village and on the West Side of Manhattan. He also became active in local Democratic politics, which furthered his business connections. It was these two pursuits—real estate speculation and politics—that would come to shape so much of his son's future life.[5]

Beginning his education at a local public school, Hugh continued his studies under the De La Salle Christian Brothers at Manhattan College, which was then located at West 131st Street and Broadway. Though the records are unclear, it seems that at some point during Hugh's time at this school his father died; with his mother already deceased, he was now left orphaned.[6] However, he was not alone or destitute. In addition to leaving him $500,000, his father placed him under the care of a successful pawnbroker by the name of McAleenan.[7] After his graduation from Manhattan College at the age of sixteen, Hugh left for a tour of Europe, where he spent time in Berlin perfecting his German, which he had begun studying as a boy. Upon his return to New York, he spent three years studying at the Jesuit-run College of St. Francis Xavier on West 16th Street and then moved on to Columbia University, where he earned a law degree.[8]

Having finished his formal education, Grant began a legal career in the offices of D.M. Porter, then one of the city's leading attorneys. However, he did not remain long there, and in little more than a year he set up his own practice in real estate law, which was especially helpful in managing the properties he had inherited from his father. About this time Grant also became a member of the Friendly Sons of St. Patrick and the Kelly Democratic Club on the West Side. It was through his work with both these groups that he came to make connections with leading Tammany officials who had previously known and worked with his late father. Building on his father's business and political associations, Grant soon was selected Tammany leader in the Nineteenth Assembly District and in 1882 was elected to the city's Board of Aldermen (the forerunner to the present-day City Council). Grant was just one of many elected officials in the city who had grown rich from the saloon business. In fact, in 1884 twelve of the twenty-four men elected to this board were saloonkeepers and a further four had received substantial financial support from those in the booze trade.[9]

After only a couple of years in elected office, Grant came to the attention of the entire city as a result of scandal. In 1884, he was one of only two members of the Board of Aldermen not accused of taking a $20,000 bribe to support a city contract for a streetcar corporation. As a result of his moral probity, Grant became the darling of the city's political kingmakers, including both the Tammany and anti-Tammany factions of the Democratic Party. In the elections of that year, he was selected by "Honest" John Kelly to be Tammany's candidate in the 1884 mayoral election. Though he lost to William R. Grace, a fellow Catholic who ran as an independent Democrat, Grant walked away from this defeat with far more than a consolation prize. The next year Tammany backed his candidacy for sheriff of New York, an office which Grant easily won and which also came with a handsome salary. This new position included a fair amount of patronage and kept him in the public spotlight for several years by allowing him prime places in the festivities surrounding the dedication of the Statue of Liberty in 1886 and the centennial observances of George Washington's inauguration in

1888.[10] With this background, education, and political connections, Hugh Grant was well situated when he ran for mayor a few years later.

Mayor Grant

After the death of Kelly in 1886, the leadership of Tammany passed into the hands of Richard Croker. It was Croker who backed Abram Hewitt in the famous mayoral election of that same year, which saw the radical social thinker Henry George come in second and the Republican candidate and future president Theodore Roosevelt a distant third. Although Hewitt won, Croker's relationship with him soon turned sour over a patronage dispute. This led Boss Croker to deny Tammany's backing to Mayor Hewitt in the 1888 election. Instead, Croker anointed the young, squeaky-clean Hugh Grant. Despite a five-way race with Hewitt running as a potential Democratic spoiler, Grant won handily, capitalizing on the poor relations Hewitt had developed with the Irish American community during his time as mayor. It was bad enough when the mayor publicly supported literacy tests and a twenty-one year naturalization period for immigrants, but his refusal to review the St. Patrick's Day Parade or fly the shamrock from City Hall on the feast of their great patron was too much for New York's Irish to bear.[11] Hewitt's political missteps played perfectly into Grant's hands, as Grant was able to parlay his father's wealth and political connections as well as his Irish ancestry to become the first New York–born, Irish American mayor.[12] Elected at the tender age of thirty-one, Grant continues to hold the distinction of being New York City's youngest mayor.

Hugh Grant's two consecutive terms as mayor are rightly remembered for several undertakings that improved the lives of average New Yorkers. His completion of the New Croton River Aqueduct was probably the most important of these accomplishments.[13] This enormous public works project secured the reliable delivery of clean water for a city that was still growing in almost geometric proportions. In addition, Mayor Grant ordered the telephone and telegraph companies to take down their unsightly and unsafe overhead lines and bury them. The recent blizzard of 1888 had demonstrated the real hazard to life and limb posed by electrified overhead wires during a storm. Even when weather was not a concern, these lines also tended to get in the way of fire-fighting apparatuses. Shortly after being sworn into office in January 1890, the new mayor notified the companies that they had one year to bury the lines. When in January of the next year they failed to meet this deadline, he ordered groups of city

This cartoon appeared in *Harper's Weekly* on October 20, 1888. The editors opposed Hugh Grant in his run for mayor because of his association with Tammany Hall and its stance against civil service reform. Despite the magazine's editorializing, Grant beat the incumbent mayor, Abram Hewitt, in this election and went on to serve another two-year term as mayor of New York City.

axmen to start swinging. This got the attention of the utilities, the lines were then buried, and New Yorkers had safer streets.[14]

In addition to responding to this threat to safety, Grant also worked to clean the city streets, whose filth was taking a toll on both public health and commerce. In preparation for this, he first visited several other cities around the country to learn of their sanitation systems, and he even had his staff research how European cities dealt with the issue. While somewhat hamstrung by state law, which regulated street cleaning on the state rather than the local level, Grant began making plans for regular and reliable street cleaning for the city. However, it was left to his successors to capitalize on the modified state laws and give the city regular and reliable street cleaning and disposal of refuse.[15]

Despite these accomplishments, Grant's time in elected office was also marked by accusations of both patronage and cronyism. One of his first official acts as mayor was the appointment of Croker as the city chamberlain, which came with the princely remuneration of $25,000 per annum. While Croker previously had held other elected and appointed positions, including those of alderman, coroner, and tax collector, this appointment certainly smacked of cronyism. The office of chamberlain involved the maintenance of complex financial records as well as the management of public monies. At least on the surface, these duties seem to have been beyond the competence of Croker, who had little formal education. In addition to this bold but legal act of patronage, there was convincing evidence that Grant had been involved in a direct kickback to the Tammany Hall sachem before becoming mayor, although cloaked in the vestments of religion. In response to questioning by a New York State Investigating Committee, Grant admitted that shortly after becoming city sheriff in 1885, he gave to Croker's newborn daughter "Flossie" (Florence), who was also his goddaughter, a gift of $10,000. It seems that Croker used this money to purchase property in her name in Harlem, an area of the city that was expected to see new real estate development thanks to the construction of elevated trains on several of the avenues. However, neither of these incidents directly involving Boss Croker, nor public revelations about last-minute pay increases to friends of Tammany working on the recently completed New Croton Aqueduct project, hobbled his bid for reelection in 1890. Grant soundly defeated Francis M. Scott, the anti-Tammany candidate, to win another two-year term.[16]

During his second term in office, Mayor Grant continued to work for a comprehensive sanitation policy. He also established a special commission to investigate the construction of underground train lines (subways). As with the overhead wires, the recent blizzard demonstrated the need for a transportation system that would continue to operate even in bad weather. Boston had already begun to plan an underground rail system in response to this same blizzard, opening its first underground train line in 1897. It took until 1904 for New York to follow suit, possibly because of Tammany's

Hugh J. Grant served as mayor of New York from 1889 to 1893. (Collection of the New-York Historical Society, #8277725d.)

fear of the competition subways would bring to the elevated lines in which its members were already heavily invested. However, despite this as well as other attempts by Grant to help manage and plan for the city's exponential growth, his reputation suffered during his second term, largely due to the exposure of widespread corruption by members of the police force. Over 80 percent of appointments to the force were controlled by Tammany along with a fair amount of money flowing back to the party bosses from loyal and grateful men on the force. As a result of these revelations, as well as increasing criticism of his close association with Croker and the rest of Tammany, Grant decided not to run for a third term in 1892.[17]

However, the ever-loyal son of Tammany wound up throwing his hat in the ring for mayor one last time. In 1894, Nathan Strauss (an early owner of Macy's department stores) was slated to run as Tammany's candidate for mayor. However, after ultimately deciding that he would be a weak candidate, Strauss bowed out. As a favor to Croker, Grant stepped into the breach late in the election. Though the reform candidate, William Strong, beat Grant at the polls, both Tammany and Strauss were most grateful to Grant for helping them at least to save face by running a stronger candidate. In fact, Strauss was so personally thankful that the Jewish businessman named his newborn son "Nathan Grant Strauss."[18]

Grant's last official public act in support of Tammany came a few years later. After the machine's defeat in 1894, Croker had returned home to Ireland, citing health problems. In truth, his departure came more in response to fears of looming investigations of Tammany now that the spirit of reform was blowing. But, with the coming birth of Greater New York in 1898 and the promised expansion in the mayor's power and patronage, Grant made a trip to Ireland to coax the former boss to return to New York. Grant made the case that Tammany needed Croker's wisdom and expertise to make the most of these new opportunities, and his attempts at persuasion proved successful. Upon his return, Croker was able to work his magic and a Tammany man, Robert Van Wyck, became the first mayor of Greater New York. (Van Wyck is best remembered for his campaign slogan: "To hell with reform.")[19] As for Grant, this mission to Ireland was the final act of his public association with Tammany, and with this his active engagement in city politics came to a happy ending.[20]

A Society Wedding

Despite Grant's busy schedule once he became involved in city politics, he was still able to find the time to befriend Julia Murphy, a young woman he would eventually marry. She had only recently made her debut into society when she met Mayor Grant, and soon thereafter they began a three-year courtship. After agreeing to give up his career in politics and to shave off his heavy black beard, the two tied the knot. Hugh and Julia would enjoy fifteen years of married life together and their union would produce three children.[21]

Born in 1873 and raised in Troy, New York, Julia was the oldest of eleven children from a prominent upstate family.[22] She received most of her education from the Madams (Sisters) of the Sacred Heart in Kenwood, right outside of Albany. Her father, Edward Murphy, was a native of that city and from a family wealthy enough to send him to St. John's College (Fordham), from where he graduated in 1857. Her mother, Julia Delehanty, was from a prominent Albany Irish Catholic family. After making his name in the brewing business, Julia's father became involved in local Democratic politics and was eventually elected mayor of Troy in 1875, a position he then held for the next eight years. In 1892, he was selected by the New York State Legislature to serve as the junior senator from New York in the U.S. Congress. Since he and his wife still had a brood of young children at home, the couple decided that only Julia would accompany her father to Washington, where in the absence of her mother she would serve as her father's hostess.[23] Upon their arrival in the nation's capital, the new senator purchased a stately home at the corner of K and 17th Streets in the Northwest section of the city which had formerly belonged to Senator Leland Stanford of California.[24] It was in this house that Julia and Hugh would be married two years later.[25]

The couple was married at eleven o'clock in the morning on Tuesday, April 30, 1895, at a lavish affair. It was quite unusual for the two not to have been married in a church. However, James Cardinal Gibbons, the archbishop of Baltimore, gave a special dispensation since Julia and Hugh wished a private affair away from the glare of nosey journalists and photographers. The ceremony took place on the second floor in a drawing room that had been sumptuously decorated with sprays of asparagus, clusters of lilies, tall palms, and white azaleas. A special altar was constructed for the occasion, and in front of it a prie-dieu was placed on top of a white fur rug. Julia wore a diamond-studded tiara given to her by Hugh. Her six sisters served as attendants, each wearing a dress made of pink mousseline de soie. The wedding ceremony itself was presided over by Archbishop Michael A. Corrigan of New York with several other priests also in attendance.[26]

After the ceremony, the assembled guests made their way to the dining room for an elegant breakfast. This room, too, was exquisitely decorated with lilacs and orchids, and each of the candelabra was festooned with orange blossoms. According to a report on the wedding in the next day's edition of the *New York Times*, "The bride's cake, set in the midst of orange blossoms and lilies of the valley, occupied a table all by itself." Thus it seems that no detail was left unnoticed at this wedding of members of two of New York State's most prominent political families. After a leisurely two-hour celebration, the new Mrs. Grant changed out of her wedding gown and donned a traveling outfit as the newlyweds prepared for their honeymoon. They were about to leave by ship for Britain and Ireland and then on for a tour of the Continent.[27]

The Grant Family Grows

After a little more than three months traveling in Europe, on August 3, 1895, the Grants returned to New York on the *St. Louis*. They tried to slip back into the city quietly by registering themselves as "Mr. and Mrs. Chambers" on the ship's passenger list. Despite this attempt at subterfuge, the press was still out in full force to greet the steamship when it docked at seven o'clock that morning. After disembarking, Mrs. Grant immediately went to her new home at 261 West 73rd Street, which had been Mr. Grant's residence before marrying. The newspapers pronounced them both to be looking very well, and the *New York Times* account remarked that Mr. Grant seemed "not so stout" as compared to when the couple left on their bridal tour.[28]

While Mrs. Grant went to her new home, Mr. Grant was met by two old friends who accompanied him by foot to his office on Broadway near City Hall. Despite his initial desire to reenter life in New York as unobtrusively as possible, the former mayor granted an interview to reporters. Since the return of Boss Croker to his native Ireland in 1894, Grant was now considered by many to be the unofficial leader of Tammany. However, during his time abroad, internal politics in the machine continued to churn and reporters wanted to hear Grant's opinion on a whole host of topics, ranging from proposed plans for the reorganization of Tammany, which was still without a boss, to bimetallism. (William Jennings Bryan was to give his famous "Cross of Gold" speech at the Democratic National Convention in Chicago less than one year later.) Reminding the reporters of his three-month absence from the local scene, Grant claimed ignorance on several of the questions asked of him and reiterated that he had no desire to be Tammany's new grand sachem. He did admit, however, to meeting with Croker several times while he and his new wife were in Ireland, but unconvincingly claimed that the two did not discuss political matters. After this meeting with the press, several Tammany leaders came to see the former mayor as he began the transition from his recent honeymoon back to his workaday life as a successful New York businessman.

While the newlyweds made their first home together at Hugh's bachelor residence on the West Side, in early 1900 they moved to a new house at 20 East 72nd Street on the Upper East Side, a house large enough that one day as their family grew they would eventually house six live-in servants.[29] Designed by the architectural firm of Rose and Stone and completed in 1894, the house was originally built for Joseph Agostini and was part of a row of three new townhomes designed and erected at the same time.[30] In 1899, it was sold to Mr. George C. Clausen, who held the property briefly before selling it to the Grants.[31] By the turn of the century, the neighborhood of their new home, which bordered Central Park, was well on its way to becoming one of the city's most fashionable districts.

While the area east of Third Avenue had become heavily congested and dirty due to the construction of elevated train lines in the late 1870s, the largely underdeveloped property west of Madison Avenue and north of 59th Street had become highly desirable. The construction of the Metropolitan Museum of Art, beginning in 1880, had attracted wealthy families such as the Astors, who began building palatial homes in the area on or just east of Fifth Avenue.[32] It was about the time this area was becoming more exclusive that the upper part of Fourth Avenue was renamed Park Avenue. However, even after this name change, steam engines of the New York Central and New Haven Railroads still chugged and belched their smoke up and down the thoroughfare. It was during Grant's time as mayor that he began the process of submerging and covering over the electrified train tracks, much to the delight of the area's new residents.[33]

Despite the continued development of the neighborhood where the Grants had recently moved, they did not spend all their time in the city. As a wedding present, Hugh had given Julia a country house in Oradell, New Jersey. Before his death, Hugh's father had begun buying property in this area of Bergen County, and with his son's additional purchases, by the 1890s the Grant family had extensive property holdings in Oradell as well as in the nearby towns of Dumont and Emerson. Like Boss Croker, Hugh had a strong interest in thoroughbreds, maintaining a horse farm adjacent to the house and eventually constructing a trotting track. In fact, his love of horses was so great that after leaving the mayor's office, Grant became involved in building the Harlem River Speedway in Upper Manhattan. Upon its completion, Grant could often be found training one of his horses there.[34]

In the years after marrying, Hugh stayed active managing his extensive real estate holdings. Because of his outstanding business reputation, he was often consulted for advice on questions of business and finance. He eventually became involved in the financial management of several financially distressed companies, such as the Third Avenue Railroad Company and the Brooklyn Wharf and Warehouse Company.[35] He also maintained memberships in several of New York's private men's associations, including the New York Athletic Club, the Narragansett Club, and the Catholic Club.[36] However, in addition to all this, Hugh also became a family man. By 1904 he and Julia had three children: Julie, Edna, and Hugh, Jr. While many of the wealthier Catholics at that time sent their daughters to the Convent of the Sacred Heart, which was run by the same order that taught Julia as a child, the Grants sent their daughters to the exclusive but nonsectarian "Miss Chapin's School for Girls," which was then located on East 57th Street. Hugh, the youngest of the three, was eventually sent to the Jesuit-run Loyola School on Park Avenue. However, the former mayor would not have the good fortune to see his children grow to adulthood. In fact, young Hugh was only six years old at the time of his father's death.[37]

The Influence of Father Hearn

Hugh Grant's untimely death in 1910 left his wife, Julia, a widow before the age of forty and with the sole responsibility of raising their three young children. She was fortunate to have the support of her family, who came to her aid immediately. Her father, the former senator, escorted Julia and her two daughters as the funeral cortege made its way from the Grant residence a dozen blocks north to St. Ignatius of Loyola Church on Park Avenue. Julia had decided to leave her son, Hugh, at home, thinking he was too young to attend his father's funeral.

The former mayor received a grand farewell with many of the city's leading citizens who came to pay their last respects at a Solemn High Mass celebrated by Father Hearn. Assisting him were Father J. Havens Richards, S.J., former president of Georgetown University, as deacon, and Father John Wynne, S.J., founding editor of the *America* magazine and a classmate of Hugh's from childhood, as subdeacon. Many of New York's most prominent business leaders and politicians also attended, including all five borough presidents. The honorary pallbearers included Morgan J. O'Brien, former presiding judge of the New York State Appellate Court and one of the city's most prominent Roman Catholics. Seated near the front of the church were more than a dozen Sisters of Charity who taught in the parish grammar school, a Christian Brother representing Grant's alma mater,

Manhattan College, and Monsignor Michael Lavelle, vicar general of the archdiocese representing Archbishop John Farley. Conspicuous by their absence were both Mayor Jay Gaynor, who claimed ill health, and Charles F. Murphy, Tammany's boss since 1902. The music for the liturgy was meticulously performed, and included Verdi's *Requiem* and Chopin's *Funeral March*. As was the custom at that time, there was no eulogy. After Mass, the body of Hugh Grant was transported to Calvary Cemetery in Queens, where a mausoleum was to be later built for its interment.[38]

After her husband's death, Julia sent young Hugh away for a time to live with C. K. G. Billings, a close friend and financial adviser to her late husband. Originally from Chicago, Billings had inherited a large fortune early in life and bought property in Upper Manhattan on the site of what is now the Cloisters (a branch of the Metropolitan Museum of Art). Here he built a sumptuous residence, which included a heated indoor pool, an oak bowling alley, and an enormous stable for racing horses, a passion he shared with Hugh's late father. Julia hoped that Billings would provide a strong male influence on her son now that his father was gone.[39] For Julia, Father David Hearn would come to take an equally important role in her life as he offered consolation and practical counsel in the years after her husband's death.

Father Hearn had not been at St. Ignatius very long at the time of Grant's death. It was only in May 1909 that he had been appointed pastor of St. Ignatius Church, head of the Loyola School, as well as superior of the Jesuit community attached to these apostolates. Born in South Framingham, Massachusetts, in 1861, Hearn was educated as a young man at Boston College before entering the Jesuit novitiate, which was then located in the Hudson Valley at West Park, New York. As a scholastic he taught mathematics at Georgetown and poetry at St. Peter's College in Jersey City. Ordained a priest in 1895, Hearn was sent to Belgium for his tertianship after a brief stint at Boston College.[40] In 1897, he was appointed prefect of studies at the College of St. Francis Xavier in New York. Only three years later he was named the college's president. While other Jesuit administrators continued to resist change, Hearn led the effort to separate the high school and college divisions at Xavier in response to the growing criticism of the course of studies in Jesuit institutions, as well as the fact that the physical space of the school was not large enough to accommodate both a high school and a college. As was common for Jesuits at the time, Hearn did not remain long in this assignment, and in 1907 he was transferred yet again, this time to Boston College to become prefect of studies.[41]

When Hearn arrived as pastor of St. Ignatius in 1909, the church building was still quite new, having been completed only eleven years earlier.

The Society had come to staff the parish in 1866 to help facilitate their ministries on the various islands in the East River. For some time Jesuits had served as chaplains on Randall's, Ward's, Blackwell's, and Hart's Islands in institutions with grim sounding names such as "Lunatic Asylum" and the "Home for Idiots." A parish nearby now gave them a residence closer to their work.[42] A basement church was completed in 1886 (and dedicated to St. Lawrence O'Toole, the original patron of the parish), but the upper church was not completed until the pastorate of Father Neil McKinnon, S.J. It was said of McKinnon that upon his arrival, he found a parish of brick and left a church of marble.[43] However, even after its formal dedication by Archbishop Corrigan in 1898, there were still some more significant final touches to be done. Much of this work would be paid for by Mrs. Grant using money that she inherited from her late husband.

At his death, Hugh Grant left his wife an estate valued at about $9.2 million.[44] At the time of the probate of the will, she was to receive $500,000 outright, and an additional $300,000 was to be given to charities of her choosing.[45] And at her death, the entire estate was to be divided among the three children in any way she saw fit. A devout Catholic, Mrs. Grant turned to Father Hearn in 1911 for advice on how to distribute these monies as well as for other counsel in dealing with her husband's estate. Her father died in 1911, so with the other important man in her life gone, it is not surprising that she turned for advice to her pastor. Hearn suggested that they "talk the matter thoroughly," and afterward he would draw up a list of recommendations. Then, "with all this before her, she could easily decide for herself and could tell her Protestant lawyer, Mr. John Bowers, that it was all her own work."[46] While in conversation, Father Hearn also mentioned that it was "time for well-to-do Catholics of position and refinement to do something for Catholic Education [and] they could not place their money with better results."[47] This would take far more than the $300,000 that the will stipulated should be disbursed, but Hearn knew that the wealth of the Grant family was quite sizeable. In planting this seed of an idea in Mrs. Grant, Father Hearn was returning to a dream that he had envisioned a few years earlier.

Back in 1905 when Hearn was president of the College of St. Francis Xavier, he had begun to lay plans to close the college portion of Xavier and make the high school division free. According to Hearn, not only was the site no longer adequate to maintain both a college and a high school, but also the neighborhood had become less residential and more commercial, making it a less desirable place to run a school. Hearn thought it best to close the upper division and combine it with the Society's other college at Fordham.[48] In addition to these very practical concerns, Hearn's proposal

Father David W. Hearn, S.J. With the help of the enormous financial support of Mrs. Grant, Father Hearn was able to found Regis in 1914 while he was pastor of St. Ignatius Church. Because of disagreements with his Jesuit superiors, Hearn was removed as president of the new school in late September 1915 and moved to Canisius College in Buffalo. He died in 1917.

for a free high school was rooted in the original vision going back to St. Ignatius Loyola that a Jesuit education should be available to all. In the 1880s, one of Hearn's predecessors as president of Xavier, Father Samuel H. Frisbee, had attempted to restore the spirit of a free education for all by offering a full scholarship to the brightest boy from each parochial school in New York City.[49] Now, twenty years later, Hearn wanted to take this modest initiative to its full conclusion.

To make this plan workable, Xavier needed to increase its high school enrollment. Thus, in 1907, Hearn wrote a letter to the parents of all the boys graduating from one of the many parochial schools in the city, encouraging them to further their son's education by enrolling him at Xavier. Without a high school education, Hearn argued, their sons would be barred from most if not all of the professions. He reminded these mostly Irish, German, and Italian parents that "the Hebrew population, even the poorest are seizing the opportunity" in sending their children to high school, so Catholics had to be careful not to be left behind. Hearn realized that the cost of a Jesuit high school education might be beyond their reach, so in recognition of this he promised that the Jesuit fathers at Xavier would do everything "short of bankruptcy" to make attendance possible for their sons. Hearn proposed that all the pastors in Manhattan encourage as many of their boys to attend the high school department of Xavier as possible, and that the pastors should contribute forty dollars per year for each boy.[50] With a higher enrollment, parish financial help, and support from the Jesuits themselves, Hearn thought Xavier would be able to offer a free high school education to all. Xavier would become the first, and the model, of offering a free secondary school education for Catholics (as the parochial schools did on the primary level). Unfortunately, Hearn's dream did not come to fruition at this time. However, thanks to the generosity of Mrs. Grant, it eventually proved to be a dream deferred.[51]

"Gratias agamus Domino Deo nostro"

Not long after their conversation, as per the dictates of the will, Mrs. Grant made gifts to various institutions, with the largest share going toward those sponsored by the Jesuits. Her gifts to St. Ignatius parish totaled almost $70,000. Some of these gifts were for church furnishings: three Stations of the Cross ($6,000); the mosaic panel behind the high altar of St. Ignatius and his companions ($7,000); and for general improvements in the upper church ($25,000). Others were for support of education and child care in the parish: St. Ignatius Day Nursery ($10,000); scholarships for boys from the parish to Xavier ($10,000); and scholarships for students from the parish to Fordham ($10,000). Mrs. Grant also made donations totaling over $100,000 toward Jesuit formation and Jesuit apostolates. Some of these gifts included: four burses for novices at St. Andrew-on-Hudson ($28,000); Xavier Society for the Blind ($15,000); a new chapel at the Jesuit seminary at Woodstock College in Maryland ($50,000); and support of Jesuit chaplains on Blackwell's Island ($6,500).[52]

In addition to these works associated with the Society of Jesus, Mrs. Grant also gave money to St. Francis Hospital in the Mott Haven section of the Bronx ($10,000) and St. Benedict the Moor Church, a parish for black Catholics on West 53rd Street ($10,000). In his record of these donations, Hearn noted that "it was wise to counsel institutions not belonging to the Society, as the public press had given notice of this clause [the amount of $300,000 to charities] in Mr. Grant's will, and many were watching what would happen." When she showed the list of her bequests to her lawyer, "the first question he asked was whether Father Hearn had seen [it]." In replying no, Mrs. Grant answered honestly since she sent Hearn a copy of the list only later, but the attorney was nevertheless surprised by her answer. However, "there could not be any feeling that on [Hearn's] part that undue influence [on her] had been exercised."[53] Mrs. Grant also strictly stipulated that all of these bequests were to be kept "absolutely secret," a requirement that would of course be attached to her founding and ongoing support of Regis High School. While respecting this request, Father Hearn predicted that the school "would attract widespread notice and people would guess." However, Mrs. Grant would "hear none of this," so her anonymity as the donor of Regis was carefully preserved until her death in 1944, when a high-ranking Jesuit in Rome asked for prayers for her by name.[54] Despite this inadvertent breach of her wishes, her name continued to be carefully protected for the next several decades.[55]

Mrs. Grant's generosity to St. Ignatius parish and the Jesuits did not end with this series of gifts in 1911. In April of the next year she gave the parish $10,000 for the construction of the "Shrine of the Patron Saints of Youth," and in the end of May, before setting sail for Europe, she sent a check for $1,000 as a "personal gift" to Father Hearn.[56] However, before her trip abroad, she and Father Hearn had begun discussing the possibility of a major gift to the Society. Hearn told her that the Jesuits were desirous of constructing a new seminary for those studying theology. The seminary at Woodstock, Maryland, that had been built in 1869 was now considered too remote and thus needed to be moved near to one of their universities, such as Georgetown or Fordham. Hearn also raised again the work closest to his heart—a free Catholic high school for boys. In fact, the school that would become Regis was actually part of a larger plan of Hearn's that in itself was an expansion of his earlier idea from when he was president at Xavier.

Hearn wanted the Jesuits to completely reorganize their system of schools in the New York City area while also expanding the number of high schools. He seemed to be promoting this somewhat out of fear of the competition that diocesan schools might mount against Jesuit ones. In a letter to the Jesuit superior general in Rome he warned of this in the strongest terms:

> In this country the high schools [public] are free and supported by the state . . . Bishops in this country have made a great fight for Catholic elementary schools. These exist almost everywhere, free like the public schools for young children. But nothing has been done yet to extend the system and have free high schools like the public high schools for Catholic children . . . I feel that before long such schools will be started by the Diocesan authorities, unless we are active and do it beforehand. If they start them, we shall lose our hold here and our university plan will suffer greatly, if not altogether destroyed. If they have the High Schools of the city, the boys might be directed into colleges they will be sure to erect and we shall get only a remnant of students.[57]

Hearn proposed that the Society make Fordham its only university in the New York City area (at this time there were four) but expand the number of high schools. He wanted to open another select school like Loyola, which would charge a hefty tuition and be aimed at the sons of "lawyers, doctors and the prosperous class." Then the College of St. Francis Xavier should be sold, and with its proceeds, a smaller parcel should be purchased farther up the West Side. With the money left over, a foundation could be established that would help make it a free school like the one he had envisioned to start with the gift from Mrs. Grant.[58] He also wanted to establish another free high school in the Bronx but gave no plan for its funding. Obviously this all never came to fruition (though the college portion of Xavier was closed in 1912 and briefly combined with Fordham's), but his plans for a free high school on the East Side of Manhattan had much better fortunes.

According to a letter Hearn wrote in 1916, "For a long time she hung between the two ideas [seminary and high school], now seeming to lean one way [and then] another." To help her with her decision, Hearn even took Mrs. Grant to see the fifty-four-acre property the Jesuits had recently bought in Yonkers where they were considering building the new seminary.[59] Upon seeing it, she said, "It is a beautiful view but once you have put up your big buildings on the little level ground there is, there is nothing left but that dreadful slope. Don't your Fathers see that?"[60] Hearn was in complete agreement that the site was completely unsuitable for a seminary. After that visit, "she never considered again the [seminary] proposition for a moment and turned with all her heart to the high school idea." It seems that with this, Hearn had closed the deal on the school.[61]

Sometime in the late spring of 1912, Hearn wrote to Rome telling them that a wealthy benefactor had proposed building and endowing a free high school for boys under the supervision of the Society. (It is not clear when it was decided to place the school under the patronage of St. John Francis Regis, but since the school was founded to educate poor boys, this Jesuit saint makes sense since most of his priestly ministry was dedicated to the poor, including children.)[62] On August 15, 1912, the Jesuit authorities sent a cable giving their endorsement to the plan, provided that the funding was assured.[63] However, while Rome approved the idea, the local Jesuit superior proved to be far from supportive. In the fall of that same year, Father Anthony Maas was appointed provincial of the Maryland–New York Province, and soon expressed his displeasure at the agreement between Mrs. Grant and Father Hearn. Maas had been rector of the Woodstock seminary since 1907.[64] He would have preferred that this benefactor give her money to build the new seminary in Yonkers. Despite this opposition from the provincial, the Jesuit General in Rome had given his approval, and for her part, Mrs. Grant remained set in her decision to establish a high school.[65]

Shortly after his arrival at St. Ignatius, Father Hearn began compiling his "Notebook of Benefactors" in order to record the major gifts to the parish. It is here that can be found Mrs. Grant's rather dramatic presentation of the first installment of her gift to start Regis. Hearn recorded the following entry for December 24, 1912, in which he speaks of himself in the third person: "Mrs. Hugh J. Grant came to the Midnight Mass in Loyola Chapel. Just before the Mass she placed in Rev. Fr. Superior's hand a sealed envelope containing a certificate on the Central Trust Co. for five hundred thousand dollars. This was the amount left to her absolute disposal by the will of her husband. It was the first installment towards the $1,500,000 for the foundation of the Regis High School."[66] Now that the first installment of the bequest had been made, on December 26 Hearn called a meeting of the consultors of the Loyola Jesuit community and presented them with Mrs. Grant's offer for their formal approval. Not only did they give it, but they also voiced support of Hearn's plan to acquire some nearby property. (Hearn already had some experience in the purchase of real estate when he bought six houses on East 83rd Street, west of the Loyola School, in his expansion of the parish plant in the early years of his pastorate.)[67] In early January 1913, Maas wrote the superior general in Rome crowing about the gift that had recently been given to Hearn and recommending that "Gratias agamus Domino Deo nostro" (Let us give thanks to our Lord God) for the incredible opportunity that had come to the Society because of this act of great generosity.[68]

With all progressing so well, Hearn began making plans to purchase some property he had his eye on for some time. There were several vacant lots across from St. Ignatius's parochial school, which "owing to the stagnant conditions of the real estate market" he thought could be had for "comparatively low rates" since "some of the owners were embarrassed and others were anxious to sell."[69] Hearn ultimately worked through a third party in Philadelphia in order to purchase property of varying sizes on East 84th and 85th Streets. The current footprint of the school was previously divided into seven separate parcels, which once included several vacant lots, the Manhattan Garage, a stable, and three private residences.[70] After all the parcels had been purchased, Hearn expressed regret that although two of the plots had been owned by Catholics, "from which we had a right to expect the property as a gift[,] [instead these plots] cost us a great deal, for our Catholics failed us."[71] Despite this disappointment, the project went ahead and soon the prestigious architectural firm of Maginnis and Walsh was selected to draw up plans for the proposed school.[72] In addition, at this meeting the consultors agreed that the school should be placed under the patronage of St. John Francis Regis.[73]

In addition to the original gift of $500,000, Mrs. Grant wound up giving the rest in four installments. She had to do this since her late husband's will did not allow her to touch the principal.[74] However, she could anticipate an average of at least $400,000 of annual income. It was from this interest that she put up the rest of the promised gift in these installments:

May 29, 1913: $200,000 in cash and $100,000 in Baltimore & Ohio Convertible Bonds
March 15, 1914: $375,000 in New York State Bonds
February 19, 1915: $350,000 in bonds
April 8, 1915: $200,000 in bonds

Remarkably in less than three years, Mrs. Grant gave $1.725 million toward the establishment of Regis.[75]

Shortly before the opening of the new school, Father Hearn sent a letter to Mrs. Grant clearly stating their agreement as to the school she was founding and how it would be supported. The letter explicitly stated that her gift was not to the archdiocese or St. Ignatius Parish but to the "Fathers of the Society of Jesus" to establish a high school "without tuition charge." Five hundred thousand dollars of her bequest was to go to the "purchase of property and erection of suitable buildings," and the remaining million or so was left "as a foundation for the running of the expenses of the school . . . [including] support of Jesuits teaching there and for the pay of any lay assistants."[76] Since the property cost about $440,000 and construction of the building came to slightly above $400,000, Regis actually opened with a foundation of about $875,000.[77] Hearn estimated that when invested, this would yield about $40,000 per annum to pay the operating costs of the school as well as to keep reinvesting a portion of the annual growth, to bring the foundation up to $1 million within a decade of the school's opening.[78]

It is possible that Hearn felt the need to express all of this in writing because of some recent controversies surrounding the establishment of the school. In the summer of 1913, Hearn had been summoned to see Cardinal Farley concerning the establishment of Regis.[79] It seems that the archbishop had heard rumors that Hearn had actually received $3 million from Mrs. Grant and the promise of much more if needed. If this were the case, then Farley wondered why in good conscience Hearn was not also establishing a free school for girls. (At this time a Catholic high school enrolling both boys and girls was virtually unthinkable. As late as 1929, Pope Pius XI was still reiterating the need to separate the sexes in schools.)[80] Monsignor Michael Lavelle, the vicar general of the archdiocese and rector of the cathedral, was also present at this meeting. He had recently expanded the cathedral's grammar school to include a high school department for girls run by the Sisters of Charity. He was hoping that some of this rumored huge sum could be used to endow his new school. Before informing the cardinal and his vicar general that this rumor was false and that the gift was of a far smaller amount, Hearn gently but firmly told the cardinal that this whole conversation was taking place as a courtesy to the prelate. According to church law, Hearn did not have to reveal any of this information to Farley, as the Society of Jesus had the right under canon law to raise funds and spend them on their apostolic works without consultation with the diocesan bishop. Hearn explained to the cardinal and his vicar general that the anonymous benefactor had given far less than this rumored amount. As far as providing a free Catholic high school education for girls, the Society, of course, was not able to do this, since by its own rule it could teach only boys. Hearn reminded the cardinal of his own attempt to offer a free education to the needy during his time as president of Xavier. Farley recalled this, and though saddened that this plan had never come to fruition, he was now very pleased and gave the foundation of this new free Jesuit high school his "hearty approbation."[81]

About this time, Hearn also addressed the Parochial School Board, a committee of the archdiocese, to allay their fears. He promised that this new school would not poach on boys who would normally have attended one of the schools in Manhattan run by the Christian Brothers.[82] This new Jesuit school would not offer vocational training in the trades (as did many of the schools run by the Brothers) but would adhere strictly to the academic curriculum, similar to the ones offered at Xavier and Fordham. In addition, Hearn stated that it was his hope that one day the archdiocese would have several free high schools "in every line of study" (academic and vocational) so as "to keep Catholic boys out of the public High Schools [*sic*]." This explanation seemed to satisfy both the School Board and the Brothers, and no further objections were raised by church authorities to the start of a new Jesuit high school in New York City.[83]

In addition to having to deal with concerns of local ecclesiastical leaders over the start of Regis, Father Hearn also had to respond to Father Franz Wernz, superior general of the Jesuits from 1906 to 1914. While Wernz approved the acceptance of Mrs. Grant's very generous gift, he nevertheless raised several animadversions.[84] First, he believed that the project had been rushed into without enough serious deliberation. Second, he felt that Hearn had paid too much for the property. (He had also thought the province had overpaid for the land in Yonkers where the theologate was to be built, a sentiment shared by many Jesuits of the Maryland–New York Province.)[85] Third, he thought there was too much unoccupied space above and below the main staircase and that there were too many classrooms, with many of them not sufficiently lighted. It was long tradition in the Society to submit building plans to Rome before construction, so it is not surprising that the general raised this third point. And finally, Wernz criticized the proposed curriculum as containing too much college work.[86] The general also stipulated that Hearn should not expend more than $400,000 for the construction of the school. Luckily, the final cost came in just slightly above this at $401,664.[87]

Conclusion

At the time of the founding of the Society of Jesus, St. Ignatius demanded that Jesuit ministries and apostolates be available to the rich and poor alike. After the first schools were opened, this norm was to be applied to them, too. A new school would be established only if it could be fully endowed.[88] Despite this lofty and laudable goal, most Jesuit schools were never fully endowed and often had to resort to other methods to make ends meet. With far different economic and social conditions to deal with, American Jesuits in the nineteenth century had decided that operating free schools was no longer possible. With Rome's acquiescence, the more than two dozen Jesuit schools founded in this century became heavily dependent on tuition and therefore remained out of the reach of most of the American Catholic community, which was still made up largely of poor immigrants. Thus it seemed that this core principle of Ignatius and his first companions—universal access to Jesuit schools—had been relegated to the history books, at least in the United States. However, the generosity of one devoutly Catholic woman brought the original vision back to life.[89]

With the encouragement of Father Hearn, who had never lost this educational ideal of the early Society, Mrs. Grant donated a considerable portion of her family's wealth to the establishment of Regis High School. And Mrs. Grant would continue to offer generous support to the works of the Jesuits, especially to Regis, until her death in 1944. After this, the tradition of generous support of Regis was picked up by her children, who (while also remaining anonymous) came to the aid of the school on several occasions in the next decades.

2 Strong Beginnings, 1914–1930

The Daily Grind

For the first few days of classes in September 1914, Frank Miller and his classmates were allowed to enter their new school through the faculty entrance on East 84th Street. But that would not last for long. On September 22, the tunnel entrance on 85th Street, which was then referred to as the "arcade," was completed, and from that point on no student was to use the front door. This rear entrance was not the only part of the building that was incomplete when classes began. Construction of the school had begun in March of that year, but the workmen were able to finish only the first and second floors by the opening of school. The two-tiered auditorium, which was three stories high and seated 1,700, was not ready until shortly before Christmas. It would take even more time to complete the chapel, since the outbreak of war in Europe had prevented the transport of the desired Italian marble. Since the Jesuit superior general had mandated that no classes were to be held above the chapel (probably in consideration of noise), the decision was made to place the library immediately above it.[1] Although the building itself was not yet complete, Regis as an educational institution was fully credentialed, having received a provisional charter from the state's Board of Regents in July 1913.[2]

Despite the fact that everything was new, Father Hearn and Father James Kilroy, S.J., prefect of studies and discipline, quickly settled the boys into a routine with all the rules and procedures clearly laid out. The first bell would ring at 8:50 A.M., and anyone not in his class at that time was considered late. The vagaries of the trains were rarely accepted as a valid excuse for tardiness, but some Regis boys soon figured out a way to deal with public transportation delays. At this time, many of the boys used the very popular Third Avenue Elevated Line to get to school. This train was so popular, in fact, that by the time it neared the stop at East 84th Street, usually there were almost fifty boys who had gathered on the last car, also known as the "Regis car." While the train made its way downtown from the Bronx, the students would chat or help one another with homework.

Once in a while, though, the conductor would announce after the 99th Street stop, that the train would run express to Midtown, an act that certainly would have left the boys late for school. Rather than have to suffer the consequences of this, it was not uncommon for one of the more brazen boys to yank the emergency cord as the train was passing through the 84th Street station. While surely inconvenient to the other passengers, this small act of subterfuge helped to assure the timely arrival of the Regis students and the avoidance of the prefect of discipline.[3]

For those boys who had arrived on time, classes would start at 9:00 A.M., and then the day would be divided into six periods of forty-five minutes each. The daily schedule also included a fifteen-minute break at 10:30 A.M. and thirty minutes for lunch. A morning prayer was said at the beginning of the day, the Angelus recited immediately before lunch, and a final prayer was offered right before dismissal at 2:30 P.M. Since the class (homeroom) teachers usually taught multiple subjects, in the interest of saving time the students themselves did not change rooms for their various courses, but rather their teachers did.[4]

During the morning break, the boys were allowed to socialize in the quadrangle under the watchful eyes and folded wings of Regis's owl. During the second week of classes, this stone bird of prey was placed in the quad above the center door of the auditorium. A resident of East 84th Street long before the building of this new high school, the owl had once surmounted the old Flemish-style Manhattan Garage that had stood on the part of the site where Regis was built. Given his long tenure and now prominent position in the new school, not surprisingly the students adopted him as their mascot.[5] After the morning break while on their way back to classrooms, the boys were allowed to talk until they entered the corridor. Then all conversation had to cease. Students were never permitted to be in a classroom without a teacher present, and teachers were reminded to always keep classrooms locked when unoccupied. If for some reason a boy had not completed his homework from the previous night, he was to see Father Kilroy before the first class. At the prefect of discipline's discretion, the boy might be allowed to make up the work. The students were told that a record would be kept of all these missed assignments to "act as a check on the boys who would be inclined to shirk their work."[6]

For the first couple of weeks of the new school year the boys had to bring their lunches, but on September 28, Regis's lunch counter opened for the first time in the basement cafeteria. Miss Louise Kelly, who worked at the Jesuit rectory across the street, ran the operation. Proceeds from this venture would be used to support the athletic association the school hoped to start up soon. If a boy brought a note from home, he would be permitted to buy "a hot lunch in some nearby restaurant." Few took advantage of this option, which suggests the financial background of most of the new school's first students.[7]

While the boys had been over to St. Ignatius Church in early October for First Friday devotions, it was not until Friday, October 16, that the entire student body gathered for Mass. The occasion was the inaugural Mass of the Holy Ghost with Father Kilroy as the celebrant. Father Hearn delivered the sermon at the conclusion of the Mass, as was often customary at the time.[8] As a treat, that afternoon the entire student body was invited by the Edison Company to visit the Electrical Exposition at the Grand Central Palace. Located on East 46th Street between Lexington and Park Avenues, this huge exhibition hall was an excellent site for such an event, and about one hundred of the students attended. This invitation may have been extended by Nicholas Brady, who was president of the New York Edison Company as well as a very generous member of St. Ignatius parish. The Regians who went to the exposition that afternoon also enjoyed free ice cream.[9]

Entrance Qualifications

In these early days, report card grades were given out eight times each year.[10] On October 26, 1914, a "Reading of the Marks" was held for the first time. Since the auditorium was still not ready, Father Kilroy went from room to room to do this. Any student who had received a 90 percent or above in every subject had his name read aloud as on the "Roll of Honor." For students who had achieved at least an 80 percent in each course, their names would be added to the "List of Merit." Grades under 75 percent were considered failures, and if a boy received two failures in a class for two months in a row, he would be expelled unless there was a health issue or some other mitigating circumstance.[11] By way of warning and to show the primacy of schoolwork above all other school activities, if a boy failed two or more subjects in one marking period, he was immediately suspended from playing on any of the school's athletic teams.[12] In the early years of Regis, there was a very high rate of attrition due to poor grades. For the class of 1921, 224 boys were admitted as freshmen but only 98 graduated four years later. For some classes, the rate of loss was even more extreme. For example, of the 320 boys admitted to the class of 1927 only 110 were awarded diplomas.[13] In the period 1914 to 1933, on average only 48 percent of those admitted as freshman graduated from Regis four years later. Interestingly, this attrition rate was not much greater than the average at public high schools, though, of course, Regis maintained much higher admission standards.[14] An oral history undertaken in the 1980s with some alumni from this period revealed that rules concerning expulsion for academic failure were strictly followed, "with very little leeway given, or any sort of second chance" to those students struggling to keep up.[15] In addition to leaving for academic reasons, a good number of boys each year did not return in the fall (often after just freshman or sophomore year) because they had found work.[16] One of the famous examples of this was John A. Coleman, who stayed for only one year at Regis after finding work to support his family. With his formal education ending with his freshman year of high school, Coleman eventually went on to found a highly successful investment house on Wall Street, and in 1943 he was elected chairman of the New York Stock Exchange. A philanthropist, Coleman in his day was one of the wealthiest Catholics in the country.[17]

As would be expected in an academically demanding Jesuit school of the time, great emphasis was placed on grades, beginning with the admissions process. When in the spring of 1914 Regis first advertised its opening in *The Catholic News*, the school announced in letters to principals of parochial schools that a minimum of 85 percent in all subjects was required. By late August of that year as more boys continued to register, this standard was raised to 90 percent to keep the size of the incoming class manageable. In addition, it is important to remember that in Father Hearn's meeting with the archdiocesan school board, he clearly stated that as was the case at Xavier and Fordham, Regis would be a "select" school offering a "Classical and Scientific Course," though for the first four decades the course offerings in science were quite scanty.[18] It is also worth noting that often in these early years, at the time of registration some boys were sent back to their elementary schools for further documentation to demonstrate that all their grades met the minimum standard. Thus, from the outset, Regis was intended for boys who could handle demanding academic work, though at times exceptions were made for a lower grade.[19]

Years later, Father Daniel Burke, S.J., a member of the class of 1919 who later served as principal of Regis from 1935 to 1940, recalled trying for admission in February 1916. (As was common at other schools at the time, students were admitted in both September and February.) When he showed Father Kilroy his report card from P.S. 45 in the Bronx, the Jesuit told him that Regis could not accept him because he had an 86 percent in mathematics. The boy returned to his elementary school and told his teacher what happened. An Irish Catholic, the woman immediately changed the grade to 96 percent, and according to Burke, who recalled this incident many years later, Kilroy accepted him the next day "without batting an eye." He also remembered Kilroy's many kindnesses to him and other students. For example, if a boy lost his wallet, the priest "would just give you fifty cents and you would pay him back the next day or whenever you could."[20] Burke also remembers the compassion of Father Thomas J. Reilly, S.J., the second prefect of discipline. In Burke's senior year the Jesuit asked him to accompany him to the home of a classmate, Thomas Quigley, who drowned just a few days after graduation while on a Regis outing to Keyser Island near South Norwalk, Connecticut.[21] Burke never forgot this tragedy, and when he became principal, he announced before a school-wide outing to Bear Mountain that the boys were absolutely forbidden to swim in any body of water in the area. After one boy did, Father Burke dismissed him from Regis, saying, "If you are going to drown, you're going to drown on your own time."[22]

By 1920, admission to Regis would require more than simply providing evidence of elementary school grades over 90 percent. In June of that year, the prospective freshmen were the first group to take entrance examinations in English, spelling, arithmetic, and history.[23] Also in these early years only boys who had attended Catholic elementary school could apply to Regis. The only exception made was for boys whose parish did not have a parochial school. This stipulation came largely in response to the American Catholic bishops who had mandated that Catholic parents send their children to parochial schools.

At the Third Plenary Council of Baltimore (1884), the American bishops directed that within two years every parish in the country should build and maintain a parochial school if one did not already exist. In addition, with only a few exceptions, the council mandated that all Catholic parents were bound to send their children to a parochial school, and by 1900 there were over 3,800 of these schools educating almost 900,000 Catholic children.[24] However, even in the days of mostly obedient laypeople and growing numbers of nuns and brothers, this lofty and costly goal was never fully achieved. In placing this requirement of attendance in a Catholic elementary school on prospective students, the Jesuits who started Regis were simply keeping in step with the wishes of the American bishops.[25] In addition, the Jesuits themselves had a very strict policy concerning the admission of non-Catholics to their schools. In 1928, the superior general, Father Wlodimir Ledochowski, in a letter to the entire Society reminded his fellow Jesuits that non-Catholics should be admitted only "with extreme care and discrimination, and with a sincere and earnest endeavor to restrict their number." In fact, he went as far as to say that the presence of non-Catholics was "not in itself desirable, and can at most be tolerated." He also issued strong caution against the hiring of non-Catholic teachers in schools operated by the Society, saying that "the large number in our schools seems to be unwarranted."[26] Thus, the decision to admit only Catholics to Regis came at a time when both the American Church and the Society of Jesus placed tremendous emphasis on providing a Catholic education to Catholic children first and foremost. The openness of Jesuits to admitting non-Catholics to their schools as a good in and of itself would come some decades later, but Regis would continue as the only Jesuit high school in the United States that admits only Catholics.

Father Hearn's attempt to turn Xavier into an all-scholarship high school stands as strong evidence for the need for affordable (if not free) Catholic education. Though at the start of the twentieth century there were a growing number of Catholic families who were able to afford the high tuitions at schools like Loyola or the Convent of the Sacred Heart, by and large the Catholic community in New York City was still quite poor.[27] Beginning around 1880, new waves of Catholic immigrants had poured into New York from Italy and Eastern Europe, joining the steady stream of Irish and Germans who continued to emigrate, though in smaller numbers than before. The Church in New York struggled to keep pace with both the spiritual as well as the material needs of these new arrivals with the building of new parishes and charitable institutions, such as hospitals, orphanages, and schools. In fact, during the first two decades of the twentieth century, the Archdiocese of New York opened eighty-one new parochial schools, which was almost equivalent to the total number founded in the diocese over the course of the entire nineteenth century.[28]

None of the early documents of Regis states that the school was founded exclusively for boys from poor families. However, the reality was that in 1914 paying tuition for a private high school would have been far beyond the reach of most Catholic families. Some Catholic families were so poor, in fact, that even their school-age (preteen) children had to work. Evidence for this can be found in the fact that some parochial schools in New York City conducted night classes for those students who had to work during the day.[29] Xavier's parochial school offered night classes for boys in fifth through eighth grades in typewriting, arithmetic, bookkeeping, and stenography. Classes began at 7:45 in the evening, which gives some indication of how long a day these boys must have been working.[30] One member of the class of 1920 had two older brothers who worked as runners on Wall Street while still in school, since the family found it too difficult to rely completely on the wages their father earned as a waiter.[31] Because of the economic background of many Catholic families, most parochial schools charged a fairly low tuition or accepted a monthly donation, which was true well into the 1950s. These schools were able to remain operational because the sisters and brothers who taught here worked for almost nothing, and the lay teachers earned equivalently low salaries. Archbishop Corrigan saw no real problem with the low wages paid to lay teachers, once commenting that many of them were more than happy to work for "pin money."

In 1914, there were six Catholic high schools for boys in Manhattan and slightly more than a dozen academies for girls (which tended to be smaller), and all these institutions relied heavily on tuition to meet expenses.[32] As stated earlier, some of these schools charged tuition in excess of $200 per year, which obviously would have made them far beyond the reach of most of New York City's Catholic families, some of whom still needed their children to work to make ends meet. In fact, at the time of Regis's opening in 1914, only about 23 percent of all fourteen- to seventeen-year-olds in the entire country were enrolled in high school. Thus, for a majority of American families, not just Catholic ones, they could not offer their sons and daughters a four-year high school education, let alone afford tuition at private high school.[33]

An article written shortly after Regis's founding mentions that in the fall of 1915, 250 boys would be admitted as the second class of Regis and would all come from the "free Catholic schools" of New York. The use of the term "free Catholic schools" again demonstrates the economic background of most of the school's first students. Father Kilroy, who was responsible for registering many of the boys in Regis's first few classes, made this same point in an interview in 1965. He said, "*De facto* those admitted were poor boys . . . for the fact that they came from a parochial school indicated that the parents were not able to send them to a private school." Regis's first prefect of discipline recalled that although the financial condition of the family was not considered at the time of admission, for him and other Jesuits who founded Regis "it was more or less taken for granted that the boys were from homes [that] were not well off."[34] Thus, in the founding of Regis as a free Catholic high school, Mrs. Grant and Father Hearn were clearly responding to the needs of poor and working-class Catholic families, and evidence for this can be found in various documents pertaining to the early years of the school.[35]

As far as permitting only Catholic boys to attend Regis, the early documents mention this in only a few places, but where this stipulation is referenced, it is made quite clear.[36] At his meeting with the archdiocesan school board in 1913, Father Hearn stated plainly that this new school was to be founded in order to "keep Catholic boys out of the public high schools."[37] Historically, as far back as the sixteenth century, Jesuit schools often did admit non-Catholic students.[38] This was also true of the early Jesuit schools in New York in the seventeenth (Latin School) and early nineteenth centuries (New York Literary Institution). However, the presence of Protestant students in these schools was a result of both the fine reputation of the Jesuits as educators as well as the general lack of post–grammar school education in New York in these early days. Once academically rigorous schools were founded under Protestant auspices (e.g., Trinity School in 1709), there was far less need for Protestant families to rely on a Catholic or Jesuit school, as excellent as it might have been.[39] In addition, by the mid-nineteenth century, relations between Catholics and Protestants had turned particularly sour for several reasons, including the failed attempt by Catholic authorities to get state support for parochial schools.[40] Given almost a half century of tensions between Protestants and Catholics, there would have been very few Protestant students in parochial schools at the time of the opening of Regis. Even if there were some non-Catholic students in parochial schools at this time, the central purpose in the foundation of Regis was to help families with less means to secure a Catholic education for their sons. In limiting Regis only to Catholic boys, the intention of the foundress and the Jesuits was not to exclude non-Catholics but rather to respond to the specific educational needs of poorer Catholic families.

Academics in the Early Years

While the 240 boys who started school on September 14, 1914, became the pioneer class of Regis High School, they were not the only students who would be admitted to this class. As was the custom at the time, in February 1915 a new group of 39 boys joined them who would have to undertake accelerated coursework to catch up with their classmates. With this addition, the pioneer class grew to almost 290 students.[41] However, far fewer would endure to graduate. On June 17, 1918, only 74 of these young men were present to receive the school's first diplomas. But in the intervening years, this group of Regians would have the distinction of being the first to do many things in the history of the school, as well as the ones to initiate many customs and traditions. Since they all shared the peculiarity of being both the first and the oldest students in the new school, they soon also began considering themselves "seniors" though technically they were just starting their freshman year.[42] Not long after starting school, the pioneer class began electing class officers for each of the six sections. Since the "F" section was made up of the shortest boys, their taller classmates began referring to them as the "babies." Rather than fight against their diminutive status, they rather embraced it wholeheartedly and chose one of the smallest among them, Frank Caragher, to represent them as their president.[43] Although aspects of student life such as sectional unity were surely important to Regis's first students, the focus for these boys over the next four years would be academics.

Although Regis was surely developing its own local customs in these early years, the school was quite similar to the thirty-five other Jesuit high schools around the nation in terms of its educational philosophy, which placed a strong emphasis on the teaching of the classics. While at this time there was a growing trend in American public school against the classics, in favor of more "practical" studies, Jesuit schools begged to differ.[44] Even the students at Regis themselves came out in support of the classical languages and their literature. In the November 1924 issue of the *Regis Monthly*, senior Victor Dowling offered several reasons for its study, even though "half of us, at least, have resolved upon a future in business." He reminded

Editorial staff of the *Regis Monthly* for the academic year 1925–26. Over the course of the past century, several student magazines and journals have been published, with several of them going out of existence for various reasons. Dormant for decades now, the *Regis Monthly* began in 1917.

his readers that the study of Latin greatly aided in the study of English, whose mastery represented "the greatest social and commercial power." He also argued that the careful examination needed to parse Latin sentences led to "keen perception and the power of analysis applicable to all matters." Finally, Dowling contended that successful students of Latin would develop "directness and clarity of expression," which again is necessary in any of the professions. While surely teenagers of the 1920s no more enjoyed drilling in Latin than do those of today, this evidence suggests that at least some early Regians believed in the importance of its study just as strongly as did their Jesuit teachers and administrators.[45] However, this opinion was by no means universal. One member of the class of 1919 felt there to be an overemphasis on Latin to the detriment of the study of English.[46]

Although the curriculum changed a bit in the first few decades, Regis's early classes spent a good deal of their time engaged in traditional coursework with a heavy emphasis on the study of Latin and Greek. For the first few freshman classes, their school day was divided up taking the following classes:

Latin (twice daily)
English (daily)
Algebra (daily)
Physical geography (three times per week)
Christian doctrine (once per week)
Elocution (once per week)

The last full period of the day was given over to a third period of Latin or another English class, and the day ended with a fifteen-minute catechism class.[47] (By the 1940s catechism was down to ten minutes each day.) In their sophomore year, Greek was introduced and was required for junior and senior years also. As far as the study of modern languages, in sophomore year students were obliged to choose among French, German, or Spanish, but unlike for Greek, they would take this course for two, not three, years.[48]

While most other Jesuit high schools at the time did not require the study of Greek, Regis mandated it for two years for all students until 1943.[49] For those who excelled at this ancient language, the school inaugurated a program that offered a more advanced and intensive study of Greek literature. Eventually called the "Homeric Academy," this seminar was started in December 1922 with eighteen seniors participating. Over the course of the school year, each member would be responsible for translating a few (up to six) of the twenty-four books of Homer's *Iliad,* and would also be held accountable for syntax, appreciation, and a general historical knowledge of the great work.[50] In the spring of their senior year, professors were invited from area colleges—including Columbia, Barnard, and Fordham as well as a few of the leading public high schools—to examine the boys on their translations.[51] The functioning of the Homeric Academy seems to have been somewhat irregular over the next decade or so, but in 1936 a young Jesuit scholastic breathed new life into it by enticing ten students to again take up the challenge.[52] This resurrection of the group proved to be a great success, and in the fall of 1937 thirty-four seniors applied for membership, with only twenty-one being selected. A new scholastic on the faculty, Mr. Walter Burghardt, S.J., who taught Greek to the upperclassmen, was named moderator. The Jesuit began the academy's new season with a series of lectures at their normal meeting time on Tuesday afternoons. In November, Burghardt was able to bring in a visiting Jesuit to give a lecture based on his recent trip to Greece. This professor brought along a series of slides made from photos he had taken on his sojourn. It is unclear if this addition to the presentation proved to be more illustrative or soporific. The students in the academy were also given the chance to display their mastery of the text in front of their classmates. For example, in January 1938 at the "Reading of the Marks" in front of the whole student body, three members would present the well-known "quarrel scene" between Zeus and Hera from Book I. This showcasing of their Greek skills would also serve to spark interest in the academy among juniors.[53]

Opportunity for advanced studies in Latin was also offered when Regis inaugurated the "Virgil Academy" in 1923. Again, a select group of seniors undertook a serious study and translation of classical texts, but here focusing on the twelve books of the *Aeneid.* At the time of its founding, the Virgil Academy began making plans to compete against teams from Boston College High School and Fordham Prep.[54]

Given the school's heavy emphasis on Latin and Greek, the time allotted to math and science was far more modest. As late as 1952, parents of incoming freshmen were reminded that Regis was designed to prepare their sons for admission to a "liberal arts college" rather than for "technical or scientific schools."[55] Given this educational philosophy, it should come as no surprise that up to 1949, mathematics was required for only two years.[56] And as far as science, the course offerings for this discipline were also fairly meager. From 1916 to 1922, one-semester courses in physical geography, zoology, botany, chemistry, and physiology were offered at different times but not concurrently. To make matters worse for those who

Members of the Homeric Academy, 1937. Founded in 1922, the Homeric Academy was a seminar for a small group of seniors who excelled in their study of Greek. The seminar was discontinued in 1984 as a result of changes in the curriculum and school scheduling that made it no longer possible for a student to take three years of Greek.

were interested in science, a member of the class of 1919 remembered the chemistry teacher to have a very heavy German accent, which made learning the topic quite difficult.[57] In 1924, chemistry was dropped for the year and not started up again.[58] However, in 1927 the state education department insisted that at least one year of science be offered at Regis, so over the next eleven years chemistry was offered as an elective nine times, with as many as forty-four students enrolled in it.[59] It would not be until the late 1940s that a minimum of one full year of either chemistry or physics would be required of all students.

It had been a tried and true practice in Jesuit schools for centuries to use competitions as part of the overall educational method, and this was no less true at Regis. In November 1915, a specimen was held in the auditorium in which a group of students who excelled in Latin were given the opportunity to demonstrate their proficiency in front of a larger audience.[60] About three dozen of the better students were seated on stage, with the rest of the freshman class as well as the principal in attendance. Father Kilroy began quizzing the boys on the five Latin declensions, and with an incorrect response, the contestant was asked to leave the stage. When time was called, Section "C" was left with the most boys still in place and so declared the winners.[61] The holding of specimens continued as the pioneer class moved through their high school years, and in 1917 a competition was held among three sections of juniors and two sections of sophomores. In these specimens, sometimes boys competed as teams and sometimes alone.[62]

While proficiency in Latin was emphasized through the holding of these specimens, the importance of the ability to speak before a crowd was stressed in other ways, too. Shortly before Christmas 1915, Section "F" of the sophomores put on an evening production of the "Ancient Mariner" to which even parents were invited. A Jesuit scholastic from Fordham was brought in to "manage a lantern" for the event, and at the end the principal pronounced it a "very creditable exhibition."[63] At the end of the school year a scholastic on staff and a Jesuit from *America* (a weekly journal of news and opinion founded by the Jesuits in 1909) were asked to judge an elocution contest. Six boys were selected from the freshman and sophomore classes to compete, with the winner receiving a medal.[64]

On March 1, 1915, the boys were given another opportunity to practice their public speaking skills, this time in honor of Father Hearn on the feast day of his patron, St. David. A representative from each section came to the stage to offer greetings to their principal, with two delivering their salutations in Latin. Another boy delivered a panegyric in Latin, which was reported to have elicited a "huzzah of applause" from the assembly.[65] In addition, there were also musical performances by students on the piano and the violin. While some of the boys may have enjoyed this assembly honoring their principal, surely the highlight of the day must have come when it was announced that in honor of Father Hearn's feast day, all afternoon classes would be canceled.[66] It is not surprising that several boys were asked to speak publicly and formally at this event, as teaching the art of rhetoric was at the heart of a Jesuit education since the very beginning.

At the time of the founding of Jesuits in the mid-sixteenth century, one of the their most important works was debate with the Protestant reformers, especially with the purpose to win back those who had been lost to

Catholicism. Central to this mission was instructing new Jesuits in effective public speaking, which also was a value of Renaissance humanism in placing rhetoric at the apex of all studies. For learned people of this time, mastery of *eloquentia perfecta* (articulate wisdom) was not just the ability to communicate effectively but also "the capacity to reason, to feel, to express oneself and to act, harmonizing virtue with learning."[67] This important part of Jesuit formation was also made central to the curriculum in the schools run for laymen by the Society and the teaching of rhetoric remained at the heart of Jesuit education in the centuries following, and this was no less true at Regis.[68]

In 1916, the school's first debating society was organized, and the following year Regis hosted its first debate to which the public was invited. This was not an interscholastic debate, but rather only involved juniors (who would have been the oldest boys in the school). At this, these junior debaters were called on to tackle the then very current topic of whether the United States should intervene in the internal unrest in Mexico. In 1918, the first interscholastic debate was held when a group of senior debaters went to a competition against Brooklyn Prep. Assigned to debate the affirmative side of the question of whether "all disputes between Capital and Labor should be settled by legally established courts of arbitration," the Regis team overcame its opponents handily.[69]

Once the school had the full complement of grades in operation, the debating societies were organized into three divisions: the Regis Debating Society for juniors and seniors; the Chrysostom Debating Society for sophomores; and the Xavier and Loyola Debating Societies for freshmen. Over time these societies grew so popular that by 1924 the junior–senior branch had to limit the size of its membership. In late September of that year, so many upperclassmen showed up for the first meeting that it had to be moved from the debating room on the second floor to the auditorium. At the next meeting in early October, again held in the auditorium, it was decided that in order to conform to the group's constitution, the size of the membership had to be reduced to sixty boys. It seems that the size of the debating room necessitated a cap on the size of the membership. Therefore, the scholastic moderator of the group, Mr. Joseph Lennon, S.J., "made known to those who would be temporarily dropped," and then the surviving members made their way to the debating room. Unfortunately, the group's popularity proved to be the undoing of some of the members.[70]

By 1940, the name of the junior–senior branch of debaters had changed to the "Hearn Debating Society" to honor the Jesuit who was so instrumental in founding Regis. While for many years the school did not offer a

Regis Debating Society, 1924–25.

course in public speaking or debate in the formal academic curriculum, this activity always played a large role in the lives of many of the students. This was certainly in keeping with the Jesuit educational tradition of a strong emphasis on building a student's rhetorical skills.

The "Yorkville Colonels" and Other Activities

By the time the first December at Regis rolled around, both faculty and students were surely longing for a respite from their academic labors. Christmas fell on a Friday in 1914, and the school's first students were required to come to school until the Wednesday before. It was decided that classes that day would end at 10:50, and for the first time the auditorium was to be used for a school-wide assembly. After Father Hearn addressed the student body, an "entertainment" conducted by some of the boys was held until noon. However, it was later decided that such a schedule would not be followed again in the future. Some parents complained that their sons could have better spent their time at their regular after-school jobs as errand boys, especially since their delivery services were now in such high demand during the Christmas shopping season. It seemed to make little sense for them to come to school for just a few classes followed by this entertainment and miss these potential wages. Thus, in 1915, while December 23 was still the last day of classes before the Christmas break, no entertainment was held and classes went until 12:15 P.M., followed by the opportunity for confessions.[71]

While this experiment in a pre-Christmas entertainment was far from a success, there would soon be other opportunities for the Regis boys to perform on stage. The first presentation of a full-scale play, however, would have to wait until the spring of 1918. In that year, one performance of Shakespeare's *Henry IV, Part 1* was put on in the school auditorium. While the original play has a few female roles, in Regis's production these roles were omitted. In later years, however, boys would play female roles, as was the custom at most other all-boys schools. The play was put on under the aegis of the "Regis Dramatic Society" with Mr. Leo Andries, a Jesuit scholastic, as the founding moderator. More than seventy-five boys were members of this dramatic troupe with a further dozen or so forming a reception committee. The "Regis High School Orchestra," under the direction of Father James Hayes, S.J., provided the musical accompaniment to the performance with pieces by Mussorgsky and others.[72] This orchestra went on to perform in even more famous venues, and in 1924 it accepted the invitation to play at Town Hall for the Holy Cross production of *Hamlet*.[73]

Over the next two decades the school would put on a Shakespearean play almost every year. By the 1930s the school's strong reputation in dramatics was recognized by even professional actors, and in 1931 Sir Philip Ben Greet, a well-known English stage actor, agreed to serve as an honorary patron of the school's production of *King John*.[74] The next year the school put on *The Merchant of Venice* with Alfred Lunt and Lynn Fontaine lending their names in support. It is not clear if any of these honorary patrons actually came to see the productions. In these early years, Regis did not limit itself only to production of plays by the Bard of Avon. As early as December 1917, a group of seniors put on short play written by Henry Lawrence, a member of the "F" section. And by the 1920s, Regians began putting on contemporary one-act dramas as well.[75]

Like drama, athletics would come to play an important role in the life of the students at Regis, though it would have a delayed start since the lower gym was not available for use until the beginning of the second academic year.[76] While it was not until the early 1940s that physical education became a required course of study, in the school's early days Regis did give its students opportunities to participate in athletics outside of class. In February 1915, the school began organizing an athletic association, and the month before, Regis sent a team to compete in a relay race against other Jesuit schools at Brooklyn College. No mention was made in the Rector's Diary of how the Regis runners performed.[77] While it is not clear how often Regians competed interscholastically in track over the next few years, runners did compete in the Princeton Games in 1922. At these races the school's best performer was junior Billy Menagh, who came in third in the mile.[78] A graduate of Incarnation parochial school on West 170th Street, Billy was universally known and acclaimed by his classmates as the fastest runner in the class.[79] Not surprisingly, he was captain of the track team in his senior year and played on the football and basketball teams.

While Billy and some of his classmates competed against other schools in track and basketball, in these early years football was only an intramural sport. It was not until 1923 that the first varsity football team was fielded, and the students greeted this enthusiastically, with almost sixty coming for tryouts.[80] However, the new team had an awful opening season. Losing all five of its games, the team was shut out three times with a humiliating defeat to Brooklyn Prep with a score of 61–0. For the entire season the Regis squad scored only 18 points while allowing 207 to its opponents. Then things went from bad to worse. In the summer of 1924, the Jesuit scholastic who was coaching the team died suddenly, so the next football season was abruptly canceled.[81]

Dreams of resurrecting the football team did not come to fruition until the fall of 1926, when the call went out for new recruits. According to the 1927 yearbook, "little men with big hearts" rose to the challenge, now playing under the name the "Yorkville Colonels" (a moniker that proved to be mercifully short-lived). Unfortunately, the team's new name brought with it no more success. Again, Regis did not win any games that year, though the scores were tighter this season, with no huge blowouts. The Colonels' only non-defeat was a tie against a team from St. Francis Academy in Brooklyn, with neither side scoring any points. A ray of hope appeared in the 1928 season with the Colonels' first win, this time over Iona Prep by a score of 7–0.[82]

The fall of 1929 brought the Regis football team its best season ever. Just two days after Black Tuesday and the start of the Great Depression, Regis played Xavier. Leading at the half with a score of 18–6, Regis withstood a furious fourth-quarter attack by Xavier, winning the game with a final score of 18–14. Two weeks later, the Regis squad continued to steamroll the opposition, shutting out Hamilton Institute, 25–0. The last game of this year, however, would prove to be Regis's greatest. While the tradition of Fordham playing Xavier on Thanksgiving Day had yet to take a firm hold, the Rams took on the team from Regis, which had retired the "Colonels" nickname and was now calling itself the "Crimson and White." With strong defenses on both sides, the first half ended scoreless. The hero of this titanic struggle was Regis's own Ed Malloy, who scored the game's first touchdown in the third quarter as well as kicking the extra point. After returning the ball to the Rams, Malloy "materialized from nowhere," intercepted a pass, and ran from the midfield to the Fordham end zone untouched. And that was not the end of it. Malloy scored one more touchdown, and when the final whistle was blown, the Rams had been shut out by a score of 20–0. For the first and only time, Regis took the championship of the Metropolitan Private School League.[83]

This football season also saw the introduction of eight official "Regis Cheers," which were printed up on small but handy index cards for use by the team's boosters. The cheers used a combination of sounds, such as "Grrrrr—," "Hoo—rah," and "Rah," and even loud whistles in one of them.[84] Far more memorable (and longer lasting) than these cheers was the Regis alma mater, composed in the late 1920s. Looking for an anthem to sing while at football games, Mr. John Diehl, S.J., a scholastic who was athletic moderator at the time, turned for advice to Mr. Daniel Burke, S.J., a Regis alumnus who was spending his regency at the nearby Loyola School. He suggested that Diehl adapt the Weston Jesuit Seminary school song, which he did by simply writing new lyrics.[85]

Unfortunately, the football team's salad days proved to be short-lived. With the loss at the end of the academic year of a few outstanding seniors, most notably Ed Malloy, the team found itself rebuilding in the 1930 season and losing all its games, including an embarrassing shutout by Fordham Prep, 52–0. And as time would prove, there would be no opportunity for a Regis comeback. Citing the late start of the next school year because of a vicious outbreak of infantile paralysis as well as the continuing difficulty in securing a place to practice, the school decided in the fall of 1931 to end football as an interscholastic sport.[86] Reluctant to see the sport disappear completely, a few classes organized intramural matches in Central Park.[87] As late as 1933, some Regians were still holding out hope that the football program would resurrect itself from the dead once again, but their hopes would never be realized. For many years, rumors circulated among the students as to the "real" reason for the sport's demise, and one of the more colorful of these held that the team was abolished due to the gory death of one of the Regis players during a game.[88] However, there is no evidence to support this, other than the overactive imagination of teenage minds. The causes of the death of football at Regis seem to have been far more ordinary.

In the vacuum left by the demise of football, a few new sports were started up, including tennis and golf. However, the athletic mainstays remained track and basketball, the latter of which the 1933 *Regian* claimed was "becoming as popular a sport as football" in the country.[89] By the mid-1930s, the varsity squad was known as the "Maroon and White," the junior varsity as the "Owls," and the freshman squad as the "Wrens." A Jesuit scholastic, Mr. Louis McKay, had organized the first interscholastic basketball team in 1916, and he and other Jesuits in training stayed very involved in the sport, often serving as coaches of the various squads over the next several decades.[90]

Over time, places were even found for those Regians who lacked talent or interest in drama, athletics, or music. In 1933, a group of boys attempted to found a "Philatelic Society," but it was not until the following year that the organization was formally recognized, largely thanks to the help of Mr. Charles McBride, one of the six young Jesuit scholastics on the faculty. Preferring this name rather than the more ignoble "Stamp Club," the members prided themselves on their hard work in collecting stamps and bundling them to the Jesuit seminary in Woodstock, Maryland, to be sold and then used to help support Jesuit missions around the world. Mr. McBride was also the moderator of the chess club, which by 1937 had thirty-five members. This group could boast its own meeting room equipped with

Basketball team, 1917–18. Organized athletics date to the earliest days of the school, with the founding of the Regis Athletic Association by Mr. Louis McKay, S.J., in 1915.

several chessboards. The club was an active participant in a chess league, which included both Catholic and public schools, sending four-man teams to the various competitions.[91] Arguably the most obscure of student organizations was a model club that was formed in the mid-1930s. Like the chess club, this group, too, could boast its own room on the third floor, where its members would display their carved boats and planes. This helped model enthusiasts find a way to bring a communal dimension to their avocation, and so offered the opportunity for fellowship for those who might have found group socialization difficult.[92]

The Taylor Thesis

The approach in 1939 of the silver anniversary of the school proved to offer more than just the occasion for a nostalgic look back at the past. It also offered the opportunity to undertake a serious evaluation and review of the education offered by Regis over its first twenty-five years, the bulk of which (1914–30) is the concern of the present chapter. In 1938, Mr. Charles Taylor, S.J., undertook such a project. After teaching as a scholastic at Regis from 1935 to 1937, during which time he was the founding moderator of *The Owl*, the Jesuits next sent him for a master's degree at St. Louis University.[93] For his thesis topic, Taylor decided to focus on his former religious assignment, Regis High School.[94] Titled "A Study of an Endowed American Jesuit Secondary School," Taylor's study was not so much a history of the school but rather a careful examination of the reasons for the "school's success in scholastic and extracurricular activities." In addition, he compiled a careful comparison of pedagogy in place at Regis against "modern educational principles" in his effort to demonstrate the superiority of the former. Not surprisingly, Taylor saw the pedagogy in place to be very much rooted in "Catholic humanism," which Taylor argued is the distinctive quality of all Jesuit education.[95]

Though Taylor does not specifically refer to this in his thesis, it could be argued that the bas-relief "Religio," which is located on the first-floor landing of the main staircase of the school, was a good artistic representation of Regis's pedagogical foundation. Installed at the time the school was built, this curious combination of figures from classical antiquity cheek-by-jowl with Christian churchmen is clearly meant to remind students of the foundations of their Jesuit education. In 1926, then-sophomore Harry Kirwin wrote a long piece for the *Regis Monthly* on the meaning of "Religio," a work of art his classmates would often "dash [past] on their way to confession" each week. Under the scene is etched the Latin phrase "Religio Ingeniorum Moderatrix et Altrix Scientiarum Parens et Magistra" (Religion [Is] the Governor of Inborn Talents and Mother/Protector and Teacher of the Sciences). Arguing for the centrality of religion at a Jesuit school, Kirwin goes to great lengths to explain how the various figures depicted in the bas-relief represent the different fields of human learning. Nevertheless, all are gathered to sit under the abstract character of "Religion" offering each her "benevolent protection."[96] Although this artwork was placed in a central location in the school to emphasize the importance of what it represented, ironically most students did not pass by it on a regular basis. Up until 1972, only faculty and seniors were allowed to use this main staircase. However, as mentioned above by Kirwin, the one exception to this rule at this time was for boys on their way to confession.[97]

After laying out the foundational principles on which the school was founded, Taylor then takes up the question of why Regis's students have performed so well over the school's first quarter century. He readily admits that given the school's high degree of selectivity, there should be little surprise at this. As an endowed high school, Regis was "independent of the pressure so commonly exerted by financial difficulties," which often require schools to accept or retain weak students out of need of their tuition dollars. However, it is Taylor's argument that this selectivity alone cannot account for the many achievements of Regians. Rather, Taylor holds that the secret to the school's success is to be found in the carefully planned program of study put in place at the school's founding, which its administrators have continued to finely tune ever since. According to Taylor, it was not enough just to gather a group of bright boys into one school; these students would need an effective method of education to bring out the best in them. The school has clearly been able to do this, and Taylor saw Regis's highly successful program of studies to be tripartite. First, the school had maintained a curriculum firmly rooted in the classics despite the disfavor it had found with some American educational theorists as early as the 1930s. Second, Regis has continually put a strong emphasis on spiritual formation, which is seen "as a dynamic force giving energy to the whole life of the student." And finally, keeping in mind Juvenal's maxim "Mens sana in corpore sano" (A sound mind in a sound body), an appropriate program of physical and recreational activities was in place for the students as well.[98]

At the beginning of his thesis, Taylor uses an interesting metaphor to describe the type of education offered at Regis. According to him, Regis "does not accept Jacksonian democracy" in the sense of a strong belief in radical egalitarianism demanding the equal and same education for all. Rather, Regis holds to the Jesuit tradition of educating the "natural, intellectual aristocracy." While the ten other Jesuit schools of the Maryland–New York Province were also rooted in this tradition and considered excellent institutions, Regis's unique selectivity has allowed it to stand head and shoulders above these others. For example, from 1922 to 1930, Regis students were required to take provincial exams, as were those boys attending the eleven other Jesuit high schools in the province. These tests were corrected at the local school and then sent for re-grading on the provincial level, where the scores were tabulated for comparative purposes. In every year and for every test, Regis produced the highest average scores. Because of this, in 1931 Regis was no longer required to submit these exams for re-grading by the province, though the students were still required to take the tests.[99]

In the spring of 1937, Regis was again included in the provincial comparison, and not surprisingly, again came out on top. The newly founded newspaper, *The Owl*, crowed over the school's accomplishment, proudly pointing out that Regis's average was "ten points higher than that of the nearest competitor." As reported in Taylor's thesis, Regis's score was only 9.3 percent higher than its nearest competitor. The author of *The Owl* article

Football team, mid-1920s. Regis's first varsity football team was fielded in 1923, but the sport would ultimately have a short life at the school, with the team playing its last season in the fall of 1930.

may have had access to different scores or may not have yet mastered number rounding. In any case, the newspaper reported that the students did not claim sole responsibility for their "triumph." Rather, the boys humbly admitted that they owed "a huge debt of gratitude to their patient instructors."[100] In addition, in 1937 Regians sat for the first time for the New York State Regents exams. This decision would allow students to qualify for college scholarships funded by the state that were directly linked to performance on these exams.[101] Despite the financial incentive involved in earning a Regents diploma, the practice of having Regians take these exams did not last long.

Another major concern Taylor raised in his thesis was the high "mortality" (expulsion of students for poor grades) rate of students. Taylor had performed a careful examination of the numbers of boys entering Regis but not graduating four years later, and computed the average mortality rate for the period 1914–33 to be 52 percent. Not surprisingly, he found this number to be troubling. Since the school already had in place what it considered to be a rigid selection process based on the entrance examinations, why were so many of these prescreened students not making it through Regis's academic program?[102]

Interestingly, Regis's mortality rate was actually not that much higher than the average rate at American public schools, which hovered around 50 percent in the years 1927–32. However, few of these schools could be or were as selective as Regis in admissions. In his analysis, Taylor has little sympathy for the opinion that this high mortality rate was an "injustice." In response to such a position, Taylor argues that "the boys were free to enter the school, and were explicitly told of the rigid requirements, and that only about half who enter graduate." For him, the answer was not to find ways to help struggling students stay at Regis. Rather, the screening process needed to be improved; perhaps the administration of IQ tests to the applicants would be a solution. He thought this might be a more precise indicator of success than the admissions exams currently in use. At the time of his writing, St. Louis University High School was experimenting with the use of IQ tests in their admissions process. Taylor did not think that the use of such tests would be a cure-all, but he considered them certainly worth trying. In 1937, even the principal, Father Burke, spoke in favor of using IQ tests. Despite this, they were never tried, and Regis has continued to use entrance exams (not intelligence tests) as part of its admissions process.[103]

The Effects of a Regis Education

In 1935, the Alumni Association began publishing a quarterly newsletter under a variety of different titles (*Alumnus News, Regis Alumni*). While interest in much of the contents of these newsletters was transitory, reading them now, decades later, can give a glimpse into the professional lives of so many of the alumni, their strong loyalty to the school, and in several cases the testimonies of some as to how much they credited their Regis education to their successes in life. A demonstration of their continued devotion to the school can be seen in the huge attendance at the various alumni events held each year. For example, at the annual "smoker" held in December 1938, more than five hundred graduates showed up, which represented almost a quarter of the entire alumni population.[104] Another example of the importance some alumni attached to their Regis education can be found in an article in an early issue of the alumni newsletter by Edward F. Bowes, '24: "We entered Regis without regard to our parents' wealth or poverty. The only entrance requirement was an ability to learn and a willingness to be taught. In return for that small requisite we received an education that could not be duplicated for any amount of money, anywhere—an education, which had it not been freely given, many of us would have had to forgo. When we graduated, colleges and employers readily conceded our scholarship. Today the public esteem which Regis enjoys is a constant source of satisfaction and pride."[105] Worth noting is Bowes's remark about how so many of them would not have been able to afford a Regis education had they been required to pay, and how many doors would not have been opened to them had they not had access to this superior Jesuit education. Some of the doors now open to them included, of course, a college education, for which many of Regis graduates received scholarships, as they had for their high school education. Not only did Mrs. Grant fund several scholarships at Fordham University for Regis graduates (see below), other Jesuit colleges also awarded full-tuition scholarships to the school's alumni. In fact, almost one-fifth of the class of 1936 were able to earn their undergraduate degrees at Jesuit colleges because of this.[106] All of this financial aid again demonstrates the economic need of the first couple of generations of Regians, especially in the years before the Second World War.

Not surprisingly the pages of these newsletters are dotted with references to Regis alumni who have entered the diocesan seminary, the Jesuit novitiate, or had been recently ordained. The boom in vocations among Regians reached such a height that by 1937 the school could boast (and did) that since the graduating class of 1918, 247 Regians (out of total alumni population of 2,035) had pursued a vocation to the priesthood or religious life (yielding a "vocation rate" of slightly more than 12 percent).[107] For the ordination class of 1937 for the Archdiocese of New York, seven of the *ordinandi* were graduates of Regis from the late 1920s.[108] One of the graduates from the school's early years who entered the priesthood eventually was promoted to the highest ranks of the clergy.

John J. Maguire, '21, was from a working-class neighborhood of the Bronx near Fordham Road when he won his Regis scholarship.[109] In terms of his class background, he was very representative of the other Regians who eventually went to the seminary, though his career in the church was not. Sent to Rome for his priestly studies, he was ordained in 1928, just having turned twenty-four a few weeks earlier. After his return to the states, the young priest was assigned to work in a mostly Italian parish on the Lower East Side thanks to his ability to speak Italian. In 1940, Maguire was chosen to work in the chancery, eventually being named chancellor of the archdiocese by Francis Cardinal Spellman in 1946. Named a monsignor two years later, he continued his rise up the ecclesiastical ranks with his promotion to vicar general in 1953. In 1959, Spellman ordained him an auxiliary bishop. After attending the Second Vatican Council, in 1965

Pope Paul VI named his coadjutor archbishop of New York, a title that sometimes did lead to becoming archbishop, though it did not for Maguire. A highly competent administrator, Archbishop Maguire was also known as Spellman's close aide, in charge of the day-to-day operations of the archdiocese while Spellman was often busy with national and international church affairs. In addition to his work in ecclesiastical administration, Maguire was also known for his involvement in issues beyond the church's door, especially in his support of racial justice, writing a letter encouraging both priests and laypeople to attend the August 1963 March on Washington (and which he directed was to be read in the parishes at Mass the weekend before). In addition to his advocacy for civil rights, he was an outspoken supporter of ecumenism and frequently participated in joint services with clergymen from other faiths. Maguire also took a special interest in the growing Hispanic population in the parishes, learning Spanish and often traveling to Puerto Rico.[110]

While 12 percent of the graduates of the school pursued religious vocations, the rest did not. However, most of them did share similar socioeconomic backgrounds with those destined for the priesthood, and because of their Regis education many rose to prominence in their chosen professions. A member of the pioneer class of 1918, George A. Brooks was from a five-flight walk-up apartment on the far East Side of Manhattan as well as a graduate of a parochial school.[111] After Regis he went on to Fordham for his undergraduate studies and then to the law school. After working at two private law firms, in 1934 he landed a job at the legal division of General Motors. In 1947, he was named head of this division and remained here until his retirement in 1965. Because of this office, his name was known to General Motors stockholders, as his signature was on millions of its stock certificates.[112] During his career at GM, he also earned a master's degree in law from New York University, after which he taught for several decades at Fordham Law School. He was also involved in charitable work, serving on the board for the Lavelle School for the Blind and the Westchester Legal Aid Society, and was among the first laymen named to Fordham University's Board of Trustees in 1964.

Like George Brooks, John V. Connorton, '30, was from the far East Side of Manhattan and was also a graduate of his parish grammar school.[113] His Regis education ultimately helped prepare him for a highly successful and varied professional life that included university-level teaching, public service, and hospital administration. After graduating from Regis, Connorton went on to earn multiple degrees from Fordham, including a doctorate in medieval history in 1944. After teaching history for a few years at

Fordham, at the beginning of World War II he joined the navy, where he eventually rose to the rank of lieutenant commander and the position of executive secretary of the Joint Army–Navy Intelligence Board. After the war, he remained in uniform, becoming special assistant to James V. Forrestal, secretary of the navy, while also helping to establish the new Department of Defense. After his time in Washington, he embarked on a new career in health care administration, eventually becoming president of the Greater New York Hospital Association. Because of his friendship with Mayor Robert F. Wagner, twice during Wagner's time in office Connorton was named to high-ranking city posts, including deputy mayor in 1965. During his time in all these different positions, Connorton still found the time to earn a law degree from Fordham in 1955. In addition to all these professional achievements, Connorton was a lay leader in church affairs, serving as Catholic cochair for the National Conference of Christians and Jews and as a member of the Catholic Interracial Council. He was married to Grace Guerin, with whom he raised six children.[114]

These thumbnail sketches of a few alumni who went on to notable success in a variety of fields can help to put flesh on the post-Regis trends of the 1,238 alumni from the first twelve graduating classes (1918–29). The only extant source for this broader kind of analysis is the first Alumni Association directory from 1958. Though by no means is a full analysis of the lives of Regians after graduation possible to do because of deaths (the oldest alumni would have been approaching the age of sixty by then) and lost alumni, the investigation that is possible can give some indication of the careers and professional lives of the graduates from the school's earliest years. The "Occupational List" section of the directory divides the alumni into more than one hundred categories ranging from accounting and thoracic surgeons to harbor pilots and trading stamps. By far, graduates who had become lawyers dominated, with 127 graduates from the classes of 1918 through 1929 still practicing law in 1958. After attorneys, the next most popular "profession" was being a part of the Jesuits, with 53 men from this period taking vows as members of the Society of Jesus. Other popular careers included civil servants (37), teachers (37), accountants (15), and physicians (37). Only eight men from this period became engineers, though it is worth noting that the percentage of graduates from the next decades (1930s and 1940s) going into the field was much higher. Unfortunately, this directory does not include the colleges or universities these alumni went on to graduate from, though with rare exception (such as to study engineering) all the graduates who went on to college matriculated at Catholic institutions.[115]

Strained Relations with Mrs. Grant

During these early years after the start of Regis, Mrs. Grant and her children remained in regular contact with the successive rector–presidents, who informed the founding family of the ongoing developments in the school. In addition, the Grants continued to provide financial support to the school and other Jesuit apostolates, while always demanding strict anonymity and eschewing any official recognition or public thanks for their uncommon generosity.

While she had provided all the funding for the construction of the new school, it was not until the end of October 1914 that Mrs. Grant actually saw the building. She had sailed for Europe on March 17, when construction on the school had just started. Returning to New York on October 28, she was given a private tour a few days later by Father Hearn, who described her as "enraptured over the wonderful beauty of the building." She was so pleased with the present state of things that at the conclusion of her tour she announced that she would give an additional $200,000 to Regis (above the initial promise of $1.5 million). With this additional money, the school would now have close to a $1 million foundation from which to support its operating costs. Thus, with her final payment on April 8, 1915, of $200,000, Mrs. Grant had now given a total of $1.725 million toward Regis, which included the purchase of property, construction, and endowment. This amount did not include smaller gifts that Mrs. Grant began giving in 1915 for causes such the altar in the chapel ($5,500), the outfitting of the library ($10,000), or scholarships for Regis graduates attending Fordham ($10,000).[116]

Although the founding of Regis was built solidly on Mrs. Grant's strong relationship with Father Hearn, she would soon have to deal with the other Jesuits who would come to administer the school. On September 27, 1915, Father Hearn was transferred from Regis to Canisius College in Buffalo, where he was made dean. Despite Hearn's removal from Regis, Mrs. Grant remained in regular contact with him, even traveling often to Buffalo to see him. When he became ill, one summer she took him to a house she had rented in New Hampshire so he could recuperate in more salubrious surroundings, but her kindness would not be enough to save his life.[117] His 1917 obituary in the *Woodstock Letters* claimed that the transfer from Regis came due to his "declining health." However, there are strong indications that his removal had far more to do with serious disagreements he had with his superiors.[118] While the plans to start a free Catholic high school were still in the discussion stages, some Jesuits, including the man who would become the provincial, Father Anthony Maas, thought that Mrs. Grant's proposed gift would be better spent by building a new Jesuit seminary in Yonkers rather than establishing a free high school. And Maas and an influential group of other Jesuits strongly believed that Hearn should have done more to convince her of this. However, the depth of their disdain for her decision to found a free high school was nothing less than amazing. In addition to conflicts with these Jesuits, a few documents from the period suggest that Hearn's removal also had to do with differences he had with the editors of *America* magazine, but unfortunately there is no evidence extant to indicate the nature of their disagreement.[119]

Shortly after Maas took office, Hearn began hearing rumors that the new provincial "claimed [Hearn] had diverted money to [founding Regis] that should have been given to Lilienthal [site of proposed seminary in Yonkers]." While Hearn did his best to keep these rumors from reaching Mrs. Grant, Maas wound up writing directly to the foundress, expressing his disapproval of this new school and claiming that "it made his heart bleed to give her men for her high school when he had so much more important work for them to do." Not unexpectedly, these sentiments from the provincial greatly upset Mrs. Grant.[120] But little did she know that this disapproval went all the way to the way to the top of the Jesuit order.

In the summer of 1914, Mrs. Grant and her children made a trip to Europe. While in Rome, they had an audience with Father Wernz, the superior general. Although the meeting began pleasantly enough with the general showering "many kindnesses . . . [toward] her," it did not end as well. Father A. J. Elder Mullan, an American Jesuit working at the Curia, was also at this meeting.[121] Toward the end of this meeting, he intervened, saying that "she was giving a white elephant to the Society and American boys were too proud to go to a free high school." Upon hearing this belittling of her generous gift, Mrs. Grant told Hearn that she nearly collapsed and had to be "rushed away from [Mullan] and Rome."[122]

Although Wernz's death on August 19, 1914, brought a change in power at the highest level of the Jesuits, the new general, Father Wlodimir Ledochowski, seemed no more disposed to Mrs. Grant's establishment of Regis than did his predecessor. Shortly after Ledochowski's election, Mullan, who had remained working in Rome, wrote to Mrs. Grant, saying that he and the new general were of "one mind" in thinking the founding of Regis to be poorly conceived. Mrs. Grant claimed that Mullan even told her that "she should not leave her money to her children but to give it to God while she lived." Reiterating his desire to see her money used to build a new Jesuit seminary, Mullan said that in her meeting with Wernz a couple of years earlier, the recently deceased general "had been on the point of asking her to drop the Regis idea and give her gift [toward building a new seminary]." After receiving this letter, Mrs. Grant concluded that Mullan and Maas were "in collusion."[123]

Mullan's letter occasioned a bitter exchange with Mrs. Grant. In response to the Jesuit's initial missive, Mrs. Grant was firm and clear. She began by telling the high-ranking Jesuit that it was "cruel" of him to tell her of Wernz's disapproval of the founding of Regis now that he was dead. She added that if Wernz had asked her to drop her plans for Regis and to build the seminary instead, she "would have gone elsewhere with her gift." She ended by asking him to show her letter to the new general "so that there could be no further misunderstanding." Mullan responded to her letter with particular venom. According to Mrs. Grant, Mullan said that he would not show her letter to the general as "he did not wish him to have a bad opinion of her." He then went on to say that although she had been named a "Founder of the Society" because of her tremendous generosity, she was really a founder in name only. Mullan claimed that only those donors who built a scholasticate (house of studies for seminarians) for the Society could be considered founders. Those who built "mere colleges" (high schools) could only hold this as a courtesy title.[124]

After this unfortunate volley of letters and Mullan's refusal to show Mrs. Grant's letter to the general, she consulted with Father Hearn about what to do next. Because he was so close to the situation and had already been criticized by members of his own order about his supposed undue influence of her, Hearn recommended that she put the question "before two grave Fathers of the Society in confession who would tell her what to do." After following his suggestions, both priests were shocked at the behavior of their fellow Jesuits and agreed that she should send copies of Mullan's letters directly to the general. In doing this, Mrs. Grant also told Ledochowski about Maas's unpleasant words concerning her intended donation.[125]

Eventually Mrs. Grant received a response from the general, who thanked her for writing and entrusting him with her confidence. He told her that what Mullan had said about founders and the Society was "absolutely false." The Society made no distinction between those who endowed colleges and those who endowed scholasticates. This brought some comfort to Mrs. Grant, but she was still left with some unresolved issues. She was less than satisfied in that the General had said "nothing to indicate that he looks on such letters or methods [of Mullan and Maas] as a disgrace to the Society." Mrs. Grant also predicted that Mullan and Maas would walk away from this whole affair unscathed and undisciplined. In this, she turned out to be quite accurate. In 1915, Mullan was recalled from

Rome and for a brief time was assigned to New York City. This situation put the foundress in an awkward situation. Aware that she knew this Jesuit from her visit to Rome and meeting with the general, some friends began to ask her if she had seen Mullan now that he was living nearby. Once in New York, Mullan did actually try to make contact with Mrs. Grant, and when that failed, he even reached out to the children. She and her family rebuffed these overtures, and thankfully Mullan was soon transferred to Philadelphia, where he spent the rest of his life.[126]

In these early years another issue caused significant tension between Mrs. Grant and the Jesuits, and this had to do with the use of the Regis building itself. In 1916, it came to Mrs. Grant's attention that Father J. Richards Havens, the rector–president of Regis as well as pastor of St. Ignatius, was allowing space in the school to be at used on occasion by persons other than Regis students. Entries in the Rector's Diary note that the Loyola School used the Regis auditorium for its production of the *Merchant of Venice* and that the parish held a dance there for the Ladies Sodality.[127] When Mrs. Grant learned the building was being used for such purposes, she wrote immediately to Father Havens, expressing her displeasure. Only shortly before this, in November 1916, the school auditorium had been used as a banquet hall for a celebration in honor of the golden jubilee of St. Ignatius Church. The school was done up quite elaborately, including a gift from Nicholas Brady's Edison Company of gold and white electric lights (in honor of the papal colors) strung in the quad. But even events that attracted high-ranking ecclesiastics such as the cardinal and the papal delegate were not to be allowed at Regis, according to Mrs. Grant, unless they were school-related.[128] After reading this letter from her, Father Havens described the foundress as in a "state of intense exasperation." She blasted him for violating the agreement that she had made with the Jesuits at the time of the school's founding that the building would be used exclusively for classes and activities of Regis students.[129]

Mrs. Grant demanded that the provincial and Havens sign a formal agreement promising never to allow the building to be used by outside groups. Havens strongly recommended to the provincial that they both sign the contract. If not, he feared that "we are likely to lose this great benefactor permanently."[130] Not surprisingly, both Jesuits immediately signed the agreement. In doing this, they gave their assurance to the "Donor of Regis High School for Catholic boys" that the building and its foundation would be used "purely for educational purposes of the Institute of the Society of Jesus." They further agreed that the building would never be used "for parochial affairs . . . or for anything akin to the Young Men's

Cast of *Julius Caesar*, fall 1939. As was custom in all-male schools at the time, boys played the female roles. In addition to this Shakespearean production, during the 1939–40 academic year the Regis Dramatic Society also performed *The Nativity of Our Lord* by Robert Hugh Benson shortly before Christmas, and the comedy *Brother Orchid* by Leo Brady in the spring.

Christian Association." Lastly, the document stipulates that a copy of the agreement is to be kept "for all time in the archives of Regis High School." While this promise is no longer adhered to since the school has for some time allowed outsiders (though usually groups associated with a Jesuit apostolate or school) to use space in the building, a copy of the contract can still be found in the archives of the school.[131]

Despite these most unfortunate interactions with a few high-ranking Jesuits, Mrs. Grant never lost her love and respect for the Society. Clearly, part of this had to do with her relationship with Father Hearn. However, even after his death in 1917, she and her family continued to remain close to the Society and to support its various works, including Regis. For example, in 1919 the foundress wrote to Father Kilroy in his new position as rector–president of Regis and the Jesuit community with a proposal for her to build a separate residence for the Jesuits working at Regis. At that time, the Jesuits teaching at the school lived with Jesuits engaged in other area apostolates in a series of brownstones on East 83rd Street between Park and Madison Avenues as well as on the top floor of the Loyola School.[132] Despite her very generous proposal, Jesuit superiors never acted on the offer. However, she made some major gifts to other apostolates of the Society. Beginning in the late 1930s she began funding a series of burses to help defray the cost of Jesuits doing graduate work at secular universities. Because of this donation, she was again named a "Founder of the Society."[133]

The family's generosity continued even after the death of the foundress in 1944. By 1951, the three children, none of whom was yet married, had donated $1.8 million to the construction of a new Jesuit seminary to be constructed in Shrub Oak, New York.[134] The Grant children originally had given a $500,000 gift to the province in memory of their mother, leaving it up to the provincial to decide where best to spend it. He suggested that the money be put toward the building of the chapel at the new seminary, and with that the children continued to give even more money toward the completion of this house of studies. For their great generosity, in 1960 Julia, Edna, and Hugh were all named "Founders of the Provinces of New York and Buffalo." In honor of this distinction, the provincial asked the 770 priests in the two provinces to offer three Masses each for the intentions of the Grant children, and for the 558 scholastics and 98 brothers to say three rosaries.[135] With this promise of a massive amount of prayer from the more than one thousand Jesuits, the provincial surely hoped that he could demonstrate the Society's deep appreciation for a family whose generosity seemed to know no limits.

Conclusion

With a student registration of 829 at the opening of the 1930–31 school year, Regis had the fourth-largest enrollment of the twelve Jesuit high schools on the East Coast.[136] While members of the pioneer class were almost all from New York City, with a few from New Jersey and Westchester, within a few years boys were coming in from Connecticut, demonstrating the school's quick rise to prominence in the wider metropolitan area (though most were still coming from working class suburban areas such as Yonkers and Elizabeth and Bayonne, New Jersey).[137] While the size of the student body had continued to increase and expand in geographic diversity since 1914, the school itself developed and matured over the first decade and a half of its existence. By 1926, the original faculty of six had now grown to twenty-six, comprising five Jesuit priests (including the rector–president), seven Jesuit scholastics, and fourteen laymen.[138] In addition, in September 1923 a new position on the faculty was created. Father Peter Dolan, S.J., was appointed the first spiritual director (later to be called school counselor) of Regis. As with other Jesuit schools that had also added this position, this appointment allowed one Jesuit to focus his time exclusively on the spiritual development of the students as well as being able to help with other personal matters (both inside and outside the classroom).[139] On a more practical level, the first telephone line was installed in the school shortly before Christmas in 1916. At the cost of forty dollars per year for eight hundred calls, the phone was placed in the office of the prefect of studies with the number "LEnox 7547."[140] At this time, the prefect of studies functioned for all practical purposes as a principal in that he was responsible for the running of the school. While the rector was the head of the entire school, for much of the school's history this Jesuit had little daily contact with the school. In fact, the students would generally see him only a few times each year.

Besides these developments, there were still other signs of the school's growing reputation. With larger numbers of eighth graders applying for admission each year (over five hundred in 1924), the entrance examination became more formal.[141] By 1930 Regis had begun sending parochial school principals a four-page "Syllabus of Entrance Requirements" detailing the areas that would be tested. Prospective students would be examined on English grammar and would also be required to write an essay in "correct and coherent English" based on a given topic sentence. As for mathematics, no prior knowledge of algebra or geometry was necessary but only a "thorough understanding of arithmetic." Gone were the days when in 1914 the pioneer class had simply to provide proof of 90 percent or above in all courses.[142]

In addition to the continuing poor performance of the football team, the first years of Regis also had their share of sorrow amid the many successes and reasons for celebration. On May 13, 1916, the first Regis student died. After a "long siege of pneumonia and pleurisy," freshman Emile X. Huerstel passed away, two months shy of his fifteenth birthday.[143] A graduate of P.S. 29, Emile was from East 134th Street in the Port Morris section of the Bronx. And in November 1923, Father William Murphy, S.J., became the first Regis teacher to die. A mathematics instructor at the school for three years, Murphy was buried at the Jesuit novitiate in Poughkeepsie with the entire Jesuit faculty of Regis present for the funeral Mass. On the first school day after his death, classes were dismissed at 1 P.M. "out of respect for the deceased."[144]

Despite these losses, these early years of Regis brought far more happy days than sad ones. In 1918, in honor of the declaration of the armistice ending the First World War, Father Kilroy canceled classes for the rest of the day. To celebrate, a group of Regians went over to the Metropolitan Museum, but they were eventually thrown out for making too much noise.[145] With the coming of economic depression and war, however, new challenges would be brought to bear on the students and their school far more serious than an unhappy museum docent.

3

"See You in North Africa!" Regis Through the Depression and World War II

> We might say that another year at Regis is underway. But "another year" simply does not hold true. . . . Our nation is fighting an uphill battle for its very existence in this Second World War . . . a victory by the Axis powers would be catastrophic, inasmuch as Christianity and our present civilization would be lost, perhaps for hundreds of years.
>
> —Editorial, *The Owl*, October 16, 1942

Regis During the Depression

When the class of 1933 began their first day of classes at Regis on September 5, 1929, little did they know that practically the entirety of their high school career would take place during the Great Depression, a time in which national unemployment rate would top 25 percent and New York City would see one-third of its factories shutter their doors. However, it would take some time for the nation to realize the impact of the stock market crash on October 29, 1929. In fact, in the entry for that day in the Prefect's Diary, Father Archdeacon simply noted, "Regular Class Order." Despite this quotidian description of one of the darkest days in American history, by no means were the school and its students ultimately unaffected by the collapse of the national economy. Since the school's endowment[1] was invested almost exclusively in gilt-edged bonds, the finances of the school took a drubbing in the early 1930s as U.S. Treasury bond yields hit zero by 1933.[2] This eventually led to cuts in both the size of incoming classes as well as the number of teaching faculty. The freshman class that arrived in September 1930 had a whopping 357 boys, which helped to yield one of the largest school populations (829) Regis ever saw.[3] In addition, during that academic year of 1930–31, there were a total of thirty-four individuals on the faculty and administration, which comprised seven priests, ten scholastics, and seventeen laymen. By the next academic year, the effects of the Depression began to affect the school, with only 156 freshmen admitted.

In addition, that fall, the school dropped the football program, which at least one alumnus recalls came as result of the belt-tightening of the Depression.[4] By the 1933–34 academic year, money got even tighter, with only seventy-two freshmen admitted, allowing the size of the faculty to shrink to twenty-six. The acceptance of smaller freshmen classes was actually happening at a time when more children were staying in school longer, since the jobs that would have attracted some to drop out of school had almost all dried up (or now would be gladly accepted by adults).[5] For the academic year 1934–35, the size of the faculty had dwindled even further to a total of twenty-two Jesuits and laymen teaching a student body of now down to 419.[6] Finally, even the school's cleaning staff was cut down to only two people.[7]

Despite how all encompassing the Depression was on culture and society in addition to the economy, little documentation remains extant as to how these events affected the students at Regis and their families at home. Neither the yearbooks nor the *Regis Monthly*, a monthly magazine produced by the students, contain direct references to or articles about the Depression. (Sadly, the school archives are missing several volumes of the *Regis Monthly*, most critically from the early 1930s.) In addition, the school newspaper, *The Owl*, did not begin publication until 1938, so it cannot be referenced for student opinions on the Depression or how it affected their lives. However, the few items that do exist can help by way of anecdotes to paint a picture of how the students personally felt the effects of the poverty caused by the Depression.

In an interview done almost fifty years after his graduation, Jerome Guszczyk, '33, could still recall having to work on both Saturdays and Sundays selling vegetables to pay for school clothes, transportation, and books for Regis. He had worked at a YMCA cafeteria, but with the deflation that came with the Depression, his wage was reduced from $2.00 to $1.50 per day. Thus, he had to find a better-paying job selling produce.[8] Because his family needed income, Joseph Flaherty, '35, was unable to go to college after graduating from Regis. (Because his family was so poor, some of his older siblings were not even able to finish high school.) Instead, he landed a job with the city, having done very well on the civil service exam. Despite his lack of a college degree, Flaherty was still able to forge a successful career, eventually joining the FBI, where he quickly achieved supervisor status.[9] Brendan Meagher, '34, recalls several of his classmates dropping out of Regis before graduation to find work and help support their families.[10] One of the best-known examples of a boy who had to leave Regis to help support his family was Robert Giroux, who dropped out in December of his senior year after landing a newspaper job. Despite his lack of a high school degree, Giroux went on to become one of the most prominent American editors of the twentieth century, nurturing significant American writers of the period including Walker Percy, Flannery O'Connor, and Susan Sontag. In recognition for his many professional accomplishments, in 1988 the school awarded him a Regis High School diploma, finally making him a full-fledged member of the class of 1931.[11]

While family circumstances forced some boys to leave Regis if the opportunity for a job had come their way, even those who had a Regis diploma had trouble finding a job during these trying economic times. Later in life, Herman H. Schutte, '31, recalled that "WW II was a picnic compared to the ten years of the Depression" when, as he remembered, some of his classmates "went the whole decade without finding a decent job."[12] During the early years of the Great Depression, some of the Jesuits at Regis, mostly notably Father Gabriel A. Zema, the school's first alumni director, tried to help graduates find a job, often calling on other alumni for help. By late 1939, this employment support was formalized when the Alumni Association decided to organize an "Employment Bureau" to help those among their number seeking work. While unfortunately the "unemployed in the ranks of the alumni far surpass the number of those who would be in a position to hear of a vacancy," it was still the hope that at least some Regians would benefit from this venture of the Association.[13] Father Zema gave his full support to this noble enterprise, but his aid for alumni would soon be called to those in even more threatening situations than being without work.

In late 1941, the nation's chronic and deep unemployment problems would find a sad resolution in the draft and voluntary enlistment of millions of men and women, including over one thousand Regis alumni. Much of Father Zema's time would be spent corresponding with (and praying for) Regis alumni as they prepared to go off to battle or while they were already in the theater of war.

Letters to Father Zema

Like Frank Miller from the pioneer class of 1918, Thomas Knichel of the class of 1938 was a graduate of the St. John the Evangelist parochial school in Manhattan. While at Regis, he had been a member of both the Sodality and the Guard of Honor for all four years. As far as academics were concerned, Tom was an average student, generally struggling in Latin but earning high grades in Christian Doctrine. However, just a few years after his graduation, this fairly ordinary Regian would come to occupy a most honored place among the school's alumni.

Five days after the Japanese attack on Pearl Harbor, Tom joined the United States Marines Corps. In early September 1942, his unit joined the Allied assault on Guadalcanal and the Solomon Islands, and during this engagement, Private Knichel lost his life. With his death, Tom left behind a wife of only three months and also earned the honorable but sad distinction of being the first Regis graduate to die in the Second World War.[14] Fifty-one other Regians lost their lives during this war that would see more than one thousand Regians serve in uniform.[15] A good number of lay teachers, too, were either drafted or volunteered to fight. In addition, a Jesuit who had been on the faculty also joined the military, becoming one of fifteen Regis alumni who served as priest–chaplains in the military.[16] Father Daniel Burke, S.J., a member of the class of 1920 who later served as principal of Regis from 1935 to 1940, became a navy chaplain in 1942. Assigned to the USS *Philadelphia*, he was part of the Allied invasion of Sicily in the summer of 1943. In November of that year, Burke came back to Regis to speak to the student body about his experiences in the war. As reported by *The Owl*, the former principal "emphasized that the perils of battle are beyond our comprehension." He also recommended that the students both pray for and write letters to "the boys on the fighting fronts."[17]

By 1942, the nation's entrance into the Second World War had also affected the boys still students at Regis. Most knew that it was very likely they would be drafted upon graduation and turning eighteen, and this recognition began to manifest itself while they were still in high school. In response to their nation at war, in the "Foreword" of the 1942 yearbook the students specifically commemorated the recent anniversaries of two important papal encyclicals (*Rerum Novarum* of 1891 and *Quadragesimo Anno* of 1931), both of which taught that there could be no peace in the world without justice. With the guidance from these popes, the seniors of the class of 1942 knew that despite the dark days that lay ahead, as they left Regis they had the advantage of the wisdom of the Church with which "to face a troubled world."[18]

As the succeeding months brought a growing number of American casualties, the 1943 yearbook contained even more references to the war and the challenges that the seniors would face after graduation. This year's senior class dedicated their yearbook to "the cause of freedom in a world at peace" but admitted that this goal would not come easily since most of them upon graduation would be "eligible for immediate service of our country." Because of this, they had "little prospect of deepening and strengthening the love that is the peace of Christ's in college," but in their self-sacrifice, they would be aiding the cause of freedom. To drive home the point that in military service they would be serving both God and country, the foreword of this yearbook was printed surrounded by full-page pictures of both Pope Pius XII and President Franklin Delano Roosevelt. Religious identity and patriotism (God and country) were clearly two sides of the same coin.[19] Fearing that they might be drafted once they turned eighteen as the law eventually allowed, some boys even went to summer school to get ahead and graduate in January of their senior year "should Uncle Sam decide that he could not get along without our help." As it turned out, the draft board did not interfere with the regular completion of their senior year at Regis.[20] However, these graduates and many other Regians would eventually serve in the military as the draft continued after World War II.

Love of country also manifested itself in other parts of the 1943 yearbook. In a copy of this yearbook given to the Regis archives by James (Jim) Marron, other young men from his class handwrote notes to Jim wishing him well and commenting on where many of them were headed. One classmate signed Jim's yearbook with the caption, "Viva le [*sic*] 69th," while another scribbled, "See you in North Africa!" above his signature. Even the captions under the pictures of many of the underclassmen had a strong patriotic or military ring to them, including quotes from Walt Whitman, Julius Caesar, and Cicero that all praised love of country and valor in battle.

One alumnus recalled how the boys at Regis would learn of the death of graduates in the war. Though he could recall no official announcement by the school over the public address system, for example, beginning in 1943 word would quickly spread among the students. He especially remembered hearing of the death of William ("Bill") Sweeney of the class of 1942. Literally a larger than life person, standing about six foot five, Bill's death drove home to this alumnus how real the war had become.[21]

During the war, Regis tried in several ways to offer support to alumni serving in uniform. Much of this effort was led by Father Gabriel Zema, S.J., moderator of the Regis Alumni Association, who also taught at the school. Born in southern Italy to poor parents, Father Zema (sometimes called "Shorty" for his diminutive stature) spent fifteen years (1935–50) teaching as a priest at Regis, and he also taught as a regent at the school in the mid-1920s. (His brother Demetrio also became a Jesuit.)[22] Beloved by his students, the Jesuit was kind to the boys beyond their life at school, even helping them to get summer jobs with the help of Regis alumni.[23] It is not surprising that his superiors tasked him with staying in touch with the school's graduates. The Regis archives contain some correspondence between Zema and about a half dozen alumni who were ultimately killed in the war. The archives also contain some letters to this Jesuit from the parents of Regians who died in the service. Using all this correspondence as a representative sampling, it seems that Zema was clearly well liked by his former students as well as their families. His preservation of these letters proves to be an important resource for demonstrating the continuing affection as well as the desire for connection Regians had for both Father Zema and their alma mater as they were sent off to war.[24]

In March 1943, George Bedder, class of 1941, wrote to Father Zema "at the first chance" he got after arriving for basic training at Camp McCain, Mississippi. George joked that despite the classical education he had received at Regis, the "Army went and put me in the engineers." He now just hoped that since "Regis, Greek, Latin, French and all really trains [*sic*] you for everything," he would be ready for whatever challenge the army might bring. He was sorry that his military duty precluded him from attending the recent "communism breakfast [*sic*]" sponsored by the Alumni Association, but he did make it to Mass that day on the army base. A few months later, Sergeant Bedder wrote to Father Zema to both thank him for the missal the Jesuit had sent him and also to express his regret in not seeing him on the soldier's recent visit to Regis while home on a furlough. However, he was happy to chat with Father Thomas Burke, S.J., the school counselor who was also quite beloved by the students.[25]

In a letter from early October, George wrote to say that he recently passed the test for acceptance into the "Army Specialized Training Program," and he attributed this to Regis, since "the Army respects a classical education." He went on to say that "languages happen to be priority number one in this program so my [Regis] education might help me more than I had suspected." George also expressed his condolences to Father Zema at the recent death of the Jesuit's mother. Reflecting on his own present situation, he wrote, "I guess you don't realize how much a mother means until you are away from home for quite some time." While he hoped to maybe get another furlough to see both his mother and Father Zema before shipping off, it is not clear if that ever happened. Sergeant Bedder was killed in action on January 30, 1944.[26]

The mother of Christian ("Chris") Becht, class of 1933, wrote to Father Zema in March 1945 to inform him of her son's death. Based in Tunisia, Chris had been killed the previous December while serving as a radio operator on a reconnaissance plane. He had originally told his parents that he was working in a ground crew, but "instead he was flying, and did not want us to worry." The entire crew of the plane was killed, and they were all buried by the "village Priest at the town of Cadaques, Spain," in the area where their plane had crashed. Mrs. Becht went on to describe her son as "a very good boy, 28 years of age, [who] never missed Mass on Sundays in his life, he had everything to live for, good home, good folks, good future, also keeping company with a good girl with intentions of marriage after the war." Before entering military service, Christian worked for the Motor Vehicle Bureau on Worth Street in Lower Manhattan.[27] Father Zema celebrated the requiem Mass for Christian at the family's parish, St. Pancras, Glendale.[28]

Not all Regians who lost their lives during the war did so because of wounds from battle. Corporal Rudolph ("Rudy") Wohlrab, class of 1940, died stateside at an Army Air Corps camp due to complications resulting from the removal of a leg tumor. His mother wrote to Father Zema in response to his inquiry about her son's death. Admitting that Rudy did not die while performing any "heroic deeds," she praised her son for working "very hard" nevertheless. After describing the progression of his illness, Mrs. Wohlrab apologized for not being more prompt in her reply. She explained, "I had started to write this letter several times, but it still hurts terrible, even just to write about everything, forgive me, Father, pray for me, please to give me a little more strength." While at Regis, Rudy had been a member of several clubs and activities, in particular the Sodality, the Guard of Honor, and the Homeric Academy.[29]

Before the peace in 1945, Father Zema began holding an annual memorial Mass in November to pray for those alumni who had died in the war. The families of these deceased servicemen were especially invited, and a breakfast was held after the liturgy. In addition to the spiritual concern for both the deceased and those they left behind, Zema also arranged for the Alumni Association to work on practical support for Regians in military service. The Alumni Association sponsored several card parties where items that had become hard to come by because of wartime rationing were raffled off. Support for this effort came from many quarters, including Father Zema's own mother, Rosa, who "sacrificed a pair of nylon stockings" in support of the Regis men fighting abroad.[30] The proceeds of these fund-raisers were then distributed in various ways. For example, a check was sent to Father Charles Brady, class of 1919, who was serving as an army chaplain in Oklahoma, to support his ministry there.[31]

While the end of the war was still off in the distance, the Association began making plans to help Regis veterans' transition to civilian life. To

Sergeant George F. Bedder, '41. This photo was sent to Father Gabriel Zema, S.J., the moderator of the Regis Alumni Association in the 1940s. Beloved by the students, this Italian-born Jesuit corresponded with many alumni, especially those who fought in World War II. Bedder was killed in action in France in 1944.

aid in this, in the late spring of 1945 the alumni raised $5,000, and soon a formal program was inaugurated to help Regis veterans with job placement and career counseling. In a card sent to alumni by the newly established "Regis Alumni Veterans' Committee," the men were reminded that the "veterans' basic problem is postwar employment." The school hoped that the older alumni could offer "young Regis vets many of whom had not worked for a salary before" guidance in vocational and career matters. By early 1946, several days were set aside for alumni veterans to come to the school during normal business hours to meet with a "competent alumnus" to help with their job search.[32]

In 1950, Father Zema was transferred from Regis, but shortly before leaving, he helped organize one last big event to honor Regians who had died in the war. Over the previous couple of years, the Alumni Association had raised over $3,500 toward the restoration of the Regis chapel in memory of their fallen brothers. To commemorate this, a large plaque was made listing the names of the Regis dead, to be placed over the entrance of the rear (tunnel) door to the chapel. In May 1949, Father Zema celebrated a Mass before the dedication and unveiling of the plaque.[33] Since attendance at this event was necessarily limited due to the size of the chapel, Father Zema sent photos of the plaque to the families of the alumni who were memorialized, and several of them wrote back to thank him for his kindness. Mrs. Helen Krall of Brooklyn wrote to thank him for the photo, which would be "fondly displayed in our home." Her son, Edward, class of 1942, had been a first lieutenant in the Army Air Corps and had been killed in action in Europe not long before VE Day. Although bestowed posthumously, Edward received the Silver Star for valor in face of the enemy, the third-highest military decoration. In this note, Mrs. Krall also expressed her deep appreciation for "the interest and kindness you have tendered to the families of our boys who have departed—you have kept the 'home fires' burning constantly." She concluded by saying that "the word 'Regis' is so warm to us all—we will never forget it—it produces boys a little different, especially their love for the faith." The archives contain another dozen letters from parents of Regians who died in the war with similar expressions of appreciation to Father Zema as well their ongoing love for the school.[34]

While surely some students who have attended public or private (nonreligious) school have maintained friendships with their teachers after graduation, the example of Father Zema and some other Jesuits from the period represents a qualitative difference between a Jesuit education and other forms. Since the priests and scholastics who ran and taught at Regis saw their role as also extending to the boys' spiritual lives by maintaining contact after graduation, it was not uncommon for priests to witness their students' marriages or to baptize their children. This is why the story of some of the more influential and long-serving teachers at the school (including laymen, some of whom are discussed later) are important to the history of Regis, in that these men (and later women) have continued to have an influence in the lives of their students long after the boys graduated. Charles Finch of the pioneer class recalls staying in touch with one of the scholastics, Mr. Charles Archdeacon, who taught him while he was still in high school when Archdeacon returned to the school as a priest and as the principal. The two would meet for walks in Central Park or go to a football game, and Finch remembers how important the Jesuit's mentorship was for him well into adulthood.[35] In addition, since there was a fair amount of turnover of the lay faculty through the period up to World War II, those laymen who stayed on the faculty for a long time came to embody much of the tradition of the new school as they began to teach multiple generations of boys.[36]

Despite these dark and dismal years, the period 1930 to 1945 also brought some reasons to celebrate and give thanks with the coming of milestones in the history of Regis. The year 1937 marked the two hundredth anniversary of the canonization of St. John Francis Regis, and 1938 was the twenty-fifth anniversary of the founding of the school. Neither went unrecognized. To commemorate the former, the 1937 yearbook was dedicated to the school's patron. Opposite a color lithograph of the saint depicted in a classic pose, the dedication page praised Regis for his "unquenchable zeal" and "firmness of purpose" in his ministry among the rural French poor, as well his "gentleness toward the sinner, detestation of the hypocrite and humble submission to lawful authority."[37] The students were encouraged to find in him "exemplified ideals" to make their own. As far as the silver anniversary of the school, the 1939 yearbook was dedicated to the memory of Father David Hearn, "by whose self-sacrifice and inspired efforts Regis High School was founded." In addition, this yearbook contained a special "In Retrospect" section with a short essay titled "Twenty-Five Years of Liberal Education." Written by senior John R. McCarthy, the piece praised the school for the type of education it had offered over the course of its first quarter century. It extolled the Jesuit pedagogical method, which stressed the study of classical languages and rhetoric as well as "character training," which of course was solidly grounded in Catholic values. This retrospective section also contained photos and short biographies of the various Jesuits who had served as rectors and prefects of studies (principals) since 1914.[38]

The last significant milestone to occur in this era came in 1943, when the pioneer class came together to celebrate its silver jubilee. Of the seventy-six who had persevered to graduation in 1918, ten had since died and another ten were in the armed forces and could not attend. However, forty-six of those who could come did. Their day of celebrations included a Mass in the school chapel celebrated by the first priest–graduate of the school, Father John P. Manning, class of 1918, which was followed by a benediction conducted by Father Zema. After this suitable period of prayer and thanksgiving, Regis's first graduates repaired to the Hotel Shelton on Lexington Avenue and East 49th Street for drinks and dinner. To their great delight and surprise, sitting on the dais were Fathers Kilroy and Archdeacon, who first greeted them upon their arrival at Regis, though surely looking a bit less spry than when in 1914 they all had first met.[39]

"Forming the True and Perfect Christian"

At the beginning of the school year in 1937, the students at Regis were encouraged to go on an adventure by train. On the last Sunday of that month, the New York Central Railroad would run a special train from Manhattan to the Shrine of the North American Martyrs in Auriesville, New York, for students in Jesuit schools and colleges in the New York City area. The train would depart from Grand Central Station at 7:15 A.M., cost three dollars round trip, and was due to arrive at its destination at ten minutes before noon. The return train would depart at five in the afternoon and was expected to pull into Grand Central at 9:40 P.M. In between was to be a day packed with spiritual activities. Upon arrival in Auriesville, the pilgrims would make a procession "up the Hill of Torture to the Coliseum," followed by a Mass with a sermon by the Jesuit director of the shrine. Immediately following came "ample time for lunch." After some sustenance, next followed Stations of the Cross and a procession with the Blessed Sacrament to the ravine to the site where St. René Goupil, a *donné* (lay volunteer), was martyred in 1642. Here, another Jesuit would deliver a relevant sermon. Though participation in this one-day pilgrimage for Regians was not obligatory, its promotion among the students was certainly a sign of the deeply Catholic culture that permeated the school.[40] Evidence of this can be found in an article in the October 1940 edition of *The Owl*, which boasted that the Regis contingent to Auriesville that year was the largest of all the high school groups.[41]

In the penultimate chapter of his thesis on the significance of a Regis education (which was discussed in Chapter 2), Charles Taylor, S.J., takes a careful look at the Catholic formation offered to the students of Regis and quotes the then current pontiff, Pius XI, in his definition of Catholic education. The pope saw the aim and purpose of Catholic schools to be "the cooperation with Divine grace in forming the true and perfect Christian, i.e., Christ Himself in those regenerated in baptism."[42] In his examination of how well Regis was living up to its goal of forming these "true and perfect" Christians, the young Jesuit looked at the various elements outside the formal classroom curriculum that constituted the religious formation program of the school.

While Taylor believed that the religious formation at Regis permeated all aspects of the students' lives, he saw the students' daily interaction with the Jesuits, especially the scholastics, to be the most important influence. Until the late 1960s, these Jesuit seminarians formed a large and important part of the faculty. For the first ten years of the school's history, thirty-eight different scholastics taught at Regis.[43] In the 1930s and early 1940s, there were sometimes as many as nine scholastics on the faculty, and it was expected that these Jesuits-in-training would spend a good deal of time after class interacting with the students. As part of a Jesuit's training, after having finished a two-year novitiate, undergraduate studies, and three years of philosophy, a scholastic was usually sent to teach in a high school or college. Thus, after about seven years of a life made up mostly of prayer and study, these young men generally were often champing at the bit when they got to their teaching assignment. In addition, since at this time most men entered the Society under the age of twenty, these scholastics were usually in their mid-twenties when they started teaching. Their youth, combined with a pent-up desire to do something practical, tended to yield young Jesuits brimming with energy and enthusiasm when they arrived at Regis or another Jesuit school. It is not hard to see how such young and bright Jesuits would serve as positive role models for the boys under their tutelage.

In addition to coming to know the students as their teachers, scholastics often served as coaches on the various athletic teams or as moderators for extracurricular activities. The scholastics also spent a good deal of unstructured time with their students. Starting in November 1915, about once a month, each scholastic would ask permission of the prefect of studies to allow the class assigned to him to stay at Regis after the official closing at 4:15 P.M. for what was known as "class in the gym."[44] (In more modern times, a similar custom is still observed, but is usually referred to as "class night.") The boys in the scholastic's class would then have the opportunity to play sports (handball in the quad, Ping-Pong on the fifth floor, basketball in the gym), and the scholastic would often join in these games as well. According to Taylor, a Jesuit's early training has usually rendered him "passable in most of the American sports, so he had not much to fear from the boys." Scholastics were also encouraged to organize field trips on Saturdays, such as to Central Park for a baseball game or to the Palisades for a hike.[45]

Taylor felt that the Jesuit's informal contact through coaching or "class in the gym" helped him to build a level of trust with his students. It gave him the opportunity to learn more about the students' "interests and

Back Row: Mr. O'Keefe, S.J., W. Churchill, J. O'Hare, J. Kelly, J. McMahon, W. Kearney, A. D'Andrea, M. Rendich, Manager.
Front Row: W. Storz, G. Rohrman, T. Farley, J. O'Donnell, Captain, R. Casella, E. Waters, J. Walsh, J. Sweeting.

Mr. Vincent T. O'Keefe, S.J., and the junior varsity team "The Owls" (1946–47). During his three years as a scholastic at Regis, in addition to his teaching duties O'Keefe also coached basketball. In doing this, he was like the scores of young Jesuit scholastics during the school's first half century who provided immense amounts of youthful energy and enthusiasm for teaching, mentoring, and coaching the students.

urges," which would make his work in Catholic formation more effective. Given the enthusiasm and energy that is generally found in the young, the scholastics were relied on to be the workhorses of Jesuit high schools of this era. Yet, even they had their limits. On the last day of classes before the Christmas break in 1921, it had been hoped that the scholastics would organize a "Jollification and Entertainment" in the auditorium for the entire school. However, the school's administration decided that these young Jesuits were already "too overloaded" to ask them to do this in addition to all their other duties, so this pre-Christmas assembly was not held.[46]

In an oral history conducted in 1979, Charles Finch, a member of the class of 1918, remembers a long-lasting friendship he first struck up with one of these scholastics. Mr. Francis Archdeacon, S.J., was one of the scholastics on the original faculty that opened the school in 1914. He later returned to Regis after his ordination and served as principal from 1925 to 1935. During this latter time, Finch, now an adult, would often return to Regis on Saturdays to visit Father Archdeacon, and the two would have long talks while they walked in Central Park. Clearly, this once-young scholastic had made a strong impression on Finch, and the latter continued to turn to the former for advice as time marched on. In the years before the appointment of the first school counselor, boys would often go to see scholastics in their free time to discuss college or career plans, which surely also helped forge bonds of respect and affection. Several other alumni also remembered the strong influence the scholastics had on them. While there is no way to quantify the personal impact these scholastics had on the Regis students, the large number of men from this period who entered religious life can give some indication. In the class of 1918 alone, four Regians joined the Jesuits, two became Maryknoll missionaries, and two others entered the diocesan seminary. Surely, the presence of young scholastics in the midst of their own religious training had a strong impact on these boys who later decided that they too had a vocation.[47]

While the scholastics certainly had a strong influence on the Catholic formation of the students, it was of course the task of the priests on the faculty to celebrate Mass for the boys at various times in the academic year. In these early years of Regis, Mass was celebrated regularly in the chapel only on Wednesday mornings with optional attendance by the students. On Fridays, the entire school was required to attend the 8 A.M. Mass at St. Ignatius. (Before the chapel had been finished, the boys were allowed to come to school a bit late on First Fridays if they had gone to Mass first in their home parishes.)[48] Classes started fifteen minutes later on these days in order to allow time for a light breakfast of buns and coffee for those boys who had fasted from the night before in order to receive the Eucharist.[49] Despite the fact that many of the boys had just been to Communion, at times the grace of this sacrament seemed to wear off fairly quickly. One alumnus from the 1930s recalled that fairly frequently food fights would break out in the cafeteria on Fridays, with the boys throwing the almost inedible free buns, which as he also recalled were usually "hard as rocks."[50] Finally, school was usually let out at noon on First Fridays, with many of the boys going out for lunch. With the Friday abstinence from meat in place, their culinary choices were somewhat restricted. One alumnus from this time recalls going on First Fridays to a nearby automat for a crock of beans, milk, and coffee.[51]

Since it was the custom at this time for Catholics to go to confession frequently, if not weekly, students were given the opportunity to see a Jesuit priest for this sacrament every week. By 1941, this was done on Thursday mornings, with the students given the opportunity of going to the lower church. However, students were never required to go to confession. They always had to option to remain in a study hall with their class teacher if they did not feel the need to approach the sacrament.[52] On days other than Thursday, students could go to confession with the student counselor in their free time. By the 1940s, his office was across from the chapel, where today there is a conference room. A student could simply go to the chapel and slip into the rear confessional. He would ring a bell and the student counselor would be alerted that a penitent was there. The Jesuit would then slip into the priest's side of the confessional. Because of this clever setup, the boy did not have to identify himself to the counselor, thus protecting his anonymity.

Despite the fact that Regians of this era went to confession quite frequently, it would be a mistake to think that they were extremely focused on their spiritual lives, and that other demands did not at times affect their decision to approach the sacrament. In January 1920, it was noted that on the regular morning for confessions, few boys took advantage of it. It was then realized that a lot of them had a mid-year exam that afternoon, which surely was occupying their time and attention. The prefect of studies decided that in the future the opportunity for confessions on days like these would take place after the exam.[53]

Mass and confession were also central parts of the annual student retreats, the first of which was held in the spring of 1915 during the week before Holy Week.[54] Lasting three days, the retreat was generally given by a Jesuit not associated with Regis. In these early years, retreats at Regis included daily Mass, three talks, Stations of the Cross and Benediction, and the rosary and spiritual reading. The entire retreat was conducted in St. Ignatius Church except for lunch, which was held in the school cafeteria. After the "general Communion" at the Mass on Saturday, a free breakfast was offered to the boys in "the 84 St. playroom." Although the total cost of the food for the first retreat in 1915 was only six dollars, Father Hearn hoped that in subsequent years the boys would "contribute to defray the breakfast expense." Despite this hint of frugality, after breakfast the school sponsored a trip for the boys up to the Jesuit property in Yonkers, where the boys played football and baseball. This was the site where some Jesuit superiors still hoped to build a new seminary.[55] The 1940 retreat master for the upperclassmen was a Jesuit with the improbable name of Father Michael O'Pray. (O'Pray worked for many years as a parish priest at St. Ignatius.)[56]

By the 1930s, the annual school retreat was held in October and still concluded with an optional excursion after. In 1936, the school began taking the boys to Keyser Island in Connecticut. Also, by this time the seniors had their own retreat, which took place in May and also concluded with an outing only for seniors.[57] It seems that some seniors may have felt that this special retreat for them was a way to convince them to enter the Society or study for the priesthood. A 1937 editorial in *The Owl* put a quick end to that. In the April issue of the paper, senior Frank Ford dedicated his editor's column to dispelling "misconceptions and misapprehensions adrift on the subject of the impending retreat of our august fourth-year men." This time for prayer was "most emphatically not intended as the initial step toward priesthood, but rather is meant to serve as a sort of light-house beacon," as the seniors were about to leave Regis and move on to make choices that would affect the rest of their lives.[58]

During the 1930s and 1940s, student associations also were an important part of the religious formation at Regis. While participation was voluntary, a large number of students did become involved in these groups, the most important of which were the Sodality and the Guard of Honor. The Sodality of Our Lady had a long and venerable history in the Jesuit order, having been established in 1563. Founded to encourage piety and the practice of charitable works among the students at the Roman College, these spiritual associations for the laity quickly spread to other Jesuit colleges in Europe. Members of the Sodalities promised to attend daily Mass, weekly confession, monthly reception of Holy Communion, as well as a period of daily meditation, and to perform acts of charity, especially toward the poor. In many ways, this Jesuit confraternity was similar to the "Third Orders," which the mendicant orders had established in the Middle

Ages. At the Society's various schools around the world, each chapter of the Sodality would have a Jesuit who directed the group's activities, and a student prefect was appointed to help supervise and lead the other members. As the centuries rolled on, Jesuits almost always established a Sodality in each of their new schools, and over time these associations were established in Jesuit parishes as well, where at times even Sodalities for women were formed.[59]

At the time of the founding of Regis, plans were quickly laid to start a new chapter of the Sodality, but these were delayed a bit until the chapel became usable. In November 1915, recruitment of students began and the first organizational meeting was held, with about seventy boys showing up. The following week, elections for officers were held and a temporary altar was set up in the lecture room on the second floor. Meetings took place weekly, and often on Thursdays the members of the Sodality would be given the opportunity to go to confession after school in addition to the regular time offered to the entire student body. Although the chapel was still not completely finished in May 1916, the group began meeting there. On Ascension Thursday, a school holiday, the Sodalists had the honor of attending the first Mass to be celebrated by the rector in the school chapel. For this special occasion, a Jesuit from *America* magazine was invited to preach. After Mass, a breakfast was held for the Sodalists, and after this, they all went back to the chapel for benediction. But by no means were the day's celebrations over.

After all these religious services, both the Sodalists and much of the rest of the student body made their way to Pelham Bay Park in the Bronx for the school's first field day. The boys participated in a whole host of sports including boating, swimming, and races.[60] This tradition of a field day at this park continued well into the 1920s, and over time, programs were even printed up listing the various track and field events, including the "Midget Candle Race" and the "Special Walking Event," possibly for those Regians who were athletically challenged.[61] While this 1916 outing is considered the school's first official field day, there was an outing that came at the end of the first academic year in June 1915. At the end of that school year, the entire student body (which of course consisted of only one class) made the arduous journey to New Dorp on Staten Island for a day of sports and recreation. Since Pelham Bay Park was accessible by subway and did not necessitate taking to the high seas, this may explain the location change.[62]

As the years went on, membership in the Regis Sodality grew and eventually was divided into several branches. In the 1942 yearbook, the entire senior class of 108 boys listed membership in the Sodality for at least two of their four years, with the vast majority listing freshman through senior years. Walter ("Tim") Hanrahan was the only member of the 1942 class to list only two years of membership (freshman and sophomore) in the Sodality. What he may have lacked in piety, Tim certainly made up in patriotism, for he was one of five men from this class to give his life in World War II. In March 1944, Tim died in an accident while in training with the Army Air Forces in Lakeland, Florida.[63] In addition to the spiritual component of the group, Sodalists also performed charitable works. For example, in 1937 the senior Sodalists taught catechism for children who attended public elementary schools, and the sophomore and freshmen members took part in organizing a drive to collect books and clothes for the poor. In 1938, there was a clothing drive for the "Colored Mission in Southern Maryland," where the Jesuits administered several parishes.[64] While the volunteer work varied by grade, the aim of membership in the Sodality was the same: "personal holiness for each student, combined with active Catholicism."[65] In 1935, an alumni branch of the Sodality was even founded, which attracted about 150 men to its first Mass and meeting. At the end of the event, Father Joseph Kirchmeyer, S.J., the school counselor, led the old boys in a renewal of the Sodality pledge they had made when they first joined the organization. For an event like this to attract such a large number clearly demonstrates the positive impact the Sodality must have made on these men when they were students.[66]

By the 1940s, the Sodality at Regis had begun to sponsor a whole host of events over the course of the school year. In the fall of 1944, the senior–junior branch of the Sodality sponsored a symposium on the subject "Catholic Youth and the Parish" and included speakers from both Regis and other Catholic high schools, including those for girls. After the speeches, refreshments were served, followed by a dance. In March, a "Sodality Day" was held, consisting of spiritual exercises, physical contests, and an entertainment staged by the members. In conducting the Sodality, the Jesuits ingeniously combined religious formation with athletics and social activities. These certainly helped to popularize the Sodality among the students in their schools. Even in an age of consensus among Catholics on issues of religion and Church, additional incentives (sports, dances, etc.) seemed necessary to keep interest strong in the Sodality.[67]

The other important student group founded to support the spiritual lives of the students was the Guard of Honor. Started in 1917, the Guard was part of a movement in the Church initiated by Pope Pius X, which encouraged more frequent reception of Holy Communion. While enthusiastic to launch a program at Regis to support this wider effort, the founder at

Father Stephen V. Duffy, S.J. (shown here in 1956), joined the Regis faculty in 1945 as a young priest and remained at the school for the next fifty-six years, teaching various courses, including religion (theology), Latin, and Greek. During his more than half century at the school, Father Duffy was well known for innovative fundraising efforts among the students in support of the missions, including his use of pools on NFL games. In his later years, although no longer a full-time classroom teacher, Father Duffy remained an important presence in the school as a tutor. Although himself an Xavier graduate, Father Duffy was known as "Father Regis" to generations of Regians. He retired completely from his work at Regis in the spring of 2001, moving to the Jesuit retirement residence at Fordham. He died in 2005.

Regis, Louis Wheeler, S.J., was told by Father Kilroy that the new group would be limited to a dozen members until "we will see how it works." Although Kilroy relented a bit on the membership cap, the initial number of Guardsmen was twenty-seven, with only a few freshmen admitted. Other than attending Mass and receiving Communion frequently, the members of the Guard generally gathered one afternoon each week in the chapel for a short meeting consisting of a brief exhortation by the Jesuit moderator, followed by some prayers led by the prefect of the Guard, who was always a senior.[68] The short gathering also opened and closed with hymns. When a boy joined the Guard, he was given a small lapel pin with the Greek word for fish (*ΙΧΘΥΣ*), which was inside the shape of a fish. The fish was one of the earliest symbols for the Eucharist, and Guardsmen were encouraged to wear this insignia with pride. New students were not allowed to join until the end of their freshman year, in order that they come to understand the "solemnity of the Guard of Honor."[69]

Well before a Regis freshman even heard about the Guard of Honor or ever actually joined during the next four years, almost immediately he would learn that prayer and spiritual formation were very important at his new school. For example, in September 1944, upon the freshman class's arrival on their first day of classes, they were separated into their various class sections, and immediately after this, they entered into a three-day retreat conducted by Father Thomas Burke, S.J., the school counselor. In addition, as part of their freshman course in religion, they were required to purchase the text *Religion and Practice: Part I,* published by Loyola University Press, as well as a Roman missal and a Regis hymnal. If these freshmen had any doubt that religion would permeate their life at Regis, these initial experiences of their new school would quickly disabuse them of this. The intellectual study of the Catholic faith and public practice of the Church's liturgy and other devotions constituted a fair portion of a boy's daily life during his four years at Regis. This would remain largely unchanged until the late 1960s, when the winds of reform began to blow through the Church and the school began to update, modify, or drop some of the elements of the religious formation program that had been in place for Regis's first five decades.[70]

Conclusion

At 8:30 P.M. on Friday, September 15, 1944, Father Taylor, Regis's principal, called the parents of the freshman class to a meeting. To underscore the importance of their attendance, in his letter of invitation Taylor noted that their presence would indicate "from the very beginning your interest in things Regian." Since they were entrusting their son to Regis "at the most critical time in his life," they had a "perfect right to see his School in its religious, academic and physical aspects." This meeting would also give Taylor the opportunity to explain in detail Regis's objectives and its regulations, so as to "obviate any misunderstandings of the School's policy." This last phrase may have been offered proactively against possible future protests of parents if their son were asked to leave the school. In fact, while this freshman class began in September 1944 with close to two hundred boys, four years later, in June 1948, only 113 would still be around. With all the departures from this class, it is not clear if Father Taylor still had to review school policy with parents despite his attempts at clarity early on.[71]

For those who did graduate in 1948 and went on to college, they entered a world far more at peace than when they started high school. And for the boys who followed them at Regis over the next two decades, their generation would come of age in a period of incredible prosperity. These flush times would help spawn a youth culture that would shape their lives and Regis, too, in ways previous generations could never have imagined.

4 A Winning Team, Father Gannon, and Anniversary Celebrations

Death of the Foundress

After the death of both her husband in 1910 and her good friend, Father Hearn, in 1917, Mrs. Grant began to lead a mostly private life. Centering herself on her children and her faith, she continued quiet support of several charities, including Regis. In addition, Mrs. Grant also actively managed the considerable inheritance left by her late husband by reading several newspapers daily to remain current on the ever-changing financial scene. In fact, her son, Hugh, Jr., claimed that before the collapse of the stock market in October 1929, his mother had already sold off most of the family's equity holdings, converting them to cash, since she believed the market to be overvalued. Thus, when the Great Depression hit, the Grant family was in fine financial shape and was more than able to maintain an upper-class lifestyle as well as to continue their significant charitable giving.[1] For example, in the period 1921–36, Mrs. Grant made a series of individual gifts to the Jesuits totaling over $350,000. Most of these donations took the form of burses to support the study of Regians who had entered the Society and were now preparing for the priesthood. In 1937, Mrs. Grant gave a further $200,000 to fund graduate studies of Jesuit priests in general. Because of these many acts of generosity, Mrs. Grant and her children were again declared Founders of the Society of Jesus.[2]

After the death of her husband, Mrs. Grant maintained a deeply Catholic home, where she lived for the rest of her life with her children, none of whom married before her death in 1944. A woman who married one of Mrs. Grant's nephews in 1949, and who was invited over often, described the atmosphere of the Grant house as almost convent-like, even after Mrs. Grant's death. In addition to the house's many religious objects, in 1914 Mrs. Grant had a private chapel built in the residence, naming it the "Chapel of the Holy Spirit." Hearn was the first to celebrate Mass here, and over the next six decades three different Jesuits served as chaplains and celebrated Mass daily, with Hugh, Jr., acting as the altar server well into his seventies.[3] The chapel was also the site for other celebrations such as baptisms and First Communions for members of the extended family.[4]

Throughout her life, Mrs. Grant's children, especially the girls, stayed strongly devoted to her. However, even Hugh's wings were somewhat clipped in her desire to keep the family together. Hugh claimed that after graduating from the Loyola School, he had wanted to attend Georgetown University in Washington, D.C., but his mother demanded that he remain closer to home. Therefore, he attended Fordham University in the Bronx and commuted.[5] While Mrs. Grant preferred to cultivate a quiet life at home, she did allow her son to travel while still in his formative years. Shortly after Hugh's graduation from Fordham in 1925, his mother sent him on a grand tour of Europe chaperoned by a well-known English Dominican writer of the time, Father Bede Jarrett, with whom Hugh remained in contact well after their trip.[6] Upon Hugh's return from his travels abroad, he went on to study law at Columbia, following in the footsteps of his father. After working at the prestigious firm of Duer, Strong, and Whitehead, Hugh eventually went on to open his own firm in partnership with another attorney. However, the war would interfere with his legal career for a time. In May 1942, at the not so young age of thirty-eight, Hugh was inducted into the U.S. Army and assigned to serve as a legal officer in the Office of the Chief of Ordnance in Washington, D.C., where he spent the duration of the war.[7] His mother even kept him under close surveillance while he was in the service, sending one of his sisters down to Washington to live with him for much of this time.[8]

While Hugh was away in the service, his mother's health began to decline, and on March 17, 1944, she was admitted to New York Hospital. Mrs. Grant remained here for more than seven weeks before dying on May 6 of natural causes. While the death certificate listed her occupation as "housewife," which was true according to the parlance of the day, this gave no sense of the enormous impact she had had on thousands of Catholic boys and hundreds of Jesuits. Because of her anonymity, most (if not all) of these beneficiaries of her generosity remained unaware of the identity of their great benefactor.[9]

When the vicar general of Jesuits in Rome, Father Norbert de Boyne, heard of Mrs. Grant's death, he cabled to express his "heartfelt condolences" and also asked for prayers from all the members of the Society of Jesus for the repose of her soul. In doing this, he explicitly mentioned that Mrs. Grant was the foundress of Regis, but since this was done in an internal communication to Jesuits only, her relationship to Regis was not made known to the wider public.[10] The New York provincial, Father James Sweeney, S.J, also promised the Grant children the offering of Masses and prayers for their late mother by the Jesuits in his jurisdiction.[11] After the death of their mother, the Grant children remained committed to her favorite charities, especially Regis and the Jesuits, and continued to make gifts to both. According to Father Edwin Brooks, S.J., who for many years served as an intermediary between the Grant family and the school, in the 1960s the family made two large gifts to Regis partially in response to some dubious financial maneuvers by Father Robert I. Gannon, S.J., who served as president of Regis from 1952 to 1960.

Father Gannon and the "Regis Problems"

Father Gannon had served as president of Fordham University from 1936 to 1949 before coming to 84th Street. In addition to his position at Regis, Gannon was also the pastor of St. Ignatius parish, president of the Loyola School, head of the St. Ignatius Day Nursery, and rector of the 83rd Street Jesuit community. With oversight over (and control of) the finances of all these separate institutions, it was his conviction that since the foundation of Regis about forty years earlier, the Jesuits who taught at Regis but lived in the community attached to the Loyola School had not paid the full cost of their room and board. For example, in the 1951–52 fiscal year, Regis paid the 83rd Street Jesuit community $22,270 for the support of the sixteen Jesuits (priests and scholastics) working at the school. However, the actual cost for their maintenance was almost $34,000.[12] With the construction of new Jesuit residence on 83rd Street, Gannon decided it was time for Regis to right this wrong.[13]

Gannon was well aware of the foundress's several attempts to build a separate residence for the Jesuit faculty of Regis and that the superior general had rejected her proposal once and for all in 1921. In response, the foundress directed that the bonds, which totaled $220,000, be added to the foundation she had already established.[14] According to Gannon, the application of these monies to the construction of the new residence was justifiable since Regis had not been paying the full cost of the support of the Jesuits who worked at the school. Before doing this, he checked with the provincial Father John McMahon, S.J., class of 1921, who gave his approval, saying that Gannon "would only be following the wishes of the donor if you take the $220,000 from the Regis Portfolio and use it for the new residence."[15] The next provincial, however, saw things somewhat differently.

In the fall of 1954, Father Thomas Henneberry, S.J., who had recently become provincial, wrote to Gannon. In this letter, he voiced concern over

Gannon's raid on the Regis endowment and raised the question of whether this had been done "contrary to the intention of the donor." Gannon immediately responded, explaining that the Grant children were in full support and saw his use of the money to be in keeping with the spirit of their mother's earlier wish to build a separate residence for the Regis Jesuits. In addition, if this first explanation was not satisfactory, then Gannon argued that the new residence could "be regarded as a safe and lucrative investment of the Regis Funds." According to his calculations, in recent years Regis Jesuits had been charged three dollars per diem for room and board in the residence attached to the Loyola School. For fifteen men, this came to $16,425 per annum. With the application of these monies to the construction of a new Jesuit residence, henceforth Regis would not be charged for room and board for its Jesuits. On an investment of $220,000, a return of 8 percent, according to Gannon, was "gilt-edged." Thus, there was no reason to be concerned that the foundress's monies had been misappropriated. The provincial wrote back, saying that either explanation proffered was sufficient and that the transfer of monies could stand. However, he added that "free board and lodging for the Regis Staff will remain the permanent policy of the House," and that all this correspondence should be safely kept in the House files "so that future Rectors may not be disturbed in the matter."[16] Despite this promise by the provincial, the evidence suggests that Regis continued to pay room and board for its faculty who lived at the residence.[17]

In addition to funding a new Jesuit residence with some of Regis's foundation, Gannon also set his sights on some other areas of the school that he desired to change. After less than four years as rector–president, Gannon determined that there were four areas that the school needed to seriously address and laid out these "problems" in a memorandum to the provincial in the summer of 1956. According to Gannon, the first area of concern was financial. While in the previous couple of years the income generated by the foundation had been enough to meet annual expenses with a bit of money to spare, Gannon feared that this situation would not last long. He felt that with increased pressure to raise lay salaries, soon the school would be operating at a deficit. In addition, if inflation were to rise quickly, this would also make the situation even graver, since the foundation was invested in bonds, which offered a safe but modest return.[18]

He titled the second cause for concern the "registration problem." Beginning with the fact that Regis was built for 800 students, he noted that the student population in recent years was hovering around 550. Thus, there was a fair amount of underutilized classroom space not considering the offices occupied by the Jesuit Educational Association on the second floor, which could always be put back into use by the school.[19] Gannon claimed that twice in recent months Cardinal Spellman "had offered to fill the space for us, mentioning the great need for facilities in the Diocese," which presumably referred to the incredible growth the diocesan schools were experiencing in the postwar era.[20] To ward off this advance by the archbishop, Regis would have to add about 275 more students, which would increase the budget by more than $63,000. According to Gannon's calculations, the foundation would need to expand by $1.6 million to generate this additional income, but no one seriously thought that raising this kind of money would be possible.[21] While president of Fordham, Gannon had tried to raise $1 million dollars in commemoration of its hundredth anniversary in 1941 and reached only $700,000.[22]

The last two problems had to do with the students themselves. As for the third or "scholastic problem," Gannon felt that "too large a number of the boys are taking it easy" and not working to their potential, arguing that a passing grade set at 75 percent "means very little work for a bright boy." Finally, Gannon raised what he called the "personality problem" of the Regis students. For his final point, it is best to read Gannon's explanation verbatim:

> Our students are drawn from the group of little boys selected by the Sisters in our parochial school and often coached for the entrance exam beyond their real capacity. As a result, we have too large a proportion of colorless boys with watery personalities and too many who have reached their intellectual top in grammar school. It is fair to assume that many "late starters" who were not high enough on the exam list would have become leaders by third or fourth year and that many other leaders never got a chance to take the examination.[23]

Gannon was an alumnus of the Loyola School, which by the 1950s had now long lived in the academic shadow of Regis, and this may have partly accounted for his sharp words.

After raising these four problems, Gannon offered a two-part solution that would address them all. First, he recommended expanding the school population to 800 (the full capacity of the building), which would answer the registration problem and preclude any move by the archdiocese to rent space for another high school. Second, he would end Regis as a tuition-free school for all students, instead charging tuition to about 30 percent of the students. According to this part of Gannon's plan, acceptance to Regis would only guarantee free tuition for a student's first year. At the end of freshman year and for the next three years, only the top 125 in each class would remain on full scholarship. The bottom 75 would have to pay $300 (the same tuition at the other area Jesuit high schools) if they wanted to remain at Regis, which presumably the bulk of them would. In addition, a student could lose his scholarship for disciplinary problems but could remain in the school if he paid tuition. According to Gannon, the charging of tuition to about 250 students could yield up to $75,000 per year, thus answering the financial problem. The annual competition for scholarships would "put a sanction on loafing and add prestige to the intellectual achievement" and so solve the scholastic problem. As for the personality problem, he recommended a "broader basis of selection, not dependent on the Sisters," but did not delineate what this new method might look like.[24]

After laying out this quite radical restructuring of Regis, Gannon thought it could begin in a modified way at once. Current students would not be subject to the annual competition for scholarships, but would remain tuition-free as long as they maintained an 80 percent overall average and "reasonable interest in scholastic extra-curriculars and good conduct." Incoming freshmen would be subject to the new plan, and breaking with tradition, new tuition-paying students would be accepted into sophomore year and then win a scholarship if they finished in the "top group." Gannon realized that the goal of raising $75,000 per year from tuition would not be accomplished immediately, but that "complete adjustment could be reached in three years." Of course, Gannon realized that his grand plan would have to be accepted by the Grant children, but stated that he felt "confident that [he] could present the total problem in a way that would not offend their sensibility and would not look like a touch."[25]

Before sending this formal proposal to the provincial, Gannon had first raised the idea in 1955 with the five consultors of the Jesuit community to elicit their opinion. (Consultors in a Jesuit community serve to advise the rector on important decisions.) According to Father William Wood, S.J., one of these consultors, the discussion between Gannon and this group proved to be "extremely tense," and soon an "irreconcilable" split developed among the five consultors. On July 1, 1956, Wood wrote directly to the provincial, complaining about the strain this had put between Gannon and the consultors, as well how the rector was proceeding with the entire matter. Wood thought it was a very poor idea for Gannon to approach the Grants before getting formal approval from the provincial. Obviously, the Grants would have to approve the changing of the essential nature of Regis, but what if they accepted this and then the provincial decided against it? This would obviously prove to make an "embarrassing situation with the Family." Wood felt that Gannon was "trying to force the whole plan through without the approval of Your Reverence by simply creating a delicate situation." Though he seemed to offer conditional support for Gannon's plan to charge tuition, he did offer explanations as to the "many fallacies" in Gannon's arguments.[26] A week later, Henneberry wrote to Gannon asking him where his plans for Regis stood, and telling him that this should be brought up with his consultors before "any approach is made to the Grants."[27]

Of the other consultors, only Father Harvey was completely against Gannon's plans, seeing it as a "harmful change in the traditional character of the school."[28] The other consultors, however, were far more supportive. Although they may have disagreed with parts of his analysis, the other three consultors (Thomas Tuite, Daniel Burke, and Peter Daly) basically agreed with Gannon's plan. Father Daly especially liked that it would "give a greater opportunity to the sons of alumni to attend Regis."[29]

Over the next months there seems to have ensued a vigorous discussion of Gannon's proposal for Regis among the Jesuit leaders of the New York Province. Henneberry was open to the charging of tuition, though he offered his own version of a plan whereby each student would be charged tuition of forty dollars per year. However, despite a general openness to the question of tuition at Regis, of course no plan was ever enacted and Regis remained tuition-free. While the archives do not contain any letters announcing a final rejection, they do contain a long confidential report to the provincial from Father Lorenzo K. Reed, S.J., provincial assistant for secondary education. Written in March 1957, this report, which may have ultimately been responsible for putting an end to Gannon's grand design, sharply criticizes Gannon, even calling for his removal. Reed served as assistant for the high schools of the province from 1947 to 1963, and during his time in office often raised concerns over Jesuit administrators who were dictatorial in manner. While by no means an advocate for administration by consensus, Reed preferred that the Jesuits in charge of the schools use a more consultative style of leadership, and he even encouraged the holding of staff meetings.[30] Clearly, he and Gannon were by means of the same mind on this. In his recent visitations of the school, Reed had heard a "woeful tale of bitterness, frustration and discouragement" concerning Gannon's leadership, and reported that none of the faculty was in favor of the "proposed change to the nature of the school." In addition, several of the Jesuits were resentful "of the Rector's lack of consideration for and appreciation of the teachers." Reed reported that some of these same men said they did not trust Gannon and even accused him of using for other purposes funds earmarked for salary increases for the lay teachers.[31]

According to Reed, Gannon was "determined not to raise teachers' salaries"; in fact, this had become an "obsession" of his. He quoted Gannon as once saying that "truck drivers should receive higher pay than teachers in our schools because it takes more skill to drive a truck that to teach in high school." His low regard for the lay faculty was of such a depth that Gannon was even ready "to turn Mr. Cyril Egan loose after 41 years of faithful service." Even when the Parents' Club had raised over $10,000 to increase faculty salaries, he refused to use the sum for this purpose, instead spending it on an expansion of the library.[32]

Reed argued that many of the problems with Gannon's administration of Regis were due to his lack of experience with high schools and not understanding the "difference between high school and college conditions." In a conversation with Reed, Gannon "repeatedly referred to the 'regular procedure of all colleges' in administering scholarships." But Reed countered, "These lads are children when they begin at Regis—some only 12 years old. . . . They can't be expected to work independently like college scholarship students." Thus, Reed thought it very unwise to have boys go against one another for a limited number of scholarships, believing that this would introduce a spirit of extreme competition in the school and would be unhealthy for the institution as a whole.[33]

In many ways, Reed's confidential report to Henneberry was very much a warning of what he perceived to be underhanded maneuvers by Gannon to get his way—first on increasing the size of the school, and then on charging tuition as well as remaining in the position of rector. Reed felt that Gannon's recent announcement at the alumni communion breakfast of the expansion in the size of the student body was an attempt "at forcing our hand" on this question, as his comments were reported the next day in the *New York Times* and were thus now out in the open.[34] Gannon had already told Father Harvey to increase the size of the incoming class, which he had done, having admitted forty-eight more students for the fall of 1957 than he had the previous year. Finally, Reed charged that Gannon had hatched a plan to stay on as rector beyond the normal six-year term. Rumor had it that Gannon had secured permission from Spellman to add towers to the church. According to Reed, once the costly project had begun, Gannon would argue that he should remain in office to see it to completion. This would, of course, keep him in place at Regis in order to put all his plans into effect.[35]

While no response from the provincial to Reed is extant, Gannon's term was not extended, no towers were added to St. Ignatius Church, and Regis never charged tuition. In 1958, Gannon left office as rector–president of Regis (and Loyola, as well as pastor of the parish) and was appointed

Members of the class of 1964 compete on *It's Academic*, a quiz show for high school students on a Washington, D.C., television station. This show (which was started in 1961 and holds the distinction of being the longest continuously running television quiz program) was hosted from its start until 2011 by Maurice ("Mac") McGarry, class of 1944. Also pictured is Father William C. McCusker, S.J., who served as principal of Regis from 1957 to 1964.

head of the Jesuit Mission Bureau. Gannon was clearly correct in calling attention to the financial precariousness of the Regis foundation, and in the 1960s future rectors would have to address this. But his plans for radically changing the very nature of the school never came to fruition. And ironically, Father Wood, who was very much against Gannon's proposal, was appointed rector in 1960 and had the pleasure in 1964 of taking a leading role in the celebrations marking the school's fiftieth anniversary of free Jesuit education, a distinction that would not have been attained had Gannon had his way.

"The Regis Zone"

In the late 1940s, the Regis basketball team would come to have an oversized place in the life of school and the memories of the men who were students here during that time. As the students traveled to distant parts of the city to root on their team or spent a large amount of their spare time shooting hoops in the quad at school, it is unlikely that they (or even their Jesuit teachers) realized how central athletics was to the overall educational program of the first Jesuit schools. Yet it very much was. The Society's first schools reflected the Renaissance humanist emphasis on "physical and intellectual instruction and exercise" that went back to the Greeks, and by the seventeenth century, the French Jesuits not only provided daily time for exercise and athletic games, but in some schools set aside an entire day in the middle of the week (Wednesday or Thursday) for walks in the countryside and participation in sports. The young scholastics were also encouraged to take part in these games, while always making sure that they did not become too violent and that the health of the youngest (and smallest) boys was safeguarded. When Jesuits had the chance to build new schools rather than putting older buildings to an educational purpose, many took the opportunity to center the classrooms around a spacious a courtyard that could be used for athletics. Regis's courtyard was used for athletics from the very first week of classes in 1914.[36] A letter from the third superior general of the order, St. Francis Borgia, demonstrates the importance that athletics had at Jesuit schools from the very beginning and have continued to have ever since. In 1568, a rector of the College d'Aquitaine had written for his counsel concerning games and sports at the school he directed. While Borgia did not think he should forbid games like chess and checkers, he surely should not encourage them. Rather, he thought the best games were those "which entail some physical exercise."[37] Few statements of superior generals have met with more ringing endorsements from Jesuit students than this one by Borgia, especially the young men at Regis who played basketball under the tutelage of Don Kennedy.

Though he never suited up to play basketball in a Raiders uniform, Mr. John ("Don") Kennedy's almost twenty years coaching the varsity team made him a giant for many of the Regians of that era for more reasons than his strapping six foot three stature. But he did not originally come to coach basketball when he arrived at Regis in 1929. Rather, he was hired to teach calisthenics.[38]

A member of the first graduating class of Brooklyn Tech in 1924, Kennedy began studying engineering at Columbia before he decided to pursue a career centered on basketball. In a 1982 interview, Kennedy recalled that he quickly grew tired of engineering, and taking the advice of an uncle, he enrolled in the now-defunct Savage School of Physical Education located on West 59th Street. Ironically, Kennedy could not play on the school's basketball team while he was preparing for a career coaching the sport, since he had already played professionally. In those days, a player was considered a pro even if he had been paid as little as two dollars a game. While still a teenager, Kennedy had already been paid for playing basketball in what was then referred to as "tin canning." According to Kennedy's recollections, in these early days of professional basketball, a group of five or six young men would pile into a car (or "tin can") and drive all over the Northeast, from Springfield, Massachusetts, to Scranton, Pennsylvania, to play any game that could be arranged. This same squad would often compete under different names, since there were no leagues in the strict sense of the term. Despite his inability to play basketball in college because of this brief career as a pro, Kennedy remained committed to the sport, graduating from Savage in 1928. He then went on to his first coaching job at New York College of Dentistry.[39]

Because this job was only part-time, Kennedy jumped at the chance to work full-time at Regis when offered a position with a salary of $1,500 per annum. However, with the coming of the Depression, he and the other lay teachers at Regis saw their salaries reduced 10 percent one year and then 5 percent a few years later. In an effort to earn some extra cash, he began coaching basketball at the former St. Michael's High School in Brooklyn. When he finally got the Regis coaching job in 1934, he actually continued coaching at the other school for several more years. He was able to do this by having the Regis team practice and play on Tuesdays, Thursdays, and Saturdays and the St. Michael's team on the other three days, with Sunday as his only true day of rest. In 1941, he gave up the St. Michael's job to coach basketball and football at the former Power Memorial while continuing to coach the Regis hoops team. However, in 1945 Power offered him the position to coach these two teams as well as baseball if he would give up basketball at Regis. Faced with this choice, he and Power parted ways, and for the next six years he coached basketball only at Regis. It was during this time in the late 1940s that Kennedy grew to be the Regis giant he remains to this day (at least among the alumni from that era still living). And then there was that 27–1 season of 1947–48.

During this period of the Raiders' great success, the team was still practicing in the lower gym, which given the room's narrow dimensions could be like playing in a boxcar. Amazingly the team even hosted some home games here when another court could not be found. They simply made do. For example, if a ball hit the wall unintentionally, it was still in play. But even in these less than ideal circumstances, Kennedy was able to get his players to play well. In later years, he even claimed that it was during this time that he invented a new defensive scheme, which went on to be used by teams around the country. In essence, it was a combination of man-to-man and zone defense, but the other team never seemed to know which was operational. Some came to refer to it as a "pickup" defense, and today it is commonly referred to as a "matchup zone." Kennedy recalls that he and his players "just called it the Regis zone," and the use of it certainly led to more victories for the Raiders.[40]

When possible, more important home games were played at one of the city's armories. However, no matter where the Raiders played, their fellow Regians came out to support them, even when they played their rivals of Tottenville High School out on Staten Island. Despite the distance, a huge number of students would come out to support the team and a fair number of the teachers, too. The faculty seemed not to mind the trip to this school in particular, since on their way home they would usually stop to slake their thirst at a favorite German brewery in Stapleton before catching a return ferry.[41]

During his twenty-one years as coach, Kennedy led the Raiders to the finals of the Jesuit Tournament ten times, winning the trophy in five of them. Under his direction the team competed in the prestigious Eastern States Catholic Invitational in Rhode Island six times, winning it twice. However, the highlight of his time at Regis came in the 1947–48 season. The Raiders finished with a 27–1 record, losing only to the Columbia University freshman team by one field goal.[42] Some of the more memorable games of the year included a season-opening trouncing of St. Ann's by fourteen points at Madison Square Garden, and later a humiliation of the Fordham Prep Rams, 61–30.

This unforgettable squad was led by twin seniors Gerry and Jack Rooney, who though both small at five foot seven played forward aggressively, as well as Joe Breen, Mike Woods, and Barry Sullivan, all of whom were six foot two or taller.[43] After the Radiers' win in the Jesuit Tournament, Father Taylor scheduled a "Victory Dance" so that the whole school could celebrate this important athletic accomplishment. After the dancing was over, the evening ended with a presentation of varsity letters and sweaters by Father Joseph Parrell, S.J., assistant principal and moderator of the team. Instead of giving these prizes to the boys, he gave them to "each player's lady friend." The crowd especially enjoyed the sight of Joe Breen's date, who was just as tall as he was.[44]

For Kennedy, this unforgettable season for the Raiders finally put to rest "the notion of Regis as a school populated by brains on stilts," which some of its rivals used to like to quip. Since its opening thirty-four years earlier, Regis had immediately earned a reputation for its outstanding academics. Now, its students would also be known for their dominance in athletics, even if only for a brief time. In fact, one of Kennedy's players would go on to become the only Regian to play professional basketball. Described in the yearbook as both "tall and athletic," Thomas E. Kelly, class of 1941, went on to play on the Boston Celtics after first serving his county in the war as a fighter pilot in Europe and then graduating from the Bronx campus of New York University in engineering, where he also played forward for the NYU team.[45] While he played on the Celtics for only a few years, both his individual accomplishment as a professional basketball player and the Regis team's success in the 1947–48 season was proof that the students could excel in athletics as well as in academics.

Despite his great success with the 1948 team, Kennedy would coach only two more seasons at Regis. In the fall of 1950, he began coaching at St. Peter's College in Jersey City, though he continued to teach gym class at Regis in the mornings. In 1953, St. Peter's finally agreed to name him athletic director and raise his salary so he would not have to hold down two jobs.[46] It was a tough decision for this Regis giant. Coach Kennedy had come to love Regis, especially some of the Jesuits who worked there, including Fathers Charlie Taylor and Dan Burke, whom he often referred to as "tops in the world." But the offer from St. Peter's represented a real advance for his career, so with his acceptance, Kennedy's association with Regis was done and an era had ended.[47] However, a few years after his departure, an improvement came to the athletic program at the school that surely would have made his life as a coach so much easier had he remained.

In January 1958, Father Gannon blessed a new gym for Regians, carved out from the auditorium, which at its construction in 1914 was said to seat 1,700. Now the much smaller auditorium was limited to just the first floor so that the basketball team could have a proper and full-sized space to both practice as well as host home games.

To some, the building of a new gymnasium right at the school was a bit of a puzzlement, because for the basketball seasons 1956–57 and 1957–58 the Raiders had in fact been playing at a brand-new gym on 83rd Street. Indeed, over the years the Regis "home court" was often in fact quite far from home. Most recently, it had been located at a public school on West 138th Street. Although a new, modern gym had been a long-desired wish of many a player and fan, and surely Coach Kennedy, too, the bifurcation of the auditorium was not the first plan. As part of the building of a new Jesuit residence on 83rd Street discussed earlier, Father Gannon had made provisions for the construction of a gym in a structure that in addition to the Jesuit residence would also include a gym for use by both Regis and Loyola. In 1954, Regians raised over $7,000 by means of a raffle to help pay for seating for the new gym. However, the Raiders would play only those two seasons at the new gym on 83rd Street.

For reasons that are not altogether clear, Gannon decided that the Raiders would no longer play in the gym they had helped finance, but rather would use a new facility in Regis itself. In 1957, Gannon began planning for the construction of a new gym in the building proper as part of a larger capital improvement project that would also include the purchase of new furniture for the library, a public address system, and a refurbishing of the auditorium. The total cost of the project was slightly more than $250,000, but for this the students were not asked to buy raffles. Rather, three unnamed persons each gave $100,000, which more than covered the cost.[48] (In a letter to the provincial, Father Thomas Harvey, S.J., who was principal until the end of the 1956–57 academic year, identified the Grants as the donors of this money.)[49] At the end of the dedication ceremony, Father William ("Cookie") McCusker, S.J., who had recently become principal in 1957, proposed that the boys remember these generous benefactors at the weekly school Mass on Friday. The Jesuit's motion was "enthusiastically seconded by the student body."

Coach John ("Don") Kennedy was not present at the blessing of the new gym, but surely he would have rejoiced with all the boys. However, that 1948 team would always have a special place in his heart. In fact, at his ninetieth birthday many of his players from that squad came together to toast their old coach. Despite the passage of almost five decades, Joe Breen would still remark about the impact Kennedy had had on them: "He loved [us]. We loved him. He made us better."[50]

Through the years, there were other teachers at Regis who, though not as physically tall as Kennedy, had nevertheless come to take on an oversized presence among current students as well as the alumni. And not a few of these were men who did not even wear a Roman collar.

"A Little Half-Sheet, Laddies"

In May 1956, Tom Henry, a member of the pioneer class of 1918, wrote to his fellow members of the Alumni Association with a special request. Since the first attempt at such an association in 1919, the most that graduates ever were asked for were nominal dues for annual membership.[51] But this time it was different. Cyril ("Cy") Egan was about to complete his fortieth year on the faculty, and the leadership of the association thought that the several thousands of boys he had taught ought to step forward to honor him for his long service. Thus, they proposed the establishment of a pension plan for the entire lay faculty in Egan's honor. In his pitch, a member of the class of 1929, J. Frank Morris, who was now a successful Wall Street banker, explained why this was needed: "Back when Regis was endowed it was planned to have an all-Jesuit faculty. But from the beginning it was necessary to utilize laymen. Fortunately for us, men of 'Cy's' caliber were engaged to complete the staff. Since the founders did not foresee lay teachers (much less a pension plan for them), we who received so much so freely have this one chance to 'update' Regis and also to honor 'Mr. Regis' himself."[52]

This pull at the heartstrings had its desired effect. Within a month of this mailing, money began to pour in. By the end of June, the association sent a check for $1,000 to Egan at his home in the Bronx as "a slight token of our affection to you—one of the grandest men that we have have had the fortune to call a friend."[53] But that was not the last of it. By 1960, more than $23,000 had been collected to start a pension plan for Egan and the other long-serving lay faculty, most notably Joseph Quintavalle, Robert Clancy, and Joseph Connolly.[54]

In June 1960, Egan retired with the distinction of having been the longest-serving teacher, Jesuit or lay, in the history of Regis. And his record of forty-four years would not be broken until 1990, when Father Stephen Duffy, S.J., began his forty-fifth year at the school.[55] Thanks to the generosity of the alumni and the pension that was started by them, Egan's life after retirement would prove to be far less lean given how little he could have saved on his own during his time as a teacher. Originally hired in 1916 at a salary of $700 per year, in 1924 Egan was given a raise of ten dollars per month for taking on the additional responsibility of also teaching elocution. Because of this modest salary, not surprisingly over the years Egan found himself moonlighting at Fordham University, St. Peter's College, and Pace University. He may have been an attractive part-time teacher for all these institutions given the versatility he had acquired on the job on 84th Street. During his long career at Regis, Egan was assigned to teach a wide variety of courses, including Latin, English, catechism, history, civics, physical geography, and "economic citizenship." He was once even asked to teach French. Shortly before his retirement, Egan performed a stint as the school registrar, but this would prove to be short-lived. When his wife heard of his new post, she presciently remarked, "Dear God, they've made you registrar—they should look at the state of your drawers." For all parties concerned, he happily returned to his true love, the classroom, for his last two years on 84th Street.[56]

In Egan's early years at Regis, it was the practice for teachers to teach up to three courses to the same group of students, but looking back on this later, Egan judged this a poor practice. By the late 1940s, it had mostly died out, though a few teachers still taught courses in multiple disciplines. (Jesuit scholastics could usually be pressed into service to teach Greek, Latin, or catechism.) During Father Gannon's time as president, he raised the idea of returning to this practice of instructors teaching the same group of students multiple subjects, possibly as a cost-saving measure. However, Egan and much of the faculty resisted this, and Gannon's plan never came to fruition.[57]

A few years before his death in 1984, Egan was interviewed by a current senior. In his wide-ranging reminiscences, Egan voiced regret over some of his classroom practices from his early days. Though common for the time, he now thought that it was in poor form for him to call students by their last names. He also recalled feeling sad when he first heard a student refer to him under his breath as "take a zero Egan," realizing that this nickname was borne from his often-used expression with students who got something wrong or came to class unprepared. He looked back on these practices as far too "macho." Despite this laudable act of self-examination, Egan may have been too hard on himself. In this same interview, Egan also recalled how many former students had stayed in touch with him over his more than four decades at Regis. Even well after his retirement, his presence at reunions was most sought after, and he continued to socialize with former students well into his late eighties.[58]

Like a vast majority of the laymen who taught at Regis in the school's first half century, Egan was a very devout Catholic whose faith permeated every aspect of his life and who counted several priests as lifelong friends. Evidence of this can be seen in something he wrote a few years into retirement. While known for his love of verse and his repeated attempts (not all successful) at writing his own poetry, Egan's best-remembered work was not in meter but rather an essay that was printed in *America* magazine in 1964, "Subway Stations of the Cross." This relatively short but quite profound reflection stands as a window into the soul of a man who was deeply committed to his Catholic faith. Taking as his starting point the Lenten discipline to pray more often, Egan argued that even the subway can be a fine place to raise hearts and minds to God. The retired Regis teacher reminded his readers that "religion must begin with people. . . . Who is my neighbor? My neighbor is an Irishman . . . Negro, Puerto-Rican, Swedish, Chinese."[59] Given Egan's deep Christian faith as well as his love of learning, it is not surprising that the homilist at his funeral, Father Joseph

Upon his departure in June 1960, Cyril ("Cy") Egan retired with the distinction of having been the longest-serving teacher, Jesuit or lay, at that point in the history of Regis.

Fitzpatrick, S.J., of Fordham University, described him as "inextricably a Christian and a teacher."[60]

In addition to Cy Egan, another lay teacher loomed large in the life of Regians in the years before the school's fiftieth anniversary. A native of the Bronx, Joseph T. Quintavalle was a member of the class of 1930. While a student, he never earned a final grade below 90 percent for any course during his four years.[61] After graduating from Fordham and teaching for a couple of years in an elementary school, in 1937 Quintavalle returned to his alma mater, where he spent the next thirty-eight years teaching Latin (and a bit of English). During the many years he taught freshman and sophomore Latin, he became famous for the line, "A little half-sheet, laddies," which he used to announce the daily (or even twice daily) pop quizzes. Quintavalle firmly believed these unannounced quizzes on the previous night's homework to be an excellent pedagogical device.[62] In fact, as late as the early 1970s during Quintavalle's final years, when these more traditional educational practices had come under question, the assistant headmaster at the time felt that success in his freshman Latin class was a great indicator of a boy's future career at Regis.[63]

Given his gentle demeanor and long tenure, Quintavalle was beloved by several generations of Regians, many of whom recall how his black teaching gown (which the lay teachers wore until the late 1960s) seemed to be always smeared with chalk dust. Fiercely proud of his Italian heritage in a school presided over mostly by Irish American Jesuits, Quintavalle would pronounce the surnames of his Italian students with perfect precision. A great promoter of the Jesuit weekly *America*, he often brought copies to class to sell to his students, and on occasion in the fall he would even bring a prized tomato, which came from his backyard garden.[64] When dedicating the 1962 yearbook to Quintavalle in honor of his silver jubilee at the school, the senior class both poked fun of his home on "Staten Insula," which was somewhat "west . . . of Gaul," but also displayed their deep affection and respect for the man who had introduced them to Latin with great patience and aplomb.[65] In a tribute to him after his death, Father Joseph Dorgan, S.J., a former colleague of his on the Regis faculty, praised him not only for his unswerving dedication to the classics but also his deep devotion to his wife of fifty-three years, Beth, and the many kindnesses he showed to his fellow faculty members during his several decades at the school. Dorgan felt that by exemplifying "pietas Christiana" in this life, his old friend was assured oneness with Christ in the next. Although he lived on Staten Island for many years, Quintavalle's funeral was celebrated at St. Ignatius Church, across the street from the school that had meant so much to him for more than four decades of his life. In addition to his wife and two sons who were present at the Mass, one of whom also went to Regis, a large crowd of former colleagues and students also came to pay their last respects, including nine Jesuits and several of his students who were ordained diocesan priests.[66]

Men like Egan and Quintavalle not only were excellent and dedicated teachers for decades, but they also did this while earning salaries far lower than what was offered by public schools at the time. Even Father Reed recognized this. In one of his regular reports on the school, he mentioned that Regis was about to lose a superb math teacher "who has reluctantly transferred to a suburban high school where he will receive an increase of almost one third of his present salary." While the salaries at Regis for lay teachers were the highest of the eight schools in the New York Province,

Reed admitted that they were still not high enough, remarking, "I wish that I could say that this salary is adequate to support a man with a family, but I cannot."[67] Thus, it is no surprise that Cy Egan had to do so much adjunct teaching in the evening or that Don Kennedy coached Regis's and another high school's basketball team at the same to make ends meet.

These men mentioned above were by no means the only outstanding lay teachers at Regis during the middle decades of the twentieth century. Some other men who had a long and venerable tenure in the classroom included Mr. Robert Clancy, who taught French and Latin; and Mr. James J. Daly ("The J"), who taught Latin and French. In addition to these men who made their career teaching at Regis, there was still another group of teachers who stayed for far shorter periods, including the first full-time female faculty, who began working at the school as librarians in the early 1950s. In an age when Jesuits still made up more than half of the faculty, there could have been a temptation to write off these lay teachers as mere adjuncts.[68] However, unlike the Jesuits who were often transferred to other assignments (especially the scholastics), this small group of lay teachers became veritable institutions among the generations of students they taught, and their affection for Regis was very much rooted in the dedicated service of these Catholic gentlemen. In addition, while their traditional piety might not have distinguished them much from many other Catholic men of the period, teachers with such a strong Catholic identity would become less and less common over the coming decades, making the impact of Egan, Quintavalle, and Clancy on the lives of their students all the more distinctive in the history of Regis.

Regarding women on the faculty, there generally were not any, save for the librarians beginning in the 1950s, with Mrs. Helen Merrigan serving the longest tenure of them. As far as classroom teachers, the only female teacher from this era, and she was only part-time, was a Mrs. Helen (Farr) Sloan, the widow of the Ashcan painter John French Sloan, who taught art for a few years. It would not be until the late 1960s with the arrival of second wave of feminism that women would be hired as full-time classroom teachers and come to represent a larger portion of faculty.

Back in the Classroom

The "School Regulations" published early in the academic year 1955–1956 were not all that different from the rules going back some years. Students were still required to enter and leave the building through the 85th Street tunnel until after 4:30 P.M., when they could then use the main door. The corridor running alongside and above the lower gym was still for the exclusive use of the faculty. However, seniors had a few privileges. They were the only students permitted to use the main staircase (though exceptions were made for beadles in their course of duty and students on their way to the St. Ignatius for Mass or confession), and of course, they had exclusive use of the Senior Room on the third floor, though the Regulations reminded them to be sure to extinguish all cigarettes before leaving the room.[69]

As had been the case since the start of Regis, the class (homeroom) teacher was the faculty member charged with the daily monitoring of the student as well as overseeing his overall (academic, moral, spiritual) formation. A guide for class teachers from the 1950s for how to conduct an annual interview with each of the boys in his homeroom class provides some insight into what this formation entailed. At the beginning of their conversation, the teacher was reminded to tell the boy that the interview was strictly confidential. Then it was suggested that the teacher ask the student to open his Latin book in order to see how the student had "prelected" for that day. The class teacher was charged with encouraging the boy to excel at Regis. Rather than relying on "the fear of being thrown out" as a motive, the teacher was to take a more practical tack. Rather than recommending study for its own sake, the guide proposed that the student be encouraged to think about what future career he might like to pursue, so the teacher could "show him that this or that subject was a means to an end." As far as character formation, the guide suggested that the class teacher point out any "personality defects," such as "faulty manners" or a "lack of dependability," so that the student could begin to address them. Finally, the class teacher was tasked with several goals in terms of the student's spiritual formation. The teacher was strongly encouraged to get the boy to join the Guard of Honor if he was not a member already. (Recall that members of the Guard promised to receive Communion at least three times each week.) The writer of this guide was of the opinion that "many youngsters do not go more often to Communion *because they have never been asked*." It was also suggested that he ask the boy if he prayed the rosary daily, since it takes "7 or 8 minutes" and they can "say it on the subway."[70]

As far as academics were concerned, students were now offered a bit of choice compared to the early years of the school. While Latin was still mandatory for all students for all four years, until 1956 at the beginning of his sophomore year, a boy was required to choose between the "Greek Course" and "Science Course."[71] If choosing the former, the Regian would begin Greek as a sophomore and continue it through senior year. As a junior, he would decide between studying French or German and continue

Guard of Honor Vice Prefect John ("Jack") Connelly (*left*) and John P. Shea, Jr., both class of 1956, at Mass before school in the Regis Chapel. The Guard was founded in 1917, and Regians who were members promised to attend Mass and receive Holy Communion several times a week in addition to Sunday. When a boy joined the Guard, he was given a small lapel pin with the Greek word for fish (*ΙΧΘΥΣ*), which was inside the shape of a fish. John Connelly, who has been teaching at Regis since 1961, still proudly wears his Guard of Honor pin.

with that modern language in his senior year. Those in the Greek Course were required to take only one science course during their entire time at Regis and would do so as seniors, choosing between chemistry and physics. Those who chose the Science Course would begin German in sophomore year (and take it for two more years), take chemistry as a junior, and physics as a senior. Beginning in the fall of 1957, this choice between two tracks of study was ended and all students were required to take Greek, and they had to take two years of French or German beginning junior year. As seniors, students were obliged to take either chemistry or physics. As far as the study of mathematics, until the school year 1949–50, only two years were required, but in the fall of 1950 a course in algebra II and trigonometry was added for juniors. Also in 1950, "Our Economic World" became a required course for freshmen, and for the first time a separate course in American history was placed in the sophomore curriculum.[72]

In maintaining its strong emphasis on Greek and Latin, Regis received high marks from the Middle States evaluation committee, which came for a three-day visit of the school in November 1955. Praised for not giving into the "modern trend" to eliminate the classics, the school was also commended for its emphasis on logical reasoning and "the practice of stressing by constant use the techniques of forceful, fluent speech." The school was also lauded for *not* including "formal study periods" in its daily order, a practice common in most public high schools but which many considered a form of babysitting and not a productive use of time.[73]

In early part of this period, speech was required for one term in freshman and sophomore year, but by the late 1950s, this was cut back only to freshman year. And finally, through the whole period of 1946–64, religion, English, and "physical training" were mandatory for all four years. As far as extracurricular activities, the menu of options remained fairly constant over this period, though there were a few new additions. By 1964, there was a varsity swim team as well as a bowling squad for those with modest athletic inclinations. For those whose interests were more cerebral, a Russian club had been established, surely a by-product of the Cold War.[74]

The demands of the curriculum described above proved to be too heavy for a fair number of Regians, and as late as the 1959–60 academic year, Father Reed voiced concern about this in his report on the school. In the fourth marking period of that year (out of eight), close to 20 percent of the entire student body had failed one or more subjects. He feared that once again some teachers were "falling back on the negative motivation of threatened failure which used to be too common at Regis."[75] In all likelihood, the Jesuit was referring to the time when Father Taylor was principal. During this era (1943–51), a student would be expelled for failures in two consecutive semesters, even if the failures were not in the same subject. In addition, the method of dismissal was rather insensitive. A member of the class of 1948 recalls several instances of Father Taylor coming into a classroom and asking one or more students to see him in the hallway. As he informed them of their dismissal, their classmates would collect their books for them, as those who were being dismissed then emptied their lockers and made their way out of the building.[76]

With the arrival of Harvey as principal in the fall of 1951, it seems there was some attempt to lessen the use of expulsion as a motivator for students. In fact, in Reed's 1955 report, he praised the school for the "sharp drop in the total number of fatalities [expulsions] which used to be so dreadfully high."[77] However, now with McCusker as principal, Reed wondered if there had been a reversal of this trend. A decade earlier in his report on the school, Reed had expressed concern over the large number of students who failed out of Regis each year. He wondered if some statistical analysis could be done so that the school could determine whether the current entrance exam "really serves to predict successful students."[78] However, by 1962, the expulsion began to decline, with the graduating class of that year having lost about 15 percent of its members since freshman year (compared to upward of 50 percent in the school's early years).[79]

Despite so much general consistency at Regis since its opening forty years earlier, some things had changed at the school in the postwar era. By 1960, the size of the student body had again grown larger. Since Regis reached its full complement of grades in the fall of 1917, its population varied widely over the decades from a high of 809 boys in 1930 to a low of 419 in 1934.[80] The 1950s saw the number again on the upswing. The school began with a population of 541 (1950–51) and ended it with 645 students for the last academic year (1959–60).[81] But as described earlier, much of this expansion came as a result of fear that the archdiocese might try to use the underutilized space in the building.

In addition to the expansion in enrollment, the geographic area from which Regis was drawing students was also undergoing change. For the class of 1918, almost 70 percent came from Manhattan.[82] By 1961, the total percentage of the student body from this borough was down to under 10 percent. By this year, boys from Queens represented the largest share of the student body at almost 24 percent. They were followed by the group from Brooklyn at slightly more than 18 percent.[83] This change is not surprising given the massive development of these outer boroughs in the first half of the twentieth century and the movement of large numbers from the crowded tenements of Manhattan to the outer boroughs. This trend continued into the 1960s. For the freshman class that was accepted in 1964, only 12 out of 188 were from Manhattan (slightly less than 7 percent), and over 42 percent were from outside New York City. Only one boy from this incoming class had not attended a parochial school.[84] On another note regarding the year 1964, of the 106 boys who graduated that June, 91 won Regents scholarships from New York State, which at that time awarded recipients a substantial scholarship if they attended college in the state.[85]

The period between the end of World War II and the school's fiftieth anniversary in 1964 also saw the beginnings of some small changes in the ethnic composition of the school. In the pioneer class of 1918, the vast majority of the graduates (seventy-two out of seventy-six) had Irish surnames, and the years after this saw the school made up of mostly boys of Irish and German ancestry. That slowly began to change with a small but increasing number of students with Italian or Slavic surnames. By 1961, almost 20 percent of the students in the graduating class had Italian surnames, with another handful of non-Irish or non-German last names in the class, too.[86] It would take several more decades before there would be a sizeable number of Hispanic or African American students at the school, though the 1950s saw the beginnings of this with a trickle of boys from these ethnic groups.[87]

As far as the economic background of the students in this period, this is hard to determine with any exactitude. As mentioned above, by the early 1960s the growing number of boys coming from the suburbs suggests that as the Catholics moved out of the city they were also moving into the middle class. However, this move up the economic ladder did not apply to all Regians. As late as 1952, Father Harvey wrote to the president of Georgetown asking for a full scholarship, including room and board, for a Regis graduate. According to the principal, although several boys had been offered full tuition scholarships, "no Regis boy has gone to Georgetown the past years" because of the additional cost of room and board. Harvey hoped that Georgetown would be able to offer "a *full* [emphasis original] Georgetown scholarship to a Regis graduate each year." For their part, the Regis administration would "take great pains to see to it that the boy honored would be a lad who would give real promise of contributing something to Georgetown beyond his own grades—by participation in extra-curricular activities, and so forth." It is not clear if Georgetown ever granted Harvey's wish, but this letter does offer some evidence that as late as the 1950s, a fair number of Regis students came from families that were in the lower middle class or the working poor.[88]

Toward Fifty Years

In 1956, the Society of Jesus celebrated the four-hundredth anniversary of the death of its founder, St. Ignatius Loyola, and not surprisingly, Regis High School, one of the Jesuits' newer apostolates, marked the milestone, too. The graduating class of that year dedicated their yearbook as an "Homage to Saint Ignatius Loyola, Organizer for God," and on the first few pages of the volume presented a synopsis of the saint's life as well as classic images of him and other early Jesuits. The remainder of the book included additional pictures of the great saint as well as brief excerpts from his writings. The school commemorated the "Ignatian Year" in other ways as well. In keeping with a custom begun a few years earlier, a Mass in honor of St. Ignatius was celebrated in late January (although on the church calendar his feast is observed on July 31, the date of his death). For this year's Mass, Father Jerome D'Souza, a Jesuit from India and a member of his country's delegation to the United Nations, was invited to preach. In his sermon, the Indian Jesuit not only "briefly sketched the key points in the life of Ignatius" but also exhorted Regians to become "true soldiers of Christ."[89]

The next anniversary Regis celebrated, though less historic, was certainly more personal. The year 1964 ushered in Regis's golden jubilee, and the school planned a variety of events to celebrate, including a retreat and a dance for the alumni as well as a reunion for teachers, past and present.[90] On November 28, a gala dinner was held at the Waldorf Astoria Hotel with over one thousand people in attendance, including many wives of the alumni. Each of the sixty-four tables had a host assigned to it, and these hosts included dozens of Jesuits, principals, and presidents of area high schools and colleges, former Regis teachers such as Cy Egan, and even Cardinal Spellman.[91] After cocktails in the east foyer of the hotel, the event moved to the grand ballroom where all were seated. Next came the playing of the school song followed by greetings or remarks by eight different speakers. The formal program ended with grace, which the assembled surely must have offered with deep thanks, since the formal program was scheduled to last for over an hour before dinner was to be served.[92] Not surprisingly, Father Gannon was the principal speaker of the evening. A most sought after speaker on the Catholic dinner circuit as well as former rector–president of the school, Gannon had some years earlier published a collection of his talks under the title *After Black Coffee*.[93] Tickets for the event cost fifteen dollars but drinks were not included.

The highlight of the spiritual commemorations of the school's jubilee was the Solemn Pontifical Mass of Thanksgiving, celebrated on February 2 at St. Ignatius Church. For this special liturgy, the school invited Bishop John J. Maguire to be the celebrant. A member of the class of 1921, Maguire was the first Regis alumnus to be ordained a bishop. The sermon was delivered by Monsignor Edwin Broderick, class of 1934, who at that time was secretary to Cardinal Spellman. Broderick began his reflection by first noting that February 2 was the "Feast of the Presentation of Our Lord in the Temple," and that all those who had gathered were observing their own "Presentation Day" by coming to St. Ignatius Church to thank God for "the grace, the light and the favors we have received in such abundance these fifty years." Beginning on a spiritual note, Broderick then went on to set the mise-en-scène. Reminding the congregation that at the time of Regis's founding in 1914 Henry Ford had just raised the daily wage of his workers to five dollars and Woodrow Wilson was still in his first term in the White House, he went on to refer to some other historical events from the period.

Given the solemnity of the occasion, the monsignor could be excused for preening a bit in referring to the "built-in respectability" that went with going to Regis, and how the "young ladies were in awe of your recital of the Greek alphabet, the nuns considered you a genius [and] the parish priest was embarrassed to preach in your presence." Playing to his audience, Broderick also took a stroll down memory lane as he recalled the infamous Regis entrance exam, the annual Novena of Grace in honor of St. Francis Xavier, jug, the senior staircase, and countless "unexpected quizzes." Given the breadth and depth of Catholic devotional life that defined their time on 84th Street, Broderick noted that it was not surprising that by 1964 nearly three hundred Regis alumni had entered the ranks of the "illustrious Society of Jesus." In addition, the school had produced a great harvest of graduates who one day would be ordained as diocesan priests. According to Broderick, since the school's opening, over 10 percent of the Regis alumni had been ordained Catholic priests. He then went on to "proudly challenge her students of the next half century to surpass, even to equal this impressive statistic."

Though he had not been a member of the Regis Debating Society, Broderick had nevertheless learned the skills of a good rhetorician and so circled back to his opening when coming to his conclusion. When Simeon encountered the child Jesus upon his presentation in the temple, St. Luke recounts that the old man asked the Lord to send him forth in peace ("Nunc Dimittis") now that he had seen the glory of Israel. In coming to the end of his sermon, Broderick asked God that he now, too, be dismissed in peace, and using Simeon's canticle, he prayed that "these young Regians presented here today may be the light to enlighten the Gentiles and the glory of our people."[94]

The golden anniversary also provided the school the opportunity to solicit funds from the alumni, something Regis had not done before, apart from modest annual dues in the Alumni Association or the drive to refurbish the chapel in 1949. Plans for this first major appeal began in January of 1963, and were laid out by Father James Carney, S.J., class of 1943, who at that time taught religion in addition to being head of the Alumni Association. It was his hope that the school could raise $500,000, and the plan was to begin with a quiet phase where the bulk of that amount would be raised from a smaller number of targeted alumni. Then the larger, public phase would begin when all the alumni would be solicited. As it turned out, the alumni raised only $230,000 for the school. Though the school did not reach its goal, this first major fund-raising was valuable beyond just the money that was raised. By the late 1960s, the shortfall between the returns from the foundation and actual expenses had begun to grow, which ultimately led to the first annual giving campaign in 1968.[95]

The celebrations marking Regis's first half-century were noticed beyond 84th Street and were also covered by several of the city's newspapers. The *New York Journal–American* ran an interview with Father McCusker in which the paper described the school as "one of the most outstanding Catholic schools in the nation." For this piece, the reporter both visited classrooms and talked to some of the school's "exceptionally bright students." In explaining why Regis had developed such a stellar reputation since its founding five decades earlier, Father McCusker mentioned that the median IQ of the students was 137, which was "remarkable because anything over 130 is considered superior." "Because the boys are so talented, the school pushes them through a demanding curriculum with some graduating with as many as 25 high school credits," whereas, according to McCusker, most schools "require only 16 to 18 credits." The principal made a point also of saying that the school provided ample recreational opportunities for the students, including four formal dances a year. Seniors have their own recreational room, "which contains several pool tables," where "they can relax and smoke if they like." However, "liquor is forbidden." The Jesuit also listed the many sports and extracurricular activities that the boys may engage in, but mentioned that debating "is one of the favorite" of these, and that the pastime has its own room displaying over 150 trophies won by Regis debaters over the years. The laudatory full-page article included six photographs of students and one of Father McCusker.[96]

A 1962 article about Regis in a Catholic magazine noted that in 1957, Regis was the only Catholic school out of a list of thirty-eight that had been "singled out in a report publicized by *Time* and *Newsweek* . . . that had produced twenty or more finalists in the National Merit Scholarship race over a two year period." In 1958, Regis students had earned a higher percentage of Regents scholarships than any other school, public or private, in the city. As Regis reached its golden jubilee, its alumni certainly had much to crow about (and to be thankful for).[97]

While the various anniversary celebrations were surely joyous occasions, there may in fact have been one that did not fit this description. In commemoration of the golden jubilee, it was announced that a full day of regular classes for all students would be held on Saturday, October 10, 1964, to allow parents "to see Regis in actual operation on a regular school day." In the letter to the parents, the principal, Father Edward ("Ned") Horgan (1964–70), invited them to come and see "what happens to your son the day after he does all that strange homework." The mothers and fathers could come "and leave whenever you want." In his gracious letter, Father Horgan promised that there would be "no speeches or collection baskets," and a complimentary light lunch would be served. Despite this warm welcome, he was clear, however, that this invitation was extended to the parents only, "since we would find it difficult to handle all the brothers, sisters, cousins and aunts of our students."[98] There are no records extant as to how much (or little) the students enjoyed this extra day of academics.

In an accident of history, the celebrations of Regis's first half century came just before a period of great dislocation and unrest for both American society and the Catholic Church. Regis was not immune to this push for reform, and over the next decade or so the school would see more change to its internal life than ever before in its history.

5 Neat and Clean with Socks and Covered Shoes

A Revised Dress Code, a New Curriculum, and Other Changes, 1964–1980

The Grants

Because of the Grant family's continued generosity to the Jesuits, especially toward the building of a new Jesuit seminary in Shrub Oak, on Christmas Day, 1960, Julia, Edna, and Hugh Grant were named "Founders of the Provinces of New York and Buffalo."[1] The Society had bestowed a similar honor on their mother many years earlier, and now the Jesuits felt that her children should likewise be recognized and thanked for their many acts of generosity.

After the provincial, Father John J. McGinty, S.J., had received permission from the superior general in Rome to bestow this honor on the Grant children, he planned to present them with an engraved parchment at a formal ceremony. However, after a conversation with the former New York provincial, Father John McMahon, McGinty changed his mind. McMahon reminded his successor that this kind of recognition was not something the Grants had ever sought or expected. Rather, McMahon "emphasized that it was only the spiritual benefit and only this would interest" them, and reminded McGinty of the "very unpretentious way in which [the family] had always presented [their] assistance to the Society."[2] Thus, all pomp was to be avoided, and the family was informed of their naming as founders simply by letter from McGinty, dated December 25 (possibly to recall the evening forty-six years earlier, when their late mother had presented Father Hearn with the first installment toward the foundation of Regis).[3]

The decision of the New York Jesuits to formally but quietly honor and thank the Grant children was well timed, for in less than ten years only one would be alive. On the morning of February 2, 1962, Julia passed away and was waked privately in the family home. Her funeral Mass was celebrated three days later at St. Ignatius Church by Cardinal Spellman, who also accompanied her body to Calvary Cemetery in Queens, where it was interred in the family mausoleum. After Julia's death, the provincial sent a letter to all Jesuit communities in the provinces marked "CONFIDENTIAL—FOR OURS ONLY," asking for the usual suffrages (prayers) for the repose of

Julia's soul. However, the letter did not mention the deceased's specific connection to Regis.[4] Next, in 1969 Edna died, which left Hugh as the only surviving Grant.[5] After her will was settled in 1971, the New York Province received $625,000 from her estate.[6] And this was only the latest gift that came to the Jesuits or Regis from the Grant family.

In 1965 and again in 1967, Hugh and Edna gave $800,000 to Regis, with the intention that the principal remain intact but that the income be used for incremental salary increases for the lay faculty.[7] In a letter to the provincial in which Hugh laid out his plans for these gifts, he mentioned that in a recent conversation they had "agreed . . . that the morale of the teachers would be greatly augmented" if they would receive annually the income from this gift.[8] After consultation with Mr. George Brooks, '18, who had been long involved with the Alumni Association and more recently with some financial planning for the school, it was decided that that "teachers with a longer period of service at Regis would receive a greater amount" of the annual distribution of the interest.[9] In addition, it seems that after this initial gift, Hugh began to give a further $10,000 each year at Christmas for the next decade as additional support for regular salary increases for the teachers. According to Father Brooks, no Jesuit superior ever went to the Grants directly for money. Since he began working in 1957 as the family chaplain, Father Brooks had also taken on the role of intermediary between the Jesuits and the Grant family when there were discussions of another possible gift.[10]

Although the decade of the 1960s brought the death of his two sisters, the 1970s were far kinder to Hugh. In 1972, at the age of sixty-eight, Hugh finally married. A close friend of the family recalled that the longtime bachelor found life quite lonely with both sisters gone, and few were surprised that he sought out uxorial companionship.[11] On February 26, 1972, Hugh married Mrs. Lucie Mackey Rollinson, a New York socialite who had been widowed.[12] A native of New Jersey and a graduate of Smith College, Lucie had previously been married to Mr. Reginald H. Rollinson, a Madison Avenue advertising executive.[13] Hugh and Lucie met at party on the Upper East Side, and the next day he phoned to "ask her to play hooky from her interior decorating business to go to a Long Island beach with him." Lucie accepted immediately.[14] After a brief courtship, they were married at St. Ignatius by Father Brooks.[15]

Though the Grant residence on East 72nd Street would have been more than enough room for the new couple, Lucie made it clear that she did not want to live there, as she found the old house stuffy. To appease his new bride, Hugh purchased an apartment at 141 East 72nd Street, in which he

Hugh Grant, Jr., and Lucie (Mackey) Grant at a party celebrating their recent wedding of February 26, 1972. Their marriage turned out to be somewhat short, as Hugh died in 1981. Lucie died in 2007.

also had a small chapel constructed. Although Father Brooks continued to celebrate daily Mass at the Grant's new residence, Lucie was rarely present. She had attended Mass a few times while they were still in the mansion but did not keep to this. Though baptized a Catholic, Lucie did not share her new husband's religious zeal.[16]

As for the mansion that he and Lucie would no longer be using, Hugh first offered it to the Jesuits. The New York provincial and several other priests came to look over the house, but eventually they refused Hugh's generous offer after determining that it would cost a "small fortune" to renovate the space and adapt it for use as a residence for several of their men.[17] The house was then put up for sale for $650,000, but attracted little interest. After the house languished on the realtors' rolls, Hugh asked Father Brooks about donating it to the archdiocese. When it was offered to Terence Cardinal Cooke, the archbishop was more than happy to accept, thinking that it "might be a useful residence for a group of priests or nuns." Shortly after this, however, when the cardinal was in Rome, Pope Paul VI mentioned to him the need for a residence for the Holy See's permanent observer to the United Nations. Ever obliging, Cooke asked Hugh if he would donate the house to the Holy See.[18] After some thought, Hugh decided that he would not deed the house directly to the Holy See, since he "did not trust the Italians" and was afraid that "once they got their hands on it, they would sell it." Rather, he would give it to the archdiocese, which would retain ownership but could loan the mansion gratis to the Holy See for use by the permanent observer, a practice that continued until 2010 when Archbishop Timothy Dolan finally deeded the house to the Holy See.[19]

In closing down their former residence, Hugh and Lucie made several gifts to the nearby Metropolitan Museum of Art.[20] Unlike the tradition of Hugh's mother, who always demanded strict anonymity when giving to charities, Lucie made sure that the museum clearly noted that these items were given by "Mr. and Mrs. Hugh J. Grant."[21]

Progressive Trends in Education

The year 1972 not only saw Hugh Grant finally marry, but also the arrival of a new principal of the school his mother had been so instrumental in founding. In September of that year, Father Robert Newton, S.J., arrived as Regis's fifteenth principal. (Newton actually was named Regis's first headmaster, a change in title that proved to be short-lived.) For the most part, the school he was chosen to administer had only recently begun to institute changes. However, after his six-year tenure as headmaster, both the curriculum and the daily life of both students and teachers had been greatly altered.

In the early 1960s, the spirit of change had again begun to blow through the American educational system. When it had first stirred earlier in the century, Regis and most all other Catholic schools had resisted progressive educational reforms, but now that the school was led by a young Jesuit with a newly minted doctorate in educational administration from Harvard University, that would no longer be the case.

Before taking this new role at Regis, Father Newton, who was still only in his mid-thirties, had already put together a substantial résumé in terms of school leadership, with experience on governing boards of several high schools, including non-Catholic institutions. He had even been involved in the educational component of the Baltimore Model Cities Program. Immediately before arriving at 84th Street, Newton had spent time in India working with the national association of Jesuit schools in that country, so his experience in terms of models of education went beyond just the United States.[22] Newton was just one of a young crop of Jesuits of this era whom the Society had sent for advanced degrees in graduate schools of education, a trend that had recent origins. In earlier times, for the most part the Jesuit superiors had selected young men of talent and intellect to lead their schools, but almost none of these priests had degrees in education. Rather, the Jesuits chosen to become administrators had generally studied one of the humanities on the graduate level. However, with a new openness to the outside world that the Second Vatican Council brought to the Church as a whole and the Society of Jesus in particular, this period witnessed a newfound fascination with the social sciences and an almost starry-eyed belief in their ability to radically improve society.

While progressive reforms had been implemented in many American schools in the decades before World War II, in the 1960s this movement was now witnessing a second spring, and this time, Catholic schools did not remain on the sidelines. Central to this movement was sharp criticism for anything in a school that seemed to "herd, brainwash, or regiment" students. Holding an exalted view of human nature, children were thought to be innately wise and capable of doing or learning most anything as long as outside authorities (teachers, a rigid curriculum, etc.) did not squelch their spirits. One of the most influential proponents of this progressive pedagogy was A. S. Neill, founder of the elite New England boarding school Summerhill.[23]

In 1960, Neill published a book chronicling his experience of leading this school, which was founded on the belief that a student's happiness is paramount. In order for a child to realize his or her full intellectual potential, it was Neill's belief that the student must be allowed almost absolute freedom. At Summerhill, attendance at class was optional, and in his book Neill boasts that in fact one boy waited thirteen years before showing up for his first formal lesson. By the end of the decade, Neill's book was selling more than two hundred thousand copies annually and had sparked the publication of a phalanx of other books that also called into question traditional pedagogical practices. This now chorus of voices for reform called for radical innovations, such as the decentralization of schools into the community using spaces such as storefronts and the use of the city (streets, parks, etc.) itself as a learning resource.[24]

The notion that schools had to update themselves eventually came to affect Jesuit high schools, too. In 1967, Father William O'Malley, S.J., then a newly ordained priest assigned to McQuaid Jesuit High School in Rochester, wrote an article expressing these very sentiments. Though the piece was mostly about the need to lessen the workload of Jesuit priests teaching in secondary schools, O'Malley also voiced concerns about Jesuit schools themselves. He warned that the Society's schools were no longer leaders in the field of education but rather "co-plodders," and feared that its schools lacked the "vision and daring" to try new things as other private schools were doing. Finally, he lamented the fact that few of his Jesuit colleagues were showing interest in the latest innovations in pedagogy, which now included "year-round classes, night classes for parents, gradeless high schools," and what is now called block scheduling.[25]

About this time, Newton was also calling for Jesuit schools to reevaluate their effectiveness in a changing world where the "rapid expansion of factual data was doubling every ten years." (O'Malley, too, was taken with this phenomenon and in his essay talked about the geometric growth in "man's accumulated knowledge.")[26] While still a scholastic, in 1966 Newton wrote an article for the *Woodstock Letters* warning his fellow Jesuits that they had better not remain unaware of the challenges that were facing their students and their schools, and that the need to update their practices and curricula could not wait any longer.[27]

In opening his essay, Newton recalled the 1964 Santa Clara meeting of administrators of Jesuit high schools during which the group reviewed current developments in the field of secondary education, such as flexible scheduling, team teaching, Advanced Placement exams, and the use of television in the classroom. According to Newton, at this point these innovations had made "little impression" on Jesuit schools, though these reforms had been around for a "fairly lengthy period." For example, a 1961 report said that about a hundred school districts around the nation had begun using team teaching in one form or another, and that hundreds more were "actively planning toward it." Despite what Newton saw as a nationwide groundswell of interest in this innovative instructional method, only seven (of the forty-nine) Jesuit high schools around the country had "indicated experimentation in this area." There was also a similar lack of interest on the part of Jesuit schools in the use of television in the classroom. The only new area in which they were keeping pace with public and other schools was in their implementation of Advanced Placement courses.[28]

Newton was also frustrated with how seemingly indifferent many teachers in the high schools were to new developments in the study of education. While there was an increase in interest with some Jesuits in the subject areas they taught (e.g., history or literature), Newton was clearly troubled that there remained "a general distrust and apathy toward the study of the various aspects of education" and the role the social sciences could play in helping the Jesuits update their teaching methods. He also criticized the "blind confidence" some of his confreres had in their "Jesuit system," which led them to dismiss anything they or their schools might learn from new approaches in pedagogy.[29]

Newton concluded his essay with a wakeup call, warning that "there exists a real danger that many . . . remain unaware or indifferent to the magnitude of the challenge that faces Jesuit schools." He felt that there were already indications that Jesuit schools had "relinquished leadership and had even fallen behind, basically because our progress has not kept pace with the rapid updating in the best of private and public education."[30] Newton had written this piece several years before he earned his doctorate in education, but he was clearly already interested in the future of Jesuit schools. And just six years after the publication of his essay, he would have the opportunity to put into practice much of what he was calling for when he became principal at Regis. However, this is not to say that Regis had not updated or changed any of its practices prior to Father Newton's arrival in 1972.

Preliminary Changes

Despite many of the changes that were in the offing, much of life at Regis in the mid-1960s had remained the same. The school still ran two annual outings in the fall and spring, with the students going by boat to Bear Mountain or Rye Beach. By 1967, the student council had taken on a larger role in organizing these events, but always with the oversight of a Jesuit scholastic moderator. For this year, Mr. Joseph Lienhard, S.J, '58, had this job in addition to teaching Latin. For the spring trip, Lienhard also oversaw the council's invitations to several Catholic girls' schools to join the Regians on the *Bay-Belle,* the boat that would bring them from the Battery up to Bear Mountain. Faculty, too, went on these excursions, but while on the boat generally stayed apart from the students to enjoy adult beverages as they sailed up the Hudson. In addition, the Homeric Academy was also still going strong, now under the leadership of Father Robert Kelly, S.J., '44, who taught classics. On May 12, 1967, the senior seminar class held its annual event, to which university professors were invited in order to examine the seniors on their translations and understanding of about five thousand lines of Homer's *The Iliad.* Still one of the most distinctive qualities of a Regis education, Greek was now studied by fewer and fewer Regians since becoming an elective.[31]

Although traditions such as the annual boat rides and the Homeric Academy were still very much a part of Regis, outside forces would soon begin to put pressure on them and other facets of the school's traditional education. In late March 1966, Regis underwent an evaluation of the Middle States Association of Colleges and Secondary Schools. In response to the visiting committee's report, the school quickly made some changes to its curriculum and practices the following September. While the committee saw "many fine things" at Regis High School and praised the leadership of the principal, Father Edward ("Ned") Horgan (1964–70), it offered some recommendations in addition to its many commendations.

In encouraging the school to diversify its course offerings and provide more opportunities for individualized study, the committee felt that more time would be needed in the class schedule.[32] To make room within the existing daily order, the committee suggested that the weekly periods for confession on Thursday and Mass on Friday be programmed "outside the academic day." Father Horgan agreed, and that following September confession period was dropped completely and the school-wide Mass was now held only every other week. The committee also recommended that "faculty members do extensive visiting to study the diversified curricula offered and the teaching methods used in the education of the gifted," and suggested Phillips Academy Andover and Phillips Exeter Academy in particular as schools worth visiting. In response, Father Horgan required every teacher to visit "at least one good school" during the course of the next academic year.[33]

As far as curriculum, Father Horgan made some modest changes in response to the committee's recommendations. Starting in September 1966, each student would now be required to take a minimum of two science courses over four years. All freshmen would take physical science and all seniors would enroll in either chemistry or physics. In addition, sophomores would be offered the opportunity to take biology. Other departments saw changes, too. In what was now briefly renamed the "social studies" instead of "history" department, it was decided that a senior elective in anthropology would continue to be offered, as it had in the previous year, again demonstrating the new interest in the social sciences. The music program was expanded to include a mandatory one-semester course in music appreciation in junior year. Finally, both freshmen and sophomores would have more time in gym, now with two periods of physical education each week.[34]

Outside the classroom, starting in September two lunch periods would be scheduled "to eliminate crowding in the cafeteria." With the addition of this additional lunch period, freshmen were now no longer required to stand while they ate. In keeping with the spirit of the times, which called for giving students more responsibility and input in their education, the role of student council was expanded to give it "full responsibility for student assemblies."[35]

Members of the class of 1967 on retreat at the former Gonzaga Retreat House in Monroe, New York. The retreat was led by Father James J. Fischer, S.J. (*second row, left*), who was then rector of St. Andrew's novitiate in Poughkeepsie. In 1980, Father Fischer was named president of Regis. Annual retreats both at school and at outside locations have been part of a Regis education since the school's beginning in 1914.

As for Regis's teachers, the Middle States report recommended across the board salary increases to improve the rate of faculty retention. Accordingly, a "substantially improved" faculty salary scale was put into effect, which was possible, as mentioned earlier, because of the sizeable donations given by the two remaining Grant children in the mid-1960s. This increase in faculty compensation was thought not only to be more just, but it was also hoped to result in a "smaller turnover in the Mathematics Department," which historically had seen many teachers come and go. In addition, Regis established a relationship with Fordham that would allow faculty to take courses at "one fourth tuition."[36]

In addition to these alterations to curriculum and student life, there were other signs that things had begun to change at Regis. While the number of graduating seniors not continuing their education at Catholic colleges still remained relatively small, these numbers were increasing, a trend the school specifically wanted to continue. When in 1970 Mr. Francis ("Jim") Ferguson was hired to help students with college admissions, he was given the specific mandate to expand the selection of colleges the seniors were applying to, especially Ivy league and other top-level secular institutions.[37] In helping seniors with their college applications, Ferguson first had the student do research on the schools they were interested in, but he generally suggested the three schools to which they would apply, exercising far more authority in this than would be common today at Regis.[38] Also, during his time as college counselor, Ferguson led the charge to drop class ranks on the senior transcripts sent to the colleges during the admissions process. In 1972, the administration acceded to the change, agreeing to Ferguson's claim that "rank-in-class provides little or no value to the college admissions office."[39] Finally, it is also worth noting one other comparison between the classes of this era, 1964 and 1973. While the former sent four young men straight from Regis into the seminary (Jesuit or diocesan), not one student followed this path nine years later, a trend much in keeping with the general plummet in priestly and religious vocations across the nation after the Second Vatican Council.[40]

Another example of both student and faculty questioning about long standing policies at Regis came on the question of grades. In an effort to de-emphasize grades and the spirit of academic competition that had long been a hallmark of a Jesuit education, in the fall of 1966 it was decided that the "Reading of the Marks" would no longer be done. Not actually a public recitation of every student's grades, this exercise, which began in the very earliest days of the school, entailed reading in front of the entire student body the names of those boys who had achieved academic awards in the previous marking period.[41] According to an editorial in *The Owl*, the senior class had been the catalyst for dropping this time-honored ritual and replacing it with "assemblies, which, for the students, are more entertaining and worthwhile."[42] In keeping with this anticompetitive spirit, in 1969 a faculty member even proposed dropping grades entirely at a student–faculty meeting, an innovation in and of itself.[43] Father Kenneth DeLuca, S.J., argued that "too much emphasis was put on the externals of education" and that "everyone gets caught up in this syndrome." His recommendation was that after abolishing marks, the size of the faculty be doubled, whereby with a far smaller teacher-to-student ratio, faculty could evaluate student performance by a qualitative rather than quantitative methods.[44] Despite this interest in change by some, Regians would still receive numeric grades regularly on their academic performance. However, the wider question of student evaluation had now been raised, and eventually the system of grades would be greatly revamped.

The new emphasis on giving students more say in their education, such as the institution of the first student–faculty meeting in 1969, began to show signs of itself at Regis as early as 1966. In the spring of that year, the first student opinion poll was administered for students in all four years, although only 330 of the forms were returned. The respondents were asked for their views on such issues as politics, the Church, sports, and life at Regis, and after tabulation, the results were posted in the bulletin board in the tunnel. As far as politics is concerned, this mostly unscientific poll showed students equally divided between support for Lyndon Johnson and Barry Goldwater if both were to face each other in another election. (By 1972, the Regis student body had moved decidedly to the left, with 31 percent of seniors choosing George McGovern in a straw poll.)[45] As far as student opinions on spiritual concerns, the survey showed that 30 percent felt the Church was moving too slowly in its modernization, while 18 percent thought things were changing too quickly. As far as student predictions regarding professional baseball, about 23 percent thought New York would win the pennant for the American League and slightly more than half thought San Francisco would win it for the National League. (As it turned out, the Yankees came in last while the Giants were beaten by the Dodgers for first place.) And finally, as far as life on 84th Street, 45 percent of respondents felt that the school did not have "extensive enough Seminars and Lectures and other 'cultural outlets.'" *The Owl* writer who reported on this poll interpreted this last finding to demonstrate the need for a "revamping of the School program," but again, it would take until the

1973–74 academic year for the administration to make large-scale changes to the curriculum. But as early as 1966, at least some students were itching for a greater say in how and what they studied, and by the mere fact of the conducting of and reporting on this poll, it seemed that the administration was at least open to beginning a discussion.[46]

Another area that had become open for discussion by the late 1960s was the length of students' hair, and eventually it became a hotly debated topic at the school, including in the pages of *The Owl.* Since the school rules stipulated that "haircuts . . . should be neat," the problem now was that the "student definition of 'neat' [had] come into direct conflict with the administration's definition of the term." However, an editorial in the paper thought that a bigger issue was at play: "The length of a sideburn is not really what is at stake here. . . . Is Regis High School, in imposing hair style regulations, dealing in an area that should not be its concern?" Not surprisingly, the answer to this rhetorical question was a resounding "Yes." According to the editorial's line of reasoning, since the student spends less than one-third of his time at school, the question of the appropriateness of his hairstyle belongs most properly to his parents, not his school. Although many parents decide not to take on this fight with their son, "parental permissiveness, regrettable as it may be, does not warrant intervention on the part of the school." The editorial concluded with an explanatory note stating that discussions on this had already begun between student government officers and the assistant principal, Father Joseph Neville, S.J.

Another sign that things had changed (and were loosening up) by the start of the 1970s could be seen in the dress code of students and faculty at Regis, with the Jesuits leading the way. In early 1970, after the provincial, Father Robert Mitchell, S.J., '43, relaxed the rules regarding dress for Jesuits while at work, now allowing ties and jackets instead of collars and cassocks, many exercised this new option. One scholastic who embraced the change wholeheartedly explained that while wearing black once served a purpose, now "it is less a religious sign than a social one." A priest on the faculty who had taken to wearing business attire justified the change by saying that clerical clothing can "symbolize a chasm between the laity and the clerical state" and thus should be avoided.[47]

With their Jesuit teachers now exercising newfound freedom in their sartorial choices, it was not long before students began demanding the right for similar self-expression. While the boys had choice in the color of their coats and ties, the mere fact that they had to wear these now became a bone of contention. In April 1970, the student council petitioned the

Members of the 1965 Hearn Debating Society. A hallmark of a Jesuit education, public speaking has been an important part of a Regis education from the school's very start.

principal, Father Horgan, for a relaxation of the dress code in anticipation of the warmer weather—no tie and jacket for the remainder of the year. After consulting with the rector, Father Charles Taylor (1966–72), permission was granted on a trial basis.[48] By the return to school in the fall, students were itching for the extension of this indult for the entire year, "since no major discipline problems have arisen as a result of this change."[49] With a new principal in place, Father James Bowes (1970–72), discussions began by way of a faculty–student committee, which asked *The Owl* to administer several polls to gauge student opinion on the question. (In general, the younger students tended to have more conservative tastes than the older ones.)[50] By early December of that year, the committee had met seven times before making its final recommendation, which came by way of compromise. Some on the committee wanted no dress code at all, while others wanted to maintain the current dress code of coat and tie, except in the warmer weather. The new dress code would be known for both its brevity and its simplicity: "Rule 1: All students are to be neat and clean in the manner of their dress. Rule 2: All students are to wear socks and covered shoes." Once put into effect, it was up to the prudential judgment of the assistant principal to determine if an individual student was violating the spirit of the rules, but students quickly began testing the boundaries, and before long a few boys were sporting shorts, T-shirts, and even overalls. It was left to a new administration, which arrived in 1972, to begin to pull the reins in a bit.[51]

As can be seen above, Regis had not remained static in the face of strong changes that had been coming to American schools since the beginning of the prior decade. It was just a couple of years earlier in the spring of 1968 when college students on the other side of Central Park at Columbia University had occupied five of the buildings on their campus to raise grievances against the administration.[52] While the atmosphere at Regis was in no way as contentious (or violent) as that at many of the nation's college campuses, Regians knew protest was in the air and that young people like themselves were demanding changes from their elders, and in many cases these elders were giving in. This struggle between change and tradition was now playing out at Regis, too, and by the early 1970s many of the customs that had been part of school life since 1914 had been greatly eviscerated or abolished altogether.

While aspects of student life had been altered (such as the greatly relaxed dress), for the most part the academic program had remained largely unchanged. But the academic year 1971–72 would see major changes in this area, too. In the fall of 1971, a year before Father Newton's arrival, a trimester academic calendar was put in place at Regis "in the hope that it would offer further possibilities for the betterment of education." In keeping with the *zeitgeist*, this change came about after much consultation and committee work and with the final change having been put to a vote by the entire faculty. With this new structure, students would have more choice in what they studied. By the late 1960s, undergraduates at colleges around the nation had won much more say in what courses they would take, and now their younger siblings were demanding similar concessions on the high school level. Even Catholic colleges saw dramatic change during this period. At nearby and also Jesuit-run Fordham University, students had demanded a series of new freedoms, including student participation in the formation of the curriculum, the end of dorm restrictions, and student representation in the faculty senate, and when this all was not immediately forthcoming, a group of students staged a "sleep-in" and a hunger strike.[53] The implementation of a trimester system at Regis would allow some student choice in the courses they took, which hopefully would avoid any potential conflict between students and administration. Regis seniors would now be able to enroll in three different English classes in the course of one academic year. This innovation also affected the underclassmen, who now saw experiments such as the sophomore history course being taught by three different teachers, "each specializing in his own particular period."[54]

This school year also brought about work toward the writing of a five-year plan that came in response to a mandate from the province. With the recent demise of the Jesuit Educational Association (whose offices were once housed on the second floor of Regis), Jesuit schools had now lost the national body that had offered direction on curriculum and other aspects of academic life in the Society's American schools (though each provincial always retained full authority over his schools).[55] With this body gone, schools were now left to chart their own future, and by the fall of 1971, the New York province had given them their marching orders. In late October of that year, Regis hosted a meeting of over four hundred teachers and administrators from the Jesuit high schools in the New York Province. Led by Father Joseph T. Browne, S.J., '43, who was now in charge of the eight high schools for the province, the meeting was called to "outline the dimensions of the problems facing our schools" and to come up with plans to respond to these challenges, which was about to claim the life of one of them.[56] In the spring of 1971, it had been announced that Brooklyn Prep would close the following year due to rising costs and the declining number of Jesuits able to staff it.[57]

By early December 1971, Regis had begun studying and planning for its own future by establishing several committees, and soon all fifty-two faculty members had embarked on a "comprehensive view of [the] education" offered at Regis.[58] Students also played a role in this evaluation and planning process by offering their suggestions. Student proposals ranged from a plan that called for all courses having a simple pass/fail grade, to the elimination of any distinction between years, "resulting in intra-scholastic enrollment in courses."[59] However, not all students were in favor of more educational experimentation and an increased amount of independent learning. One senior complained of the "mandatory independent study" by history and modern language teachers since, he argued, "many students, through no fault of their own, cannot handle the responsibility of determining what and when to study." Some seniors now had only ten classes per week (down from thirty as juniors) and found it difficult to use all the unstructured time efficiently.[60] Despite this one student's call for restraint, the handwriting was on the wall: progressive educational changes were coming to Regis.

After almost six months of work, on April 4, 1972, the "Regis High School: 5 Year Plan" was finally published. More than sixty pages in length, the document included footnotes detailing the exact faculty vote on each proposal (yeas, nays, and abstentions). In addition to each department's list of proposals it hoped to implement, the plan also included a series of school-wide "implementable items" such as issues dealing with admissions policy and the Jesuit identity of Regis. In the former area, it was now a goal of the school to employ a full-time admissions director, who would be charged with ensuring that "for the foreseeable future, the current norm of 75 per cent 'poor' to 25 per cent purely academic be retained" in the composition of each entering class. Since Regis did not have a rubric in place to determine the economic background of applicants, another implementable item was to establish an ad hoc committee to determine the definition of "poor."[61]

Each of the academic departments had to draw up its goals for the next five years, and a review of some of these items provides a sense of the overarching educational philosophy in vogue at the time. The English department, for example, wanted to establish an "attitude towards learning" that would encourage "individual endeavor" and discourage "passive acceptance—a reversal of the past student/teacher relationship." The emphasis now was on "individual student activity" and not on "passive coverage of a body of knowledge."[62] The "Department of History and Social Studies" was setting out into new waters, and in doing so was reflective of the wider intellectual trend that was placing new importance on the study of non-Western cultures. As part of its new goals and objectives, the department also planned that students would now have "a sympathetic understanding of other civilizations . . . beyond [their] own traditions."

A few years earlier, educational experimentation at Fordham University had led to the establishment (albeit short-lived) of a stand-alone academic program in which the only requirement for students was the study of Urdu, so that they would "break out of the confines of Western thought."[63] Though the change in the history curriculum at Regis was nowhere as radical, it was most definitely a strong break from the classical education that had reigned at the school since the beginning. The change that students probably noticed the most was the moving of "American Civilization" from junior to sophomore year. Placing it earlier in the curriculum was done in the belief that "historical studies should commence from the better known and more easily understood material." Thus, the study of modern European history would now be done in junior year. Finally, the course choices in the newly named history and social studies department surely put new emphasis on the second part of its name with the offering of sociology and cultural anthropology as senior electives.[64]

Even departments that taught the hard sciences saw the need for change in the coming years. As part of its goals, the math department asked the school to purchase a "Nova 1200 Data general computer with at least three teletype input machines." Since this computer used the BASIC computing language rather than FORTRAN, the operation of it by teachers could "be taught in about 15 hours." While the use of the computer would be "limited only by the imagination of the teachers and students," it was the math department's goal to begin offering a senior course in BASIC as soon as possible. The members of the math department thought that possibly the science department would also make use of the computer, though the latter did not mention it in its set of goals. In fact, the science department's part of the Five Year Plan was notably brief. The department was quite satisfied with the changes that had come in response to the 1966 Middle States report and the institution of a minimum of two years of science for all students before graduation. The only real recommendation made was for the offering of more elective and Advanced Placement courses.[65]

The Newtonian Revolution

When Father Newton arrived at Regis in the fall of 1972, this Five Year Plan was still fresh on the minds of both faculty and students, especially its many recommendations for change. However, he took his first year in office slowly, getting to know the school before making systemic changes. This was probably wise since his predecessor, Father Bowes, had lasted only two years as principal. Acknowledging that Bowes led Regis during some trying times, even an editorial in *The Owl* described his tenure as similar to "steer[ing] a ship which always seemed to be riding on rough waters."[66] In fact, both he and Father Neville, who had been assistant principal since 1962, left Regis at the end of the 1971–72 academic year. In recent years, Neville had had to deal with much of the student unrest, especially over rules governing when students could leave the building.[67] Thus, Newton's deliberate approach seemed quite called for given the challenges of his immediate predecessors.

As part of taking a long overview of the school during his first year, Newton hired an outside expert to study the space utilization of the building. With the changes to the curriculum and pedagogy he planned to implement, Newton believed this preliminary step to be crucial, since alterations to both would affect the way students and faculty interacted with one another and the space in which this would all happen. In the winter of 1973, Mr. Richard Strother, an architect who specialized in planning and designing schools, was brought in from Cambridge, Massachusetts, to perform this study. After determining that after almost six decades of use the building remained structurally quite sound, he saw no reason why the interior space could not be greatly reconfigured, so he recommended tearing down many of the interior walls so as to divide the building differently. A change like this would help to meet the needs of the new patterns of student–faculty interaction, which would de-emphasize lecture-based learning. With this in mind, the architect recommended removing faculty desks from the third-floor teachers' room and distributing them around the building in instructional areas (resource centers), which would allow for easier and more frequent interaction with students. The trend was toward individualized studying, and a reconfigured interior for Regis seemed necessary for this goal to be realized.[68]

Individualized learning would ultimately be the hallmark of the educational reforms instituted by Father Newton, and brainstorming on space considerations for this new type of pedagogy was an important first step. But individualization was only one part of it. Newton's plan to overhaul education at Regis would include four other major components: unstructured time, modular schedule, the establishment of resource centers, and an advisor system. Changes such as these would come to substantially reshape the way Regians had been taught since the school's founding, and on the eve of these changes, *The Owl* described the school as about to undergo "the greatest change in its history." Before the final execution of these changes, Newton even included a few students in part of the deliberative process, asking the outgoing student council president to nominate four students to join the final deliberations of the faculty. After the students offered their input, in May 1973 the final plans for a new academic program at Regis were announced, with a few details still to be worked out.[69]

As far as the academic day itself, Regis would be moving to a modular schedule made up of twenty-minute units or "mods." This new schema for organizing the day would allow more space in the schedule for "self-initiated learning." Moving away from an older style of pedagogy, which was characterized by a "teacher dominated, force fed learning situation," students would now have far more discretion on how they spent their time learning. In the educational parlance of the day, the trend was away from "closed teaching systems" to "open learning systems," in which the content of the curriculum was shifted from something "narrow, fixed, [and] determined by outside authority to [one of] breadth, flexibility, [and] adaptation to [the] individual involved."[70] To help students navigate these new educational waters, an academic advisor system would be set up. In this, each teacher would be assigned to advise fourteen to seventeen students, with each student meeting with his advisor at the beginning and the end of the day. A great deal of importance was placed on the academic advisor. According to the document that defined the advisor's role:

> Ideally, the advisor will be the faculty member in the school who through daily contact with the individual student comes to know him best. The primary aim of the [academic advisor] system is to provide for the student someone who takes a special interest in his academic and personal adjustment and development at Regis. Though it is expected that the student will find in his classes, in extracurricular activities and informal ways faculty members to whom he relates easily, the advisor is the faculty member who (as delegate of the Headmaster) exercises responsibility for the day to day development of the student at Regis.[71]

While some of the other changes instituted by Newton were amended or dropped completely by subsequent administrators of the school, the role of the faculty advisor has remained largely the same up to the present. However, in its early days, the program certainly had its critics. Two years after its inception, an editorial in *The Owl* stated simply that "the advisor system does not work" and that it did not offer any "specific value" to students. The unnamed student who penned this piece felt that Regians did not need anyone supervising their work, and that in the end, the teacher had simply become a "scolder" for a student who was struggling in a particular class.[72]

When the students returned from summer vacation in the fall of 1973, not only did they find they now had academic advisors, but they also found a greatly reconfigured building, most notably with the creation of resource centers. The wall that once separated rooms 507 and 509 was gone, now creating a much larger space that became the math resource center. As for resource centers for English, social studies, and theology, the space of the library was given over to create one super-sized resource center for all three departments. To accommodate this, the library was relocated from the second floor to the third by the joining of several rooms. Unlike the resource centers, where serious conversation was allowed between faculty and students, the library was designated as a silent study area.[73]

A central goal of the establishment of resource centers was to increase student–teacher interaction. However, despite the rearrangement of the physical space of the building, it took more effort to get some teachers to actually sit at the desks provided for them in these resource centers. For example, as part of Newton's evaluation of his recent visits to theology classes in the spring of 1974, he noted that the theology section of the combined resource center on the second floor had "the least faculty presence."[74] Also as part of this new rationalization of space, classrooms were now grouped largely by department (e.g., English on the fourth floor and math and science on the fifth floor).[75] The progress of these renovations had slowed a bit near the end of July after a fire broke out in the old handball room in the basement, causing extensive smoke damage on this level as well as on the first floor. Despite this setback, a good bit of the building had been reconfigured to meet the demands of the new academic program.[76]

In addition to the new walls and new rooms, students also found that they were now expected to learn in a new way. In the recent past, only seniors had found themselves with a fair amount of free time to work independently, but now this progressive model of education was being introduced to the lower grades, too. While as recently as the 1972–73 academic year, "students in the first three years were scheduled into structured classes for virtually all of the 40 possible periods during the week," in place now was a "gradual introduction of unstructured time from freshman through senior year." With a week divided into ninety mods of twenty minutes each, freshmen would have fifteen to twenty unstructured mods, sophomores and juniors eighteen to twenty-five, and seniors could have up to thirty-four unstructured mods or more than eleven hours per week to work independently.[77] Even with built-in blocks of unstructured time, teachers were still permitted to release students from regular classes if they thought it was in the student's best interest to work independently rather than in a classroom setting.[78] Students were even allowed to leave the building as long as their plans outside were "worthwhile and constructive."[79]

In addition to the makeover of academics, the guidance department also saw some significant changes. Beginning in the fall of 1973, guidance periods were created in the student schedules so that, according to Father Leo Daly, S.J., the class could delve into topics "not strictly academic . . . such as ideals, values, and personal character." It was even planned that soon juniors would be given psychological exams to "evaluate personality and interest." It was hoped that this would help the student "get his head straight as to what he wants to do in life." Under this new plan for guidance, this department would also take over the student retreat program.[80] In addition to days of recollection for freshmen and sophomores, a new junior retreat was to be established in addition to the senior retreats. These upperclassmen retreats would take place at off-site locations, including retreat houses and even private homes. To coordinate this expanded retreat program, a Jesuit working in the guidance department was named the school's first chaplain. In addition, in an effort to strengthen the services offered by this department, Newton approached Father Louis Padovano, S.J., a psychiatrist who maintained a private practice on Fifth Avenue, about working as a consultant with students in need as well as possibly offering presentations to faculty on adolescent psychology and development.[81] While Padovano never did become involved, eventually Regis did enter into a relationship with a psychiatrist whom the guidance department would refer to when necessary. In 1986, a full-time psychiatrist was added to the faculty.

Finally, in another effort to broaden the educational experience as far and wide as possible, Regis began holding "X" days. As an "eXperiment" in learning, these days, during which no regular classes were held, were established to allow faculty and students the opportunity to engage in activities for which there normally would not be enough time. The first was held in mid-February 1973, and students were allowed to either come to school and work independently all day or participate in one of the activities planned by faculty members. The offerings by faculty proved to be fairly diverse. For example, Mr. Robert Weimann of the science department led a group of boys to the New York Aquarium at Coney Island. The social studies department showed a documentary film at Regis on traditional family life in India, which was followed by a question and answer period led by a representative from the Indian consulate. Another group went to the visit the Catholic Worker House on East 1st Street.[82] However, some of the proposed trips did not work out well. Father Paul Callahan, S.J., of the classics department had planned to bring a group of boys to the Metropolitan Museum of Art to view a series of short films, but since the museum required a minimum of forty to hold the program, it had to be cancelled since the students were slow in registering for this excursion. On the other hand, there was no lack of student interest in a student-initiated plan to go see the film *The Exorcist*, which had been released just a few weeks earlier. However, Father Newton eventually nixed this, explaining that the movie was of "a very questionable nature, not only psychologically but also in terms of its explicitness."[83]

While the changes to the academic program at Regis began slowly in this period, with the year 1972–73 seeing the greatest amount of alteration, the spiritual component to a Regis education had experienced far more revamping in this same period.

In late June 1964, Father Owen W. Daley, S.J., who taught theology and German, led a group of students for six weeks of language study in Austria, marking Regis's first study abroad program. While this program lasted only about a decade, since then there have been other foreign study experiences for Regians sponsored by the school (including some that have had an exchange component) to countries such as Germany, Spain, France, and Australia.

"The Holy Ghost Reception Committee #9"

Founded to encourage more frequent reception of Holy Communion, membership in Guard of Honor at Regis remained strong well into the 1960s. As late as 1962, a current student in the Guard told the story of having been tapped on the shoulder on the subway by a man who had noticed the distinctive Guard pin on his lapel. The older gentleman proudly identified himself as both a Regis alumnus and a fellow Guardsman, and was also quick to add that he had not missed Mass on Wednesday since he had graduated from Regis many years earlier.[84] The Guard of Honor, as well the Sodalities, weekly Masses, and confessions, were all part of a strong and vigorous religious formation program that had helped the school produce so many devoutly Catholic men for decades, as this story of the Guardsman on the subway anecdotally demonstrates. But as the move to update the academic program of the school came to full speed by the early 1970s, there was also a desire by the Jesuits on the Regis faculty to modernize much of the school's spiritual life, too, and interestingly this trend actually predated the progressive educational reforms.

The December 18, 1958, issue of *The Owl* ran a small story about changes recently instituted by the Guard of Honor. At this time the Guard had begun experimenting with two new practices to "put more variety into their weekly Wednesday morning Masses."[85] In order to encourage more active participation in the liturgy, at the time of the offertory prayers each member of the congregation was now invited to bring up a host to be consecrated. Another innovation came in early December of this year, when the Guard's moderator, Father Eugene Prior, S.J., celebrated a Mass *versus populum* (facing the people). While neither of these liturgical experiments was especially radical, they did demonstrate that at least some of the Jesuits on the faculty were interested in the modern liturgical movement and wanted to expose their students to it also.

With the calling of the Second Vatican Council in 1962 by Pope John XXIII, the updating of the liturgy would only be one of many changes that would come to the Church. As did most other religious orders of both men and women, the Society of Jesus took very seriously the challenge of the council to "scrutinize the signs of the times."[86] Not long after the council's conclusion in 1965, the Society as a whole began to reevaluate its practices, customs, and ways of proceeding so that its members could more effectively preach the Gospel to a world that seemed to be changing more rapidly than anyone could have ever imagined. As a school founded by the Society and staffed by a large number of its priests and scholastics, Regis would come to be affected by the changes and experimentation the Jesuits now began to undertake.

Shortly before the coming of all these changes, there seemed to be no end to the growth the American branch of the Society of Jesus had been experiencing since the end of World War II. In 1950, its numbers had reached 6,897 (priests, scholastics, brothers, and novices), and a decade later, in 1960, its membership had soared to 8,338. But this would mark its zenith. By 1970, the ranks of the American Jesuits had shrunk to 7,055, and in this same year, only four men entered the novitiate for the New York Province.[87] (Not too many years earlier, four to six young men would enter the Society the summer after graduating from Regis.) While the causes of this decline were complex and continue to be debated by historians, there can be no argument that as the level of experimentation and change by American Jesuits heated up, the order's ranks began to thin out. The impetus for this reform in the internal life and ministry of the Jesuits came initially from the "aggiornamento" called for by the Vatican Council itself, which leveled this challenge at all religious in the Church. However, with the election in 1965 of Father Pedro Arrupe, S.J., as the twenty-eighth superior general of the Society of Jesus, the Jesuits now had a man who embraced this call to reform and update wholeheartedly. After his election to this office, as a major superior Arrupe now had the opportunity to participate in the fourth and final session of the council. Speaking several times to the assembly, the Basque Jesuit said that the Church needed to become "at home in diverse cultures and learn from them."[88] While Arrupe made this challenge to the Church as a whole, it can be argued that few took it as seriously as the Jesuits themselves, surpassed perhaps only by American nuns.

As part of the general's call to enter into a deeper dialogue with modern culture, practically every Jesuit house of training (novitiate, juniorate, philosophate, theologate) in the United States moved from a rural or suburban setting to an urban one, or at least one close to a major university. Most of the Jesuit priests who had taught at Regis since the school's opening in 1914 had gone to Woodstock College in rural Maryland, and were formed in its highly disciplined, semimonastic setting.[89] But in 1970, in response to Arrupe's challenge, the school relocated to Morningside Heights on the Upper West Side of Manhattan to be close to Columbia University and Union and Jewish Theological Seminaries. In addition, it was hoped that this new location would afford the young Jesuits in training the opportunity to live alongside the poor and so learn from them as they moved toward priestly ordination.[90] By the early 1970s, a fair number of the Jesuits who were studying at Woodstock also taught part-time at Regis, and what they were experiencing and learning on the Upper West Side soon began to make itself felt across the park on the Upper East Side.[91]

In this era of renewal and experimentation, one of the first parts of the spiritual life at Regis to change was a name. The course that had been called "Religion" or "Catechism" in 1966 had its name changed to "Theology." And this new nomenclature was just the beginning. By 1974, the course offerings in the theology department had changed dramatically. In this year, students were allowed to choose either "yoga or sex," as one headline in *The Owl* phrased it. Actually, that year seniors could choose among six senior theology electives, which included liberation theology, human sexuality, and a course with the provocative title of "Mind Control and Meditation."[92]

The desire to update the spiritual life of the school went beyond just the academic. In an effort to make students' Catholic faith more meaningful to them, one young scholastic began experimenting with the liturgy itself. Put "in charge of seeing that the Sophomore Mass happened [*sic*]," Mr. Anthony Meyer, S.J., decided that they would use only hymns that "the kids wrote themselves." To play these original compositions, an impromptu band was put together, which one student in keeping with the times gave the whimsical name the "Holy Ghost Reception Committee #9." Meyer described the style of liturgical music created and performed by these teenagers as not "rockish" in style but as "the music of Everyman."[93] And music was just one part of the Mass to undergo a radical transformation. For one school liturgy, students made the crucifixes, altar cloths, and even candlesticks fashioned out of used soda bottles. In addition, a "collapsible cinemascope screen, eight feet high and twenty-four feet wide," was set up to allow a continuous display of images to be projected during the Mass. Using multiple projectors, images from the Vietnam War and wheat fields were projected continuously throughout the liturgy.[94] This practice of experimentation and novelty with liturgy continued well into the 1970s. For example, as part of the school's observance of Ash Wednesday in 1975, students took part in a service that started in the auditorium with a session of mime along with poetry reading, and then moved to the chapel for excerpts from T. S. Eliot's *Murder in the Cathedral* including also a "Greek-type chorus, Dancers and Priests to give a performance of great intensity and strength," this para-liturgy ended with the distribution of ashes by two Jesuits.[95]

While the cause and effect relationship is difficult to discern from the extant sources, what is clear is that the move toward experimentation with student spiritual life at Regis came roughly at the same time that the formal religious activities that had been in place since the school's earliest days were either abolished or fell into desuetude. By 1967, the Sodalities had completely disappeared, and other groups were soon to follow, with the Guard of Honor making its last appearance in 1972. In that year, the group was described as having the distinction of being "the only overtly religious activity at Regis." Their central activity was a weekly Mass on Wednesday open to the entire school, but despite this, attendance was "usually light."[96]

While the 1968 *Regian* did include a "Religious" section, there were no specific activities listed, but rather about fifteen pages of candid photos of students engaged in spiritual activities such as at Mass or on retreat.[97] The 1970 yearbook contained no "Religious" section at all. However, even five years earlier, there is evidence that change was afoot. While the Sodalities were still listed among student activities in the 1965 yearbook (as well as the Guard of Honor and the Sanctuary Society), the purpose of these groups seems to have changed dramatically. Whereas the 1955 *Regian* described the Sodality's dual purpose as "sanctification of self and neighbor," the 1965 yearbook reported that "community action" was "the heart of this year's Sodality."[98] This is not to say, however, that charitable works had not been undertaken in earlier years. In 1955, the Sodalists' activities included visits to hospitals on Welfare (now Roosevelt) Island in the East River and Nativity Mission Center on the Lower East Side, as well sponsoring a Thanksgiving food drive. By the mid-1960s, the focus of the spiritual formation had clearly changed, now with far greater emphasis placed on "community action" over traditional religious practice.

This newfound interest in community action or service actually had its origins in the Sodality, which, as demonstrated, did sponsor opportunities for members to engage in charitable works. By 1964, however, a separate activity named the "Community Action Program" (CAP) had been established. Under the direction of Father Owen Daley, S.J., the group soon claimed a membership of more than two hundred, and in these early days the students focused themselves on tutoring elementary-age children in the city.[99] Soon CAP's activities expanded to include visiting patients at several different Manhattan hospitals, as well as taking small children from the New York Foundling Hospital on excursions around the city. In 1967, CAP even put together a program in which two Regians spent two weeks working in Appalachia at the end of the school year.[100]

Started about the same time as CAP, forums were established for the first time at Regis in the mid-1960s. Started in order to make "Vatican II's theme of dialogue with every segment of society meaningful to Regians," these facilitated discussion groups were more academic in nature and less hands-on than CAP.[101] An article in *The Owl* described the goal of the forums as trying to break "down the padded walls that make Regis the comfortably closed and self-sufficient society that it is."[102] By 1970, there were five separate forums in place at Regis, the largest of which was the International Forum, which sought to provide students with "opportunities . . . to familiarize themselves with the problems and cultures of other societies." In addition, there were also the Liturgical, Interracial, Christian Family, and Ecumenical Forums.[103] Though there is no evidence that the forums and CAP were meant to replace the Sodalities, in many ways they did, but without the heavy emphasis on prayer and other traditional Catholic devotions.

A review of the pages of *The Owl* through the decades of the 1950s and 1960s provides a good barometer of the changes in student spirituality as well as the overall attitude toward religion by Regians. In the 1950s, many of the twelve annual issues of newspaper included short articles on the religious life at Regis, some of which were even admonitory in tone. For example, the lead editorial in the May 1953 edition spoke of the need for Regians to deepen their devotion to the Blessed Virgin Mary. By the early 1960s, however, the frequency of articles on spiritual topics decreased to about two per year, and this downward trend just continued as the years went on. By 1972, the closest thing to an article on spirituality was an editorial offering an excerpt from a play by William Saroyan that students might find useful during Lent, "traditionally a time for personal reflection and self-evaluation."[104]

By 1976, the tone of at least some student articles in *The Owl* had turned somewhat hostile toward spirituality. To commemorate Lent for this year, the paper ran two student opinion pieces in response to the vague prompt "God and themselves." The senior writer began by explaining that his way of communicating with his "person–God" may seem ridiculous to some-

A Mass at Regis during the 1967–68 school year. In the heady days after the Second Vatican Council, the celebration of the Mass underwent all sorts of innovations and experiments both in the United States and around the world. At this particular Mass at Regis, students participated heavily in the preparation for it, including the performance of "rock and roll hymns," the fabrication of candlesticks made from discarded Coke bottles, and the playing of symbolic words and images during the liturgy. (Photo: Ed Lettau, *The Sign*, September 1968, 22.)

one else, but that his response nevertheless remains, "Screw Mass, I'd rather walk in a forest or open field . . ." He actually did conclude his reflection by saying that he continued to see himself as a member of the Catholic Church, though some of the "structures and details" of it he saw as "ridiculous." However, not all students that year evinced such an attitude toward their faith. The junior asked to respond to this same prompt offered a very different reflection. While the academic standards for students had remained relatively high, he felt that "the spiritual life of the Regian does not receive as much care." Realizing that the Church overall was having a hard time maintaining connection with young people, he still felt Regis could do better. While the school continued to offer daily Mass in the chapel, he felt that it was scheduled "too early" and was certainly in need of some "perking-up." He even wished Regis had one Mass each month for the entire school, possibly on First Fridays. It is not clear if the writer knew that the school used to have weekly Mass for the entire student body until a decade earlier. The junior concluded his piece with the ominous warning that if the spiritual life of the students was not taken up by the administration, then "we may soon hear much talk of spirituality as the area where Regis fails."[105]

Like this junior writer for *The Owl*, the 1976 report of the Middle States visiting committee also raised some questions about the spiritual life of Regis. From the committee's reading of the students, it seemed to them that the values being communicated to the boys were more "human" than explicitly "Christian or Catholic," and in their recommendations thought that an ongoing study committee be established "to examine further the Catholic/Jesuit dimension of Regis High School."[106] An earlier report by a provincial visiting team also raised some serious questions as to the school's support and encouragement of religious practice by the students. The team worried that apart from the Mass of the Holy Spirit, Mass for graduation, and weekly Masses for freshmen, "all the liturgical celebrations are along private lines by individual teachers and individual classes." The visitors thought that while "perhaps this is sufficient for the present needs," a tremendous responsibility had been put on the faculty to initiate all the "contacts of worship" for their students, and they wondered if this would continue to be effective over time. The team went on to encourage the school to find new ways for students to participate in Mass. In 1966, the weekly Mass for the entire student body had been dropped, and just six years later outside observers were voicing serious concern over the loss of regular and frequent celebrations of the Eucharist by the Regis community. In keeping with the spirit of the times, the team thought that new, innovative ways should be experimented with to attract students on a voluntary basis to attend Mass or even to go to confession while at school. Over the next decades, different attempts were made to increase voluntary attendance at Masses and to make these experiences more meaningful to students, but nothing would ever come to equal the consistent and regular approach to religious practice and prayer that had been the case at Regis during the school's first fifty years.[107]

The school newspaper is also a good source for uncovering the development of the retreat program at Regis. Whereas in 1954, *The Owl* described a three-day senior retreat held at a Jesuit retreat house upstate, during which more than thirty students remained mostly silent, engaging in daily Mass, Benediction, and several spiritual conferences led by a Jesuit,[108] a 1967 article in *The Owl* demonstrates how much had changed in the intervening years. By this year, the senior retreats were described as:

> something of an experiment. The students participating in the Retreats had a good deal to do with the actual running of them . . . contemporary and Biblical literature . . . passages were used to initiate group discussion . . . one such discussion was started by readings from the book of Job and the liner notes from Richie Haven's album "Mixed Bag." . . . Contemporary music . . . of the Beatles, Phil Ochs, Simon & Garfunkel and others illustrated the difficulties of the modern cut-off generation and asked what was to be done. Unfortunately, they had no answers. It was the job of those making the retreat to probe these problems. . . . The change from last year's "silent" Retreat was designed to make the seniors feel that the retreat was "their thing," something they would participate in and not merely have preached at them.[109]

The May 1974 sophomore retreat also demonstrated that innovation and experimentation were continuing. While this retreat held at Regis contained "no formal lectures or gripe sessions," it did include lots of offbeat activities, such as a paper sculpture session during which "an individual would shape out of newspaper a form that would be one of a person's best qualities, and the group would try to guess what it was"; a class in body movement, including ballet, yoga, and acrobatics; and an exercise in silence, which was held for five minutes.[110] However, despite these attempts to make the retreat relevant and interesting to the students, by 1976 the sophomore retreat had fallen on hard times, with one teacher describing it as "a losing proposition." Father Newton supported changing the format again to make it "more satisfactory" to the sophomores. In this same year, the Middle States visiting team also looked at the retreat program at the school. It voiced concern that based on student questionnaires, it seemed that these retreats "are valued primarily for their beneficial results in the area of human interaction." And even the various opportunities afforded students for service raised similar concerns. Again, these were seen by the students as "humanitarian endeavor ('a good thing for people') rather than a strict response to the Catholic/Jesuit dimension" of the school."[111] This question of how well Regis is communicating Christian values in a particularly Jesuit context has continued to be a cause of concern since the mid-1970s, and has come up in each of the three Middle States reports since.

Life After Regis for the Classes 1964 to 1980

As mentioned earlier, beginning in the mid-1960s, a growing number of Regis seniors applied to and eventually attended non-Catholic colleges and universities. For example, for the class of 1964, fewer than 10 percent of the graduates did not go to Catholic colleges or universities.[112] By 1973, the situation had reversed entirely. For the senior class of that year, only 40 percent of graduates went to Catholic colleges, with 20 percent going to Ivy League schools and 14 percent to state colleges.[113] This trend continued to accelerate in the coming years, with only 21 percent of the class of 1977 continuing their education at Catholic institutions.[114]

This increase in the numbers of Regis graduates attending secular colleges was not accidental. While students had once been greatly discouraged from applying to these kinds of institutions since the earliest days of the school, this prohibition had been by no means absolute. Exceptions had been made for those boys who wanted to study engineering, as well as on occasion for those whose financial situation made it difficult for them to turn down a scholarship from a non-Catholic college.[115] But by the late 1960s, this policy against applications to non-Catholic colleges was dropped (with students now actually encouraged to apply to these institutions), and not surprisingly the college choices of graduating seniors changed dramatically.

This willingness of Regis and other Catholic high schools to allow their students to attend non-Catholic institutions of higher learning came largely as a result of the Second Vatican Council's encouragement to cultivate a greater openness to and dialogue with the wider world. Before this, American Catholicism very much had a "ghetto" quality to it. As the sociologist Will Herberg described it, "The Catholic Church in America operates a vast network of institutions of almost every type and variety . . . from baseball teams, to sewing circles, from bowling leagues to religious study groups.... There are [also] Catholic hospitals, homes, and orphanages; Catholic schools and colleges ... Catholic associations of doctors, lawyers, teachers, students, and philosophers."[116]

In a more recent study of American Catholicism, James D. Davidson, also a sociologist, described the Catholic Church before the 1960s as trying to create a "fortress ... to protect Catholics from a hostile society and socialize them" into a traditional approach to faith and morals."[117] Though it is far beyond the scope of study of this book, one can only speculate about the many ways attendance at non-Catholic colleges affected Regis graduates beginning in the late 1960s, but maybe the most notable would be the increased likelihood of meeting and marrying a non-Catholic woman.

For the class of 1976 the breakdown of the total number of applications submitted to colleges and universities were as follows: Catholic, 25 percent; highly competitive, 20 percent; other, 20 percent; Ivy, 19 percent; state and city, 15 percent; technical and military academies, 1 percent. Of course, where the students applied affected where they eventually were accepted and attended. As recently as the graduating class ten years earlier (1966), ten went to Boston College, but not one student did in 1976. In 1966, forty-nine went to Fordham, but ten years later that number had dropped to thirteen. In addition, now Regians were not only attending non-Catholic colleges, they were also attending some of the most elite secular colleges and universities, including the University of Chicago, Princeton, Colby College, Johns Hopkins, Swarthmore, Cornell, Dartmouth, and Bowdoin. Though in the past Regis may have been an integral part of the "fortress Catholicism," now that these walls had been dismantled, these highly selective institutions quickly realized the quality of Regis graduates and began admitting them.[118]

For the class of 1979, 26 percent went on to attend Ivy League schools and 25 percent to other highly competitive colleges. Overall, this class had an acceptance rate of 78 percent to all the institutions to which they applied, another sign of the quality of the students and the respect Regis was accorded by colleges and universities. This class was representative of other classes from this era in winning many awards and scholarships. Seven students were named National Merit or Achievement Scholars; 105 won New York State Regents Scholarships; and 398 won other academic scholarships (partial or full). This class was awarded about $1.5 million worth of scholarship for their entire college career, or about $3,000 per student per year. (For the 1980–81 academic year, the average tuition, not including room and board, at four-year colleges was $3,500.)[119] In addition to now attending a far greater diversity of schools, a growing number of Regians were going to college far away from the New York City area. For the classes of 1964, 1965, and 1966, only seventeen students in total went to schools outside the Northeast or the mid-Atlantic. However, fifteen of these students went to Notre Dame, but there has long been something unique about attending Notre Dame for Catholic boys, despite the distance. For the class of 1979, 13 percent went to colleges in the Midwest, South, or Far West.[120]

As far as life after college, again using the class of 1979 as an example, the vast majority of the members of this class went on to successful careers in fields such as law, medicine, and higher education. However, one area in particular has stood out. Unlike for the men who graduated from Regis in the school's first thirty graduating classes, for whom law dominated as a profession, the top career area for this class was business and finance, with more than twenty of the alumni from this class working at investment firms and other financial management organizations by 1998.[121] In many ways, this change reflected the overall change in the U.S. economy, with Wall Street becoming the driving engine of so much economic growth, especially in the New York metropolitan area. Finally, in regard to Regis graduates from this period who entered the priesthood or religious life, while some from the classes of 1964 to 1980 may have tried this vocation for awhile, few stayed with it. By 1998, only eight men from this period had entered the priesthood or religious life (six Jesuits and four diocesan clergy).[122] This was a far cry from the number of vocations produced from the classes of 1918 through 1937, which had 247 men in the priesthood or religious life by 1958. The times certainly had changed.

Conclusion

The year 1980 not only marked an end to a decade, in many ways it also brought about a close to an era. With the Vietnam War fading in people's memories and much of the radical fervor of the fifteen prior years having spent itself, the country and the culture began to settle into a new homeostasis. This "return to normalcy" was helped by the fact that boomers were getting older, marrying, and settling down. This societal trend was also largely true at Regis, though one event in the calendar year 1980 remains emblematic of the unrest and dislocation of the previous era.

While a few boys had died during their time at Regis because of illness or accident, 1980 saw the first, and only, Regis student ever murdered. Steven Zwickert was only sixteen when his life came to a tragic end a few weeks before his graduation. An alumnus of Resurrection Ascension parochial school in Rego Park, Steven had skipped the eighth grade before beginning at Regis in the fall of 1976. Active in school plays at Regis and at his parish, he also played the guitar as part of his church's folk group. After escorting a girl to the Dominican Academy's junior prom, Steven was only a couple of blocks from his home in Queens when he was shot once in the chest in an attempted robbery. Since he had died in the early morning of Ascension Thursday, Regis was closed, apart from a few seniors taking Advanced Placement exams. However, the next day, the students and faculty filled four separate Masses in the school chapel to pray for Steven's soul, and for consolation and strength for the Zwickert family as well as for themselves. For the funeral on Saturday at Steven's home parish, his classmates lined the middle aisle and sang the alma mater as his coffin was carried in. In addition to a score of reporters and television cameras, more than nine hundred friends and family came to pay their last respects.[123]

In little more than a week after Steven's murder, a sixteen-year-old turned himself in.[124] Though he acknowledged a role in the attempted robbery, the young man claimed that his .38 caliber revolver had gone off accidentally. Steven's death and the trial of his assailants came at the same time that New York State was debating stricter gun control laws. For Steven, this discussion and any possible resolution came too late. But his untimely death remains a symbolic reminder of the social unrest and dislocation many Americans and Regians experienced in the late 1960s and 1970s.

6 The Return of the Missing Owl

Financial Concerns

Though secure in its perch above the center door on the south of end of the quad for more than forty years, in the late 1970s the iconic Regis owl disappeared, seemingly the victim of a teenage prank. Despite the valiant efforts of the assistant headmaster, Mr. John Tricamo, its whereabouts could not be determined. Realizing the significance of the old bird to many of the alumni, Father Raymond Swords, S.J., president of Regis from 1976 to 1980, asked Tricamo to redouble his efforts to find it. After much careful detective work, Tricamo was able to make contact with a person who knew the owl's whereabouts. Eventually Tricamo met this person at an out-of-the-way location in an outer borough. The exchange took place in the dark of the evening as the owl, swathed in burlap, was transferred from one car to the other. Though secure once again, the owl was not returned to its former roost. Instead, it was placed under lock and key in the Jesuit residence on 83rd Street. Not long after this, when the quad was done over in 1983, three new owls were cast in replica of the original, and these knockoffs were placed above the doors leading into the auditorium on the north end of the quad. With the establishment of the Regis Archives in 2007 in the rear of the library, the original owl was given a permanent and secure home back at Regis, where it now sits forlornly in a corner, deprived of its former place of honor.[1]

While Father Swords's goal to get back the Regis owl was important, his task to stabilize the finances of the school itself was far more critical. In fact, this Jesuit was brought in as president in 1976 largely for that reason. A native of New England, Swords spent many years as a professor at the College of the Holy Cross teaching math as well as serving as director of admissions, before being named president of the college in 1960. After a decade in this office, Swords left Worcester to become a chaplain at Boston City Hospital, but he would not stay in this job for long. After just two years, Swords was asked by his provincial to go back to school work, now as head of Cranwell Prep, a Jesuit high school in Lenox, Massachusetts, which was then in crisis. Despite his business savvy and hard work, Swords had the sad duty to close the institution in 1975 due to rising costs and declining enrollments.[2] But before he could return to chaplaincy work, he was asked once again to come to a Jesuit institution in need. Father Swords came to Regis at a time when the school had been struggling for several years with expanding deficits. And this time his attempt to keep a struggling Jesuit high school open would prove to be a success.[3]

It is important to recall that before the late 1960s, the school was able to meet its budget simply by relying for its funding on income from its investments and occasional large gifts from the founding family. However, in many ways its expenses were artificially low. While there were always a significant number of laypeople on the faculty who drew mostly modest salaries, the province was given a per diem to support each Jesuit teaching at Regis, with no direct funding for other expenses such as health care, continuing education, or retirement. The province had to rely on other sources for these needs. As the number of full-time Jesuits on staff began to decline in the early 1970s, this led to strains on the budget as more (and more expensive) lay teachers were hired. In addition, the school began to solicit the alumni for support, but it took some time for this giving to become a reliable source of income. (Before the late 1960s, the founding family had been adamantly against the school raising money from alumni or other sources other than them.) Although annual alumni financial support of the school has been quite strong since this time, it has never to been to such an extent that the school has not had to liquidate some assets each year to make ends meet. Because of this regular selling of these, Regis has never had a true endowment, from which by definition only a limited percentage of the annual growth is withdrawn each year. Thus, in the years immediately preceding Swords's arrival, the finances of the school had become increasingly bleak.

In a period of six years, the school's operating budget had more than doubled: for the fiscal year 1968–69 it was $352,000, and by 1973–74 the budget was over $726,000. The biggest single year over year increase came between fiscal years 1970 and 1971, when expenses jumped 34 percent. And spending was up in every "cost center" in the budget, from salaries to fuel and postage.[4] For example, the starting salary of a first-year teacher with a bachelor's degree increased 60 percent between 1967 and 1973.[5] Much of this increase was due to raises in teachers' salaries, which came as a result of both the school's commitment to increase compensation for the sake of justice as well simply to keep pace with the rapid inflation of the period, which by 1974 had topped 11 percent. In addition, with the declining number of full-time Jesuits on the staff, lay teachers (who commanded higher salaries) had to be hired in their place, which added further pressure to the already straining budgets.[6]

Regis was not alone during this period in facing tough economic times. From the late 1960s onward, the national economy had sputtered through two recessions and an energy crisis. As a result, Regis and most of the other Jesuit schools around the country were seeing a lot more red ink on their ledgers than in the past, as their expenses grew much faster than their income. In fact, according to Father Carney, by 1969 only eight Jesuit high schools in the nation had operated in the black that year.[7] For the fiscal year ending June 30, 1971, Regis finished with a $140,000 deficit, but by 1973 this number was over $285,000.[8] By 1975, the annual deficit had been reined in to slightly more than $196,000, but clearly this could not go on forever.[9] To bridge these gaps the school had to spend down cash reserves as well as liquidate some assets.[10] Luckily for the school, additional revenue sources began to flow in the early 1970s to cushion some of the blow.

As mentioned earlier, Edna Grant had died in 1968, and in late 1970 her estate was finally settled. Much of Edna's estate was left in trust to her brother Hugh, with the bulk of its distribution to come after his death. However, there was an initial distribution of monies, and from this Regis received slightly more than $190,000, which was to be added to the endowment (restricted), and a further $159,000 in cash, which the school could place in its reserve account to meet immediate needs (unrestricted). In addition, the school also received 756 shares of IBM stock, which at that point were valued at over $240,000.[11] And revenue from Edna's estate continued to flow to Regis for several more years. In 1972, the school received $62,000 in unrestricted funds as well some additional restricted securities.[12] In 1973, the school again received disbursements in the amounts of $51,995 (unrestricted) and $172,556 (restricted).[13] Finally, Hugh also gave the school several large gifts during this period. According to his daybook from the period, at Christmastime in 1975 he planned to give a $100,000 gift to Regis. In the audited financial statement for the following year (ending June 30, 1976), a bequest for $101,116 was recorded, with the extra monies presumably coming from interest.[14] Around Christmas 1976, he again made a gift of $100,000 to the school, and as was noted in a letter from this period, both these gifts were intended to help the school pay the annual increases in teachers' salaries. In 1977, Hugh's generosity increased tenfold. At Christmas that year, he gave Father Brooks a check for $1 million as an "out and out gift to Regis with no restrictions at all." In giving this, Hugh again stressed that his donation was to be treated strictly anonymously, in keeping with the family's tradition. In a letter to the Jesuit provincial in which he reported on Hugh's most recent gift, Father Brooks stated clearly that he "did not think this gift would have been possible without the wonderful help and cooperation Father Swords gave me."[15] In addition to Regis, Hugh also continued to be generous toward the Jesuit province, and in 1980 gave $1 million for the province infirmary at Murray-Weigel Hall on Fordham's campus in the Bronx.[16]

While this annual income generated from Edna's trust and Hugh's occasional gifts might have been seen as manna from heaven, the school's leaders realized that they could not forever depend on the generosity of the Grant family, no matter how well-timed their munificence tended to be. In response to the financial challenges of this period, in 1971 Father James Carney, the alumni director, led the Alumni Association toward the goal of raising $100,000.[17] Alumni actually donated over $110,000, a huge sum given that as recently as 1967 the alumni had only raised slightly more than $16,000.[18] Until the mid-1960s, alumni giving to the school was minimal at best. For many years, the graduates were asked to contribute just a five-dollar annual fee to remain active in the Alumni Association, with the bulk of this used to support the group's activities, in addition to a small gift usually given annually to the school to fund a particular need (e.g., new kneelers in the chapel or a mimeograph machine). This began to change, however, shortly after the golden jubilee in 1964. In that year, a special "Loyalty Fund" was established, which raised $230,000, with over 1,800 of the graduates participating. In 1965, the Loyalty Fund was not continued, but it was revived in 1966 (along with annual dues), and the alumni began raising increasing amounts for the school over the next few years.[19]

As finances became more of an issue, the administration began to turn to the alumni not just to raise money, but also to help the school manage its savings. From the time of Mrs. Grant's original series of gifts, the school's endowment had been invested primarily in gilt-edged bonds, which of course are quite safe but historically have only generated a modest rate of about 2 percent per annum. As early as 1970, Father Taylor realized that this was no longer tenable and received permission from the provincial's office to begin exploring how a Finance Committee might help the school make use of the services of a professional fund manager.[20] With the help of Father Carney, four alumni (Gerald E. Murray, class of 1949, Michael F. Page, class of 1946, Richard J. Powers, class of 1943, and Barry F. Sullivan, class of 1949) were asked to study the feasibility of engaging such a service. In its report, the ad hoc committee offered a series of recommendations to Father Taylor, including the appointment of a "Short-Term Finance Committee, with School and Alumni participation" and "an intense review of the School's expense situation." On the whole, these alumni did not think that the school's financial situation was hopeless, but rather that changes were necessary "to assure the long-run viability of the school."[21] Father Taylor moved quickly on these recommendations and appointed several men (Jesuits and Regis alumni) to form a permanent Finance Committee by early 1972. Of the original members of the ad hoc committee, only Barry Sullivan remained; he was also joined by Father John (Jack) C. Connelly, S.J., Father Eugene F. O'Neill, S.J., Theodore J. Moynahan, class of 1934, and Thomas F. O'Toole, class of 1952.[22]

After several meetings, the committee issued its final report in September 1972 to Father Murphy, who had just recently replaced Father Taylor as president of Regis. In it, the committee gave its full "unanimous recommendation" that endowment funds (which were then valued at about $7 million) be placed under the management of a private investment manager, and also recommended a particular firm after reviewing proposals from "about a dozen investment advisors."[23] Although it believed an investment target of 12 percent per annum might be "very difficult to achieve," the committee still felt that this should be the school's goal "in order to satisfy Regis' longer term financial requirements which are likely to be substantially higher than at present."[24] Unfortunately, the early 1970s was a terrible time to get into the stock market, with the Dow Jones industrial average bottoming out for the decade in December 1974. Over the course of this decade, the value of the Dow increased by less than 0.5 percent. Despite this wise move in managing the school's endowment more actively, the time in which this took place could not have less propitious. Ultimately, it would take both increased fund-raising, mostly from the alumni, and a more austere approach to spending that would get Regis through these tough economic times. In addition, about the same time that the school decided to become more aggressive in its investments, it also tried cutting expenses to bridge this growing gap between revenue and expenses. In 1970, the administration decided to admit thirty-five fewer students in each class in the hopes that this could lead to a reduction in the size of the faculty, but this decrease in the number of teachers never actually transpired.[25] However, the school's total enrollment did fall, with the school population bottoming out at 476 students for the 1973–74 academic year, a low that had not been seen since the Great Depression.[26]

While the bad news remained that operating costs continued to rise annually, the good news was that alumni contributions were up also. In 1975, the alumni had raised over $205,000 toward the annual fund, up from $77,000 in 1971. The Parents Club also continued to offer financial support for the school, mostly from the proceeds of their annual card party, which netted almost $24,000 in 1974. (Unfortunately, the contributions from the Parents Club remained mostly static in the early 1970s.) But it was the alumni who really stepped up and increased their giving. In the spring of 1975, the Alumni Association began asking the graduates to consider naming Regis as beneficiary in their wills, with the promise that all that was bequeathed would remain in the investment portfolio and not be spent to close operating deficits. It is interesting to note that in its appeal to the alumni, the association promised to remain steadfast in its policy not to publish the list of donors, explaining that this is done in the attempt "to keep the spirit of the original founding family who desired anonymity where their munificence was concerned." For reasons that are not altogether clear, the income from investments held in trust by Hugh for Regis were not distributed every year between 1971 and Hugh's death in 1981. However, when they did come, these infusions of cash and other assets in the 1970s were surely a help to the school, as the decade brought mounting financial pressures.

Crisis Averted

With the arrival of Father Swords in September 1975 came even tighter fiscal control. For the first fiscal year that Swords served as president (July 1, 1975–June 30, 1976), the operating deficit was slightly above $250,000. By 1977, Swords had this number down to $114,000. Amazingly, by 1978 he had the school running a surplus of $11,000, and by 1979 this surplus had topped $100,000. In an interview with *The Owl* in 1978, Swords spoke plainly that the school was in a "critical" situation, and "if we were to keep invading the endowment at the rate we have been doing for the last five years, I would estimate that Regis would be obliged to close its doors in eight to ten years." He admitted that after two years in office, costs had already been "cut to the bone," and he did not think any further cuts were possible or advisable.[27] He did praise the students for their support of the school, especially their coordination of the school's first "walkathon" in May 1977, which was largely student led and organized, and which netted over $5,000.[28] (By 1981, the walkathon, which had by then become an annual event, raised over $24,000.)[29] Faculty who served in that era recall that Swords made a point of stressing how important it was to economize, even mandating that teachers keep a written record of long-distance calls made from the school phone and be billed for them if they were of a personal nature.

Despite his eagle eye on the bottom line, Swords did not skimp on necessary projects. For example, in the summer of 1977, several capital improvement projects were done around the school costing over $12,400, including the painting and caulking of two hundred windows around the school, significant repairs to the boilers, and replacement of the wood in some gym bleachers.[30] However, it was not just the nickels and dimes saved here and there that took the school from the red back into the black. Under Swords's leadership, new sources of funding were found and existing ones expanded, and spending was kept in check. For example, in 1979 the school raised over $48,000 from corporations and other foundations, and in this year the parents raised close to $60,000, which was more than double what they had raised in 1974. As far as spending, it did increase under Swords's time as president, but at a much more modest rate, and he was able to do this with the nation's inflation rate hitting highs it had never seen before (13.5 percent in 1980). For example, as far as instructional costs went, teachers' salaries and benefits only increased by 9 percent between 1976 and 1979.

For help reining in costs and widening financial support of the school, principally from the alumni, Father Swords was able to rely on counsel and support from an expanded Board of Trustees, which now included laypeople. Since the start of Regis six decades earlier, the school always had a Board of Trustees, as per regulations of the New York State Board of Regents. However, the five or six men on this board had always been Jesuits, as was the custom of most other Catholic schools run by religious orders, which had all priests, nuns, or brothers serving as the legal owners (or trustees) of the school. For many years, the Board of Trustees of Regis (and many other schools) met only once annually, in keeping with corporation bylaws. With rare exceptions, it was the Jesuit provincial who had the lion's share of authority over schools like Regis, and these boards were almost ceremonial in nature.[31] However, many Catholic institutions around the country, beginning with colleges and universities, began to expand their boards of trustees to include laypeople. In 1969, Fordham first included laymen on its board, and soon Catholic high schools followed this trend, too.[32] In 1975, the Jesuit Secondary Education Association (JSEA) issued a report written by Father Charles M. Whelan, a Jesuit at Fordham

Law School, on the importance of appointing laypeople to schools sponsored by the Jesuits as well as the legal relationship between these schools and the Jesuit province.[33]

With the winds of change in the air in terms of school governance, in late 1975 Father Murphy expanded the school's Board of Trustees to thirteen members, naming six laymen, including Barry Sullivan, who had been serving on the financial committee of the school. The newly expanded board met for the first time on December 16, 1975, and at that meeting elected as chairman Lawrence X. (Larry) Cusack, class of 1938, who served in this capacity until 1982.[34] In these early years of the expanded board, the Jesuits maintained a majority of seats to symbolize "the important principle that Regis is a Jesuit school and that although lay involvement is an essential characteristic, it is, nevertheless, lay involvement with a recognition of Jesuit primacy."[35] Although Swords did not inaugurate this newly expanded board, he was in full support of it. In fact, in a letter to Cusack in 1977, Swords strongly stated his support of laymen on these boards in a discussion of Cusack possibly stepping down as chair and Swords taking that office. Swords wrote, "I feel strongly that the Chairman of the Trustees should be a layman . . . because laymen are by background and experience more suited for the tasks and the responsibilities of the position." He also wisely thought that the chairman and the president should not be the same person, since the "President should be accountable to someone; it is true that he is accountable to the entire Board of Trustees, but if he is Chairman of that Board this accountability is in danger of being weakened . . . since he [as chairman] may be able to control and influence the Board more than is healthy." As a sign that Swords really did believe that the chairman, as well as the board, had real power and responsibility, the custom of the chairman presiding at graduation along with the president began at this time also.[36]

While Father Swords was very supportive of lay involvement in the board, Hugh Grant was not. Before expanding the membership to include laymen, Father Murphy consulted the foundress's son for his approval, as well as to ask him if he would consider serving as a member. After thanking him for his gracious invitation, Hugh begged off, citing his age. However, he did go on to offer some serious reservations. Based on his personal experience as a board member of a Catholic college, he cautioned Murphy to remember that "the owner of the School is the Society," and its success or failure would be ultimately of more concern to the Jesuits than it would to any layman, since the school could never "affect him personally (like the welfare of his children)." Since laymen think "along secular lines," it was his prediction that it was inevitable that the lay board members would come into conflict with Jesuit board members. He counseled that the "number of lay members be kept to an absolute minimum."[37]

It was also the newly expanded Board of Trustees that led Regis through its first major capital campaign, which proved to be a great success because of the generosity and participation of the alumni. In the spring 1979 announcement of the campaign, Mr. Myles V. Whalen, class of 1948, and Father Swords laid out the reasons behind the initiative. They explained that for many years there was no reason for the school to raise money, since "the original endowment provided by the founding family in 1914 generated enough interest, year after year, to cover our operating expenses." However, as detailed above, expenses had increased dramatically and the "interest from the endowment was insufficient for our needs." That had forced the school to liquidate part of the endowment to meet expenses, and it also led to the establishment of the annual fund. Whalen and Swords were happy to report that for the 1977–78 fiscal year, the school was able to operate in the black "for the first time in several years," with sufficient income generated from the following sources: the annual fund (30 percent), investment income (36 percent), and the rest (34 percent) coming from friends of the school and small foundations. However, the school looked forward to continued increases in operating expenses, which would far exceed any annual growth that would come from the endowment—thus, the need to raise $9 million by 1987, with the goal of the first phase set at $6 million. As any well-planned capital campaign begins, Regis's announced that the school already had $2.9 million in hand or in pledges from eight alumni and two other sources that the fund-raising literature described as "foundations." Not surprisingly, these unnamed sources were in fact Hugh Grant. Between 1977 and 1980, Hugh had given four gifts totaling $2.1 million.[38] These donations came as a result of Hugh's regular giving to the school through much of the 1970s, which were simply counted as part of the "quiet phase" of this capital campaign. It is also worth noting the incredible generosity of the eight alumni, including Mr. William J. Hasey, class of 1935, who donated $350,000 worth of stock from a pharmaceutical company of which he was once president.[39]

While Regis's first capital campaign began with hopes of great success, the school struggled to meet the goal of the first phase, set at $6 million.[40] However, once again the founding family would come to save the day. On March 20, 1981, Hugh J. Grant, Jr., died at the age of seventy-six in Delray Beach, Florida, where he and his wife had been spending winters. His body was flown back to New York City for a funeral Mass at St. Ignatius

Church on March 25, which was celebrated by Terence Cardinal Cooke, the archbishop of New York. Father Brooks, the longtime family chaplain and priest who had witnessed his marriage to Lucie, delivered the eulogy. After the liturgy, Hugh's remains were entombed in the Grant family mausoleum in Calvary Cemetery in Queens, where the remains of his parents and two sisters had already been placed.

In Hugh's obituary, which ran in the *New York Times* on the day of his funeral, it was mentioned that the late son of Mayor Hugh J. Grant had been a benefactor to the archdiocese, the Society of Jesus, the Metropolitan Museum of Art, "and other institutions."[41] Given his family's strict demands for anonymity in regard to its support of Regis, it was not surprising at all that the school was not mentioned. However, at his death, a large sum would again come to the school, but interestingly not from wealth that was owned strictly by Hugh. Rather, before the death of his sister Edna in 1968, she had left a large part of her share of the family's fortune in trust for Regis with her brother, with the school to get the annual income. Upon his death, the principal was to be given outright to the school. By the time of Hugh's death, the part of Edna's trust that was to be given to Regis was valued at $2.28 million and was soon disbursed to the school, with another large sum going to the archdiocese as well as smaller amounts to other Catholic institutions.[42] This enormous gift more than helped the school to reach its goal of the first phase of the capital campaign. Much of Hugh's fortune, however, was left in trust to his wife, Lucie, with the proviso that its contents would be disbursed to Regis and other beneficiaries upon her death. In addition, income generated by these monies would also benefit the school until the settlement of the trust, which would come at the death of Lucie.[43]

Evolving Admissions Policies and Procedures

As detailed in the previous chapter, great change came to student life and academics at Regis in the late 1960s and 1970s. This period also saw readjustment to the admissions process for eighth-grade boys applying to the school, which even for awhile allowed seventh graders to apply as well. For decades, the admissions policy and procedures at Regis had not changed whatsoever. Recall that at the time of the founding of the school in 1914, admission was limited to Catholic boys who had attended a parochial school (though exceptions were made for boys whose parish did not have a school) and who had earned a 90 percent grade in all subjects. (The minimum average had at first been set at 85 percent but was quickly raised, since so many boys had shown up seeking a place.) However, as soon as

1920 this original policy would see change. That year the first entrance examination was used to select the members of the class of 1924. Prospective students came to Regis on a Saturday in mid-June for the exam, and the only criterion to sit for it was that the boy had graduated from a parochial school, though the exception for boys whose parish did not have a school remained. Places in the next freshman class would be offered solely on the results of this examination, and the use of various standardized tests was used for the next five decades to select the members of each new incoming class. It is interesting to note that in these early years of using the exam, generally more than half of the students who sat for it were accepted. For example, in 1922, 430 boys took the exam and 250 were offered admission.[44] Today, this percentage is far lower. But just as the late 1960s brought change to academics and student life, it would also have an effect on the school's admissions policies and procedures.[45]

In September 1968, Father Horgan announced at a special school-wide assembly that Regis would now begin to consider financial need in some cases as part of the admissions process for the next freshman class. He told the students that this change in policy came as result of a wider plan for Jesuit high schools made on the province level, which was to include changes on both the university and the secondary levels.[46] Popularly known as the "Demong Drive Decisions" (because of the address of Jesuit property in Syracuse where superiors met for a series of meetings), this plan called for some dramatic changes to the Jesuit educational apostolate.[47] As far as higher education, the province was planning to make Jesuits available to teach at secular colleges and universities, a practice that was rare to nonexistent before this time. In addition, the province was in touch with minority groups to discuss the possibility of the Society helping them to set up a "community-owned-and-operated college" somewhere in the New York area. As far as the high schools, experiments were slated to begin with lay participation in the administration of the schools as well as the more controversial discussion of the possible "phase-out" of three high schools from Jesuit control.[48] As part of these potentially sweeping changes to Jesuit schools, it was hoped that the Society's schools and men could be more responsive to the needs of the poor and groups who historically had not benefited from a Jesuit education.[49] Regis was specifically named in this plan, since it offered "a unique opportunity to the province" in the latter's effort to better educate "the economically disadvantaged in the New York metropolitan area." The Demong Drive Decisions originally mandated that beginning in 1969, Regis's admission policy "insure that 75 per cent of the incoming class each year [comprise] academically qualified boys, whose families could not otherwise afford a quality education." It was also hoped that Regis and the other high schools would no longer accept only candidates "who want to come to us," but would also "*find* [emphasis original] the boys we want to come to us." Finally, the province's schools were charged with raising capital to fund more scholarships for boys from "underprivileged minority groups."[50]

A fair number of students reacted negatively to the proposed change to the admissions policy when it was announced, fearing that "Regis as it stands today will deteriorate and eventually collapse." However, an editorial in *The Owl* cautioned against this unwarranted panic, reminding Regians that Father Horgan had said publicly that there would "no substantial change" in the academic qualifications of the next freshman class.[51] Because of the lack of extant documentation, it is impossible to determine if this new policy had a real impact on the selections for the incoming freshman class in 1969. However, by 1970 the school announced that "about half" of the class that was admitted for the fall of that year came from "lower income families" which was further defined as boys coming from "lower middle class families." In an interview with *The Owl*, Father Robert McGuire, S.J., a guidance counselor who was involved in the admissions process, said that Regis was doing heavier recruiting from grammar schools in poorer areas to meet the new goal of admitting boys from more modest backgrounds. He also proudly stated that the new admissions procedures now took a more "human approach." In addition to taking into consideration a boy's performance on the entrance exam, the admissions procedures also included a review of his grammar school grades and his economic background. This new approach for awhile also included separate interviews with the boy and his parents by two Regis faculty members.[52] However, in 1982 the formal interview with the parents was discontinued and replaced with "a brief, informal meeting" with them before a formal interview with their son.[53]

With this change in the admissions procedures and the new emphasis on admitting boys from poorer backgrounds, in 1971 the school appointed Father Thomas Murphy, S.J., as its first director of admissions, and he held this job for only one year before becoming the president in the fall of 1972. He was replaced by Father Gerald Rippon, S.J., who stayed in the position for a decade while also moderating the Hearn Debating Society. It was during Rippon's tenure that the new admissions procedures were finalized and the first Scholarships Committees were established to review the applications of the semifinalists. (In these early years, the Admissions Committee was known by this name.) The members of these first Scholarships

Committees included Father Rippon and Father Stephen Duffy, S.J., as standing members, a third Jesuit and two lay faculty members. While the committee played a central role in selecting the next freshman class, they technically only made recommendations to the headmaster, who still had the final say in the awarding of the Regis scholarship.[54] In addition to overseeing the final selection of the students, Father Rippon also handled all the other parts of the process. This included sending announcements to the then more than five hundred Catholic parochial schools in the area, and by this time it also included a greater outreach to Catholic boys in public schools. It was Rippon who organized Regis's first open house, though in its first year this day was not designed for potential students. Rather, on All Saints' Day in 1974, schools from around the metropolitan area were invited to send representatives to an informational session held at the school. It was not until October 13, 1975, that the first true open house was held for interested students and their parents.[55] Finally, because of a direction from the archdiocese, in the fall of 1974 seventh-grade boys were allowed to sit for the exam and two were actually admitted for the following year's freshman class.[56]

In the mid-1970s, on average, about 1,300 boys sat for the Regis Scholarship Exam, which the school obtained from an outside agency that also did the scoring. But performance on the exam was only one part of what came into play in terms of being chosen as a semifinalist. (Only semifinalists were invited in for interviews.) In addition, the boy's grades from grammar school, the results of other standardized tests, recommendations from his grammar school, the actual application, and, finally, as stated above, the student's "financial rating" were all also considered. Documentation from the period states that those scoring in the highest percentiles were "virtually always" named semifinalists. Consideration was also taken into account for a student who had had a "bad day" on the exam but whose scores on other tests were very high. This process of selecting semifinalists was performed by the headmaster and the director of admissions, who generally chose about 320 of the original 1,300 to be semifinalists. After being named a semifinalist, both the boy and his parents were interviewed by two Regis faculty members, who spoke with them separately.[57]

For those students claiming financial need, at least for a few years they were required to submit their parents' previous year's income tax return. A separate Financial Review Committee composed of three faculty members was established to authenticate real need, and were given a worksheet compiled by the school (based on poverty figures as published annually by the Department of Labor) to evaluate economic need. To be considered "poor," a family of four had to earn under $8,500. To be considered "really struggling," the family had to subsist on between $8,500 and $11,500. To be classified as "struggling somewhat," the income range was set between $11,500 and $14,500. Even families not considered "low income" but for whom paying a high school tuition "would impose some difficulty," could ask for special consideration. Families earning above $22,000 were considered to be "not in need."[58]

When the Scholarships Committee finally met each year to make their decisions, it based its determination on the same set of criteria that had been used for the selection of the semifinalists, but now looked into this much smaller pool of applications with far greater precision. Through this period, the committee generally offered 140 acceptances (scholarships) each year and created a ranked waiting list of 20 more names. A document from this period states that the Scholarships Committee was instructed to accept "as many students from poor, struggling families as possible" and that students from this economic class "should be the majority of those who win scholarships." Father Newton, who was headmaster during this era of the new admissions process and of course very much involved in it, often said that economic need was to be seen as "positive consideration" when determining admission.[59] In the scoring sheet prepared by Father Newton and given to the Scholarship Committee for use on the freshman class that would be selected for the fall of 1978, financial need was given a "relative weight" of 10 percent. Academic performance was given a weight of 75 percent, and "personal characteristics," based on the interview, recommendations, and application, was assigned a weight of 15 percent.[60] Since the income range for determining a family's financial need was fairly broad, and with no documents from the various committees from this era still extant, it is impossible to determine to what extent and to what degree the members of the incoming classes really came from homes of economic need. In any case, the period of the 1970s really did bring about a change in consciousness on the part of the school's administration about the need for Regis to admit more boys from poor households, and Mr. Frank Walsh, who served on this committee several times during this period, recalls that the question of financial need was of serious importance in the committee's determination of each freshman class.[61]

Because of poor health, Father Rippon gave up his role as director of admissions in 1981, and for more than a decade the position remained vacant, leaving the admissions procedures to be handled by the principal's office and the registrar. In 1993, Mr. Eric DiMichele, who had been on the faculty since 1982, was named the next director of admissions. Shortly after assuming this role, DiMichele began holding several regional information nights in the outer boroughs and the suburbs. With the continual closing of parochial schools in the New York City area, which began in the early 1970s, the stream of Catholic eighth-grade boys who knew about Regis and would have been encouraged to apply was not so steady anymore. Thus, DiMichele and the school administration recognized the need to get the word out about the school, including to parents of boys in private, non-Catholic schools, which historically had sent few to no boys to Regis. The number of students coming from Catholic elementary schools has seen a slow but steady decline over the last twenty years. In the class of 1995, almost 72 percent (95 boys) graduated from parochial schools. For the classes entering between 2008 and 2012, those coming from Catholic elementary schools has dropped to about 50 percent, and the evidence suggests that this decline will only continue.[62] The geographical origins of the student body have also been changing during this time, especially in the last two decades. Whereas in 1991 more than 65 percent of the entire student body lived in New York City, only 47 percent of the incoming freshman class that arrived in 2012 live in New York City.[63]

In addition to the concern that Regis should be educating more boys from economically disadvantaged backgrounds, by the mid-1970s the issue of race also became a topic of concern in terms of the makeup of each incoming class. The school and Jesuit schools in general had come a long way when just a bit more than thirty years earlier Jesuit high school students in the New York area, including Regis, were asked in a debate competition to consider the issue of whether "Jesuit schools should accept colored students."[64] Times surely had changed. In fact, in Father Swords's first presidential address to the student body in September 1976, he said that he believed there should be a "better balance in the school between minorities and non-minorities."[65] Based on the school's determination of race and ethnicity for the period 1981–97, the black or African American population ranged in terms of percentage from a low of 3.2 percent (sixteen students) in 1981 to a high of 8.1 percent (forty-one students) in 1986. During this period, the percentage of Hispanics enrolled at Regis showed steady growth, climbing from 7 percent (thirty-four students) in 1981 to 12.2 percent (sixty-two students) in 1993. The percentage of Asian students showed similar growth, with fifty-eight students or 11.4 percent of the total school population by 1993. This change in the racial composition of the school in many ways reflected the demographics of the Catholic population of the New York City area, with the low number of African American or black students due to the relatively small black Catholic population of the region.[66] Finally, the class of 2016, which arrived in September 2012 and will be the ninety-ninth senior class to graduate from Regis, had the following racial/ethnic composition, not including whites: Hispanic/Latino (15.2 percent), African American (4.3 percent), Asian American (10.9 percent), Middle Eastern (4.3 percent).[67]

The Alumni Mentor Program and REACH

As part of recognizing the school's need to remain faithful to its founding mission of educating boys who otherwise could not afford a Catholic education, in the fall of 1993 a small group of faculty and administration began some brainstorming. These conversations began in the context of the Student Support Services Committee in their discussions of ways to help Regis students who seemed to be struggling from early on in their careers at the school. The idea was raised of starting sort a summer program for some boys before their arrival as freshmen, to "provide kids with habits and skills they aren't getting at home, with perhaps some interventions for parents as well." It was hoped that such an undertaking would "translate into measurable improvements during the school year." Soon the conversation developed into starting a wider summer program for elementary-age students, which would include boys (and possibly even girls) who might not attend Regis.[68] Over the next couple of meetings, the name "Project Excelsior" emerged for a possible "two-summer educational program [for] a small group of academically well-motivated boys and girls from economically distressed areas of New York City." Father Kenneth J. Gavin, S.J., class of 1962, who was named president of Regis in 1992, felt that such a program would be very much in keeping with the Society of Jesus' preferential option for the poor. In addition, he felt that while some of the graduates of this program would attend Regis, "the program will make every effort to see that its graduates are admitted to high quality high schools in the New York City area."[69] Some years earlier, in the 1979–80 academic year, a program with similar goals had been tried under the name "Insignis" (Latin for "outstanding"). Back then, it was Regis seniors who did the work as they volunteered to tutor children in thirteen Catholic elementary schools in the South Bronx and Harlem. The brainchild of Father Charles J. Beirne, S.J., principal, and Dr. Michael Mincieli, class of 1960, guidance counselor, the plan involved these seniors "trying to help raise the verbal and math scores of fourth, fifth and sixth graders over a period of years," with Regis faculty mentoring these novice teachers.[70] Although Regians have continued tutoring inner-city kids, now in both Catholic and public schools, through various programs sponsored by the school, none of these efforts was carefully focused or designed to really increase the number of boys entering Regis from disadvantaged backgrounds.

After these initial discussions in the fall of 1993, the committee did not meet for several months, though informal conversations among the members continued. By April 1994, Frank Walsh had drawn up a memo outlining the three different "loosely defined" camps that had emerged as to the central purpose of an "Excelsior" summer prep program. First, there were those whom Walsh described as the "feeder-folk," in that they supported a program that would be designed to help at least some of its participants gain acceptance to Regis who otherwise would not have qualified for admission. Borrowing a term from philosophy, Walsh named the second camp the "*Ding an sich* crowd," since its supporters thought the proposed program should be a "thing in itself." They believed the work and mission of such an undertaking should "stand on its own merits" and be "quite distinct from Regis," though it would reflect the school's commitment to service by involving some students and teachers with "schools, parishes and communities with which we have lost connection." This second group was not against possibly "recruiting" some of the program's participants.[71] However, it would still be a few more years before a new program of whatever type would be up and running.

In addition to establishing a separate program for middle school boys, this committee also took up discussions regarding the possible need for a full-time tutor at Regis whose focus would be on struggling students, especially during their first and second years. Mr. Kevin Driscoll, class of 1991, arrived in the fall of 1995 with the title "alumnus mentor." For the first years of this mentor program, one alumnus who had graduated from Regis four years earlier was hired to conduct after-school tutoring as well as to teach one or two courses. For their work, these fresh college graduates were given a stipend and health insurance. In 1998, the Alumni Mentor Program (AMP) expanded to include two Regis alumni, including Mr. Brendan McGuire, class of 1994, who was hired specifically to establish a pilot tutoring program for inner-city boys. Working with Frank Walsh, the two began gathering middle-school-aged boys from the Bronx and northern Manhattan at a classroom in St. Nicholas of Tolentine School in the Bronx. While this attempt lasted the year and was generally successful, McGuire's commitment as an AMP mentor was for just one year, and Frank Walsh wound up going on sabbatical in the fall of 1999. However, that next academic year, Father Vincent Biagi, S.J., principal, eventually approached with a proposal Mr. Brian FitzGerald, class of 1994, who was the other AMP mentor the same year as McGuire. And it was FitzGerald who eventually did most of the research, which led to the establishment of the program that would come to be known as REACH.

After finishing his year in AMP in the spring of 1999, FitzGerald moved on from Regis to travel abroad, but the following March, Father Biagi, who had just become principal that previous fall, wrote to him with a proposal. Recently the Board of Trustees had given the administration permission to establish an "outreach program" to economically needy but gifted students. In his e-mail, Biagi offered him the opportunity to spend a year doing research on what shape this program should take, since at that point the administration was still quite vague on this. Would it be a self-contained middle school such as Nativity on the Lower East Side? Or would it be more like a Prep for Prep program, in which needy students were given enrichment work on weekends and during the summer but attended other schools. Biagi had already composed a list of leading educators in New York whom he wanted FitzGerald to interview.[72]

Brian FitzGerald wound up accepting the offer, and that fall plunged himself into the task while also teaching two courses and coaching baseball. Thanks to the contacts made by Father Biagi, beginning that summer of 2000, FitzGerald began interviewing some leading educators in the New York City area, including Dr. James Borland, the dean of Columbia Teacher's College, Dr. Frank Macchiarola, president of St. Francis College in Brooklyn, leaders of the Prep for Prep program, as well as numerous officials in the education offices of the New York archdiocese. He also talked with educators who were running model schools for poor but talented children, including Brother Brian Carty, F.S.C., principal of De La Salle Academy on the West Side, as well as principals of traditional parochial schools in depressed, urban neighborhoods. FitzGerald quickly found resistance, especially from archdiocesan officials, to any mention that Regis might establish its own middle school, in the fear that such a move would "drain the best and the brightest" students from existing parochial schools, many of which were already struggling to keep their enrollment numbers stable.[73]

In speaking to more than two dozen people, FitzGerald received advice that ran the gamut, from the absolute need to start a separate "feeder school" for Regis (which might need to start with fourth grade), to recommendations that it be an intensive after-school and summer program that might not necessarily advance many or most of its graduates on to Regis. After months of research and interviews, FitzGerald typed up a detailed set of notes while also apprising a subcommittee of the Board of Trustees of his findings at each stage. Deciding to move on from Regis in the spring of 2001, FitzGerald passed his findings on to Father Christopher Devron, S.J., who had been hired to implement a program now that all the fact-finding had been accomplished. Under Father Devron's leadership, REACH (Recruiting Excellence in Academics for Catholic High Schools) was founded in the fall of 2001, and the first cohort of about thirty-five boys began their studies in the summer of 2002. As it turned out, the program would not be a middle school but rather a Saturday and summer program that would admit bright but economically disadvantaged boys in the summer after fifth grade. In addition to being Catholic, to be admitted into REACH the boys needed to come from homes where there was demonstrated financial need. For example, in 2011, 61 percent of all REACH students came from families that qualified for the federal free and reduced lunch program, while 80 percent of REACH families had an income below the household median income for New York City ($53,466).[74] In the fall of 2001, Father Devron began contacting all the pastors and principals in the four boroughs as well as some on Staten Island and southern Westchester, asking them to encourage talented fifth grade boys from economically disadvantaged families in their parish or school to apply for this new program. Thanks to the generosity of Father Joseph McShane, S.J., class of 1967, then president of the University of Scranton, every cohort has spent three weeks each summer on the university campus, where their days are filled with academics and their late afternoons and evenings with sports, enrichment activities, and community-building exercises. Upon their return from Scranton, the REACH students continue their summer studies with three weeks of classes at Regis itself. Each fall, the boys have begun the academic-year portion of the program by coming to Regis for twenty Saturdays of academic work. Since REACH's inception in 2002, several Regis teachers have taught in the program (both in the summer and during the school year), and Regis alumni who were still in college have worked as tutors and counselors during the summer program. In addition, current Regis students have also acted as mentors to these elementary-school-aged boys.[75]

Since its start in 2002, 236 boys have graduated from REACH and eighty have been awarded Regis scholarships, which represents a 33 percent acceptance rate, far higher than the overall acceptance rate to Regis of 15 percent. In addition to those boys accepted to Regis, a further ninety have been awarded full or partial scholarships and have enrolled in the other Jesuit high schools in New York City (Fordham, Xavier, Loyola, and Cristo Rey). A smaller number have won scholarships to other New York City Catholic high schools as well as the selective or specialized public high schools. As of the fall of 2011, eighty-one college-aged REACH alumni had matriculated at a college or university, including such highly selective institutions such as Cornell University, Massachusetts Institute of Technology, the College of the Holy Cross, and the University of Notre Dame.[76] Finally, by the spring of 2012, the core administrative and teaching staff had grown to four positions, with each of these educators also involved in teaching at Regis itself, including Mr. Todd Austin, the REACH director since 2006, who offers courses in the theology department.

Student Spiritual Life in an Era of Fewer Jesuits

In October 1979, Pope John Paul II made his first visit to the United States while also becoming the first pope to visit the White House. (In 1965, Paul VI visited the United States, but his sojourn lasted only fourteen hours.) As part of the massive media attention the papal trip garnered, two Regis students appeared on network news shows as part of their effort to provide a glimpse into the attitudes of young Catholics toward both the new Polish pope and the Church in general. Andy Infosino, class of 1981, was chosen to appear on NBC'S *Prime Time Sunday*, and the network even had a camera crew show up at his home in Oakland, New Jersey, to accompany him in on his commute from the suburbs. While Andy's comments on the new pope were congenial in describing him as "exud[ing] youth and vigor," the attitudes of his fellow Regians toward Catholicism during this period were far less enthusiastic.[77]

That previous spring a random group of forty graduating seniors had been selected to take a religious survey. Composed by the National Catholic Educational Association (NCEA), the survey asked respondents a series of questions on their understanding and views of the Catholic faith as well as their practice of it. The test was administered by Father James DiGiacomo, S.J., a member of the theology department as well as a popular writer and speaker on the topic of catechetics as well as young people and religion. Not surprisingly, the Regians scored high on their factual knowledge of Catholicism, but their attitudes toward Catholic doctrine and practice were far from uplifting. Only 5 percent of the seniors agreed with church teaching on contraception, with almost three-quarters rejecting it. In terms of religious practice, 55 percent said they attended Sunday Mass regularly, and 10 percent said they never attended church. In trying to understand and contextualize these results, DiGiacomo said that despite these depressing numbers, the responses of Regians were actually generally better than those of other Catholics their age, and it was his opinion that in general Regis's survey results reflect the "current condition of the

Church." However, he hoped the findings of this survey would help the theology department to respond more effectively to the situation and adapt the curriculum accordingly.[78]

A decade after this NCEA survey, the school began administering the JSEA's Student Profile Survey to freshmen, and then again the same survey to these students in their senior year. Since its inception in 1989, this survey has also been given to the same population of students (freshmen and seniors) at the other forty-five Jesuit high schools around the country. Using a Likert scale, students are asked to choose a response along a continuum from "strongly agree" to "strongly disagree" or "never" to "very frequently" to a series of questions regarding intellectual and personal development; perspectives on civil liberties and civic responsibility; and religious attitudes and behaviors. After more than a decade of use, in 2003 Dr. Ralph Nofi, the school's clinical psychologist, put together a detailed report analyzing trends in student responses. In regard to their religious attitudes and reported behaviors between their freshman and senior year, Nofi found that after their time at Regis, seniors have shown a "significant positive change in developing a sense that their individual moral failures can have an effect on the wider community"; an increased sense of the communal dimension of the Eucharist; and greater confidence about the degree to which they put Christian values into practice in their daily living. But that was all the good news. Over a ten-year period Regis seniors have consistently expressed weakening practice in prayer, Sunday Mass attendance, and the use of confession, as well as a declining attitude toward the importance and relevance of the Church in their lives. There was even a notable diminution of belief in the centrality of the Resurrection. In comparing these results with students from other Jesuit high schools as well as Catholic teens in general, the attitudes and practices of Regis seniors are in keeping with these other groups.[79] Not surprisingly, Regis students reflected the general weakening of beliefs and practices that has been true in the United States of all younger Catholics since the 1970s.

The school reacted to Nofi's findings in several ways. First, Father Biagi commissioned a new look at the structure and focus of the freshman retreat, which resulted in its expansion and a greater emphasis on the Eucharist as the center of Catholic spirituality and Christian service. Second, the freshman orientation was changed to include an opening prayer service based around the qualities of a graduate of a Jesuit school (generous, loving, open to growth, religious, and committed to justice) as articulated by the JSEA and adopted in various forms by Jesuit high schools around the country.

Third, the question of religious identity took on greater importance in the formal structures of the school as a whole, including a fair deal of discussion as part of the 2006 Middle States report and the establishment of the Religious Formation Committee, a permanent body of faculty and administrators, which meets regularly to review religious life at the school.

About the time that DiGiacomo administered the NCEA survey in 1979, there were still a large number of full-time Jesuits involved in the life of the school. In fact, the school year 1982–83 began with eighteen priests and scholastics as members of the faculty or administration. Early that year, this group came together to discuss the spiritual life of the school and ways the Jesuits could continue to support as well strengthen it. At this meeting, eleven of the eighteen voted in support of the motion in favor of "a special presence for Regis Jesuits at the 8 am liturgy in the Regis chapel." Others discussed the advisability of introducing at these Masses "dialog homilies," or having a special bell rung to invite students to the Mass, though no votes were taken on these suggestions. As part of this conversation, the Regis Jesuits recalled past practices that the school had supported to strengthen student spirituality, such as May sermons on Mary delivered by students and daily visits to the Blessed Sacrament in the chapel. While these practices were no longer popular, new ideas were discussed, such as the offering of new prayer resources and aids to both students and the lay faculty. The question of how to include lay teachers in the promotion of Catholic spirituality and prayer among the students came up at this meeting and would continue to be a topic of concern for the school administration and the Jesuits right up to the present. For the first fifty years or so of Regis's existence, there had been always a large number of Jesuits on faculty, and these "professional" religious seemed to handle the spiritual life of the students quite well. With the Jesuit teachers' thinning ranks, it was readily apparent to the school and the Jesuit order's leadership that the lay faculty would soon be responsible for this central aspect of the school's mission.[80]

During this meeting of the Regis Jesuits, the group also discussed retreats at the school, especially the new retreat for sophomores called "Quest," which began in 1979. In the era after Vatican II, the retreat program at Regis had gone through a fair amount of flux. By the late 1960s, the school had eliminated the traditional preached retreats held at Regis, which had been a spiritual mainstay since 1914, and began a period of experimentation. By the mid to late 1970s, the retreat program had come to consist of weekend retreats for small groups of upperclassmen in a house owned by an alumnus in Spring Lake, New Jersey, an Easter retreat for sophomores (now replaced by Quest), and a day of recollection for freshmen.[81] While Quest was praised for opening up each student's "affective side," it was now felt that a second-stage retreat was needed. Finally, it was also discussed that the lay faculty should be invited to become involved in them, too.[82]

As the number of Jesuits on the faculty continued to decline, the lay faculty began to take on more and more responsibility—not only for retreats but for much of the spiritual life of the students—and in the fall of 2000 a layman was named the school's first campus minister. In the 1970s, the office of the school chaplain had been created to oversee the spiritual life of the students, and from its inception, this role had been filled by a series of Jesuit priests. After the last Jesuit to fill that post left the school in the spring of 2000, lay people have since held the position, which is now referred to as "campus minister" rather than "chaplain," though the duties have remained largely the same. Today the campus minister is charged with coordinating the various retreats offered to students, including the mandatory ones in freshman and sophomore year as well as a choice of optional retreats for upperclassmen. With generally fewer than five priests on the faculty since 2007, careful coordination of the schedule has been necessary to make sure that at least one priest is available to go on retreat for the celebration of the sacraments, though even this is not always possible.

The smaller number of priests on the faculty, along with the relatively small number in attendance, led in the fall of 2006 to the decision to drop daily Mass in the school chapel. However, during the Lent and Advent seasons, Mass has continued to be celebrated on Wednesdays, with these liturgies generally attracting a crowd of at least a dozen faculty and students. Since the dropping of the weekly Mass for the entire school in the late 1960s, the entire student body has gathered for Mass at St. Ignatius Church a few times each year, usually centering around a major holiday such as Thanksgiving and Easter along with the Mass of the Holy Spirit, which takes place early in September. Finally, in regard to the hearing of confessions, the campus minister schedules formal opportunities for this sacrament once per year, with additional opportunities for this on both the freshman and sophomore (Quest) retreats. To help with this, Jesuit priests who reside at the 83rd Street community but do not work at Regis often lend a hand.

Over the last two decades or so, both the Jesuit administrators of Regis as well as the leaders of the New York Province have realized the increasingly central role lay faculty will play in the life of their schools as their numbers continue to decline, and have tried ways to prepare these men and women for positions of leadership in the schools. For the most part, these opportunities for further development have been coordinated on a national level by the JSEA, and have taken the form of intensive programs such as the Seminars in Ignatian Leadership and the JSEA Symposia and Colloquia on Jesuit Education. Since the 1990s, these seminars have brought together two dozen or so teachers and faculty at locations around the country twice a year for five days of training. The seminar runs for three years, culminating in a certificate in Ignatian Leadership. Several graduates of this program have moved on to administrative positions in Jesuit schools, though many have remained as classroom teachers. The symposia and colloquia are convoked every few years, involve a far larger number of attendees, and have focused on specific topics such as "Evaluation: A Key to *Cura Personalis*" (Regis University in Colorado, 2003) and "Jesuit Mission: Sent to the Frontiers" (Santa Clara University in California, 2010).[83]

In addition to committing itself to the ongoing training of faculty in Ignatian pedagogy and the spiritual traditions of the Jesuits, in 2012 the school itself began its first sponsorship process with the New York Province. Although the Jesuit province had continued to sponsor the school long after it no longer formally owned it, Regis began a process that several other Jesuit high schools around the country had undergone some years earlier. In preparation of a formal visit of a committee appointed by the province, the school began a series of self-studies looking at how effectively the academic, extracurricular, and overall life of the school reflected the values of a Jesuit education.

Over a period of three days, a team comprising six educators from other Jesuit high schools as well as officials from the provincial office visited the school and met with dozens of faculty and staff members as well as some students. After much conversation and review of the self-studies prepared by the faculty and administration, the team was happy to recommend to the Jesuit provincial, Father David Ciancimino, that the "Sustaining Agreement Between Regis High School and the New York Province of the Society of Jesus" be renewed for five years, after which another self-study would take place.[84]

Other Changes to Curriculum and Student Life

The 2011–12 review process for this sustaining agreement with the Jesuit province required a fair amount of preparation and the production of lots of paper. However, this paled in comparison with the decennial process for reaccreditation with the Middle States Association of Colleges and Schools, which the school had been undergoing since 1955. Though the initial accreditation of the school from this association goes back to the 1920s, it was not until this year that a visiting team of teachers from other schools was sent to Regis to perform their own evaluation before issuing a final report on behalf of the association and the notice of reaccreditation. This process has continued now for more than fifty years, with the most recent coming in 2006. A review of these self-evaluations prepared by the school as well as reports of the visiting team demonstrates that some aspects of academic and student life at Regis have continued to develop and change since the 1980s, though by a far smaller degree than they had in the late 1960s and 1970s.[85]

One of the areas of academic life to see the most significant change in the last thirty years was the classics. Beginning in the academic year 1985–86, Latin for the first time was no longer a required subject. In justifying this change, the writers of this section of the Middle States self-evaluation argued that because of the Latin requirement, "both the history and modern language programs have suffered." As far as history was concerned, the Latin requirement in junior year had "prevented the scheduling of Modern European History." In regard to the study of modern languages, the self-evaluation noted that a growing number of students had been arriving at Regis in freshman year "with a considerable amount of language studies behind them." Because of the mandatory study of Latin and the other demands of the curriculum, these boys had to wait "in most cases two years before resuming the study of the language [they] had begun." With the arrival of the freshman class in the fall of 1986, each student was now given a choice of embarking on a three-year study of Latin, French, Spanish, or German. In this first year where the students were given an option, about half of them chose Latin. (By 2012, only one quarter of the incoming freshman class had elected to study Latin.) In their junior year, students could elect to begin a second language, and at this time could choose among classical Greek, Italian, or Russian. If a student chose not to study a second language in his junior year, he was then required to take physics.[86] In the fall of 2001, the study of Chinese became another option for incoming freshmen, and in this first year of its offering, thirteen boys signed up. By 2004, Mr. Pedro Acosta, who had been hired to teach this new course, was now teaching four levels of the language.

In addition to the language department, the teaching of science also underwent some change and updating over the last two and a half decades.

Father Arthur C. Bender, S.J., '67, and his freshman advisement group in 1993. In addition to spending one year on the faculty in the academic year 1979–80, Father Bender has been teaching at Regis since 1991.

As a result of a critique in the 1986 Middle States evaluation, by the 1996 visitation the number of sections of both biology (freshman) and chemistry (sophomores) had been increased from four to five, thus decreasing both lab and class sizes.[87] In addition, students in both these two courses also received an additional twenty minutes of instructional time during each five-day cycle of classes. As far as senior electives, the offerings included advanced courses in biology, chemistry, and physics and an introductory course in psychology. For those students with a strong interest in the sciences, in 1986 the department began offering an independent course ("Science Research Project"), for which students would undertake their own study of a particular topic under the mentorship of one of the members of the science department as well as with the guidance of outside scholars and researchers.[88] Finally, in 2006, all students were required to take three full years of science (with physics in their junior year), regardless of whether they had elected to take a second language in their junior year.[89]

There were also some other changes to the curriculum that have come during the last three decades, either as result of recommendations by the Middle States visiting teams or because of the desire by the faculty and administration to amend or expand course offerings. As for the latter, an

American Studies course was added for sophomores, which, since its inception in 1991, has been taught by teachers from both the English and history departments.[90] While a course in film had been required for sophomores since the 1970s, in the 1980s a senior elective in film was added as well as a required course in art history for juniors. During the mid-1980s, the school expanded its use and teaching of computers with the hiring of Mr. James Phillips as full-time teacher, whose duties in addition to teaching music also included the instructing of computer applications to freshmen and a senior elective in computer programming. Upon Phillips's arrival, the school had only one mainframe computer and a few terminals. Only a handful of Apple IIe computers were available for student use, with just one computer course offered, a senior elective taught by Mrs. Diane Walsh of the science department.[91] Given how quickly computers were becoming a part of daily life, Phillips was given the funds to start a computer lab with the purchase of ten Apple IIG computers.[92] This expansion of the use of computers by students, faculty, and administration has continued since. By 2012, the school had over a hundred computers around the building for use by students, with a further ninety reserved for faculty, administration, and staff. In addition, by this year SMART Boards had been installed in most classrooms.[93] Finally, in 1998, the school made its first appearance on the Internet with its own website (http://www.regis-nyc.org/). Since its launch, the site has had several makeovers, and it now includes an intranet component that allows parental access in addition to its use by faculty and students.

While the school has continued to reshape its course offerings and requirements during these past three decades with little controversy among students, Regians did have a lot to say when a new marking system was instituted in the fall of 1983. Having abandoned numerical grades, which the school had used since 1914, the first iteration of new system had just five gradations: honor, merit, satisfactory, unsatisfactory, and failure. Ms. Patricia Opper, who taught science and was part of the committee that recommended the change, explained that the new system had been introduced in an effort "to get away from the 'numbers chase'" and the "arguing over a point or two between students and teachers." Letter grades, which remain in use in many other high schools, were deemed to not to be the right solution, since they "could easily be equated with number grades." After the institution of this new system, some students began to wonder whether they had been consulted enough before its implementation. When these concerns were raised with the assistant headmaster, Mr. Frank Walsh, he explained that while student input was important, it was ultimately up

In the 2004–5 academic year, the varsity basketball team won the the B division State Federation Championship in Glens Falls, New York, beating the best of the private and public schools of New York. Because of this win, they were invited by the New York Knicks for an insider's tour of Madison Square Garden. In addition to this honor, the team also was champs in the Catholic High School Athletic Association, and the head coach, Mr. Kevin Cullen (*back row, far right*), was named coach of the year by the *New York Daily News.*

to the faculty to decide what system of grading would be most appropriate for its students.[94] Not long after the new system was put into place, a sixth gradation (high honor) was added to the scale.[95] The topic of the grading system and the possible need to revamp it has come up now and again since the 1980s, though no major changes to it have been instituted since.

In 1981, another change to the curriculum came with the institution of required Christian service for seniors, for which time out of the regular school day was carved out. Regians had long been doing Christian service (or "works of charity and mercy," in the parlance of the Catholics before the Second Vatican Council) since the founding of the school through organizations such as the Sodalities, but for the most part, this work took place outside of school hours and was never considered to be a formal part of the curriculum. However, beginning in the late 1960s, new emphasis was placed on the importance of service and the pursuit of justice at Jesuit educational institutions, especially after the Jesuit Superior General Pedro Arrupe's statement that the main objective of Jesuit education was to form "men for others; men who live not for themselves but for God and his Christ."[96] In light of all this, the Regis administration eventually decided that a formal service component be included in the formation of Regis students. Thus, in 1981 all seniors performed service on Tuesday mornings by their participation in a variety of activities. By 1983, senior Christian service could be divided into four major areas: tutoring, hospital visitations, programs for the elderly, and Head Start programs.[97] Because of its strong commitment to the service component of a Regis education, in the early 1980s the school also began allowing seniors to spend their entire third trimester engaged in Christian service, and in 1987 half of the senior

In 2010, Regis installed a green roof, which at the time of its completion was the second largest in the city. The new roof was made of four to eight inches of growing material and was planted with native wildflowers and grasses. Because the sun does not touch the actual roof membrane, it is expected to last about twice as long as a conventional roof. Its benefits are many, including the lowering of the building temperature on the upper floor as well as the absorption of storm water. The school's science teachers have begun to use the roof as part of their environmental science and ecology curriculum, and an apiary was installed to facilitate biodiversity in the neighborhood.

class elected to do this.[98] Those boys could still take Advanced Placement exams in May by meeting with the teachers outside of the school day to keep up with the material. In addition, for the last three decades seniors have also been allowed to engage in full-time professional internships in their third trimester in fields ranging from finance to media. Those seniors who elect to remain in a full-time academic program in their third trimester have continued to perform service once per week, as they had for the first two trimesters. For their last months in the school, these seniors who stay at Regis have been able to choose from a wide variety of classes, ranging from culinary arts and nutrition[99] to the highbrow analysis of noteworthy television series such as *The Wire* to *Mad Men*.[100]

Alumni Since 1980

In looking at trends in colleges chosen by Regis seniors for the years 1980 to the present, as compared with the era 1964–80, the change is far less dramatic than the comparison of the latter era with those who graduated in the fifty years before 1964. Nevertheless, there has been some development. Once seniors were allowed and even encouraged to apply to non-Catholic colleges, this began to dramatically affect where Regians went to college. As mentioned in Chapter 5, whereas up until the mid-1960s, it was rare for a graduate to go on to a secular college or university, only 25 percent of the class of 1976 moved on to Catholic colleges, a statistic in keeping with other classes from the mid-1970s. However, trends in college choice at Regis have continued to develop.

Of the 1,066 students who graduated between 1993 and 2001, 59 percent went on to Catholic colleges. The explanation for this reversal of the trend against Catholic colleges is not clear, as there is no extant survey data as to why students chose to apply to and attend certain colleges and not others. However, it is worth pointing out that during this period, thirty-five students enrolled at Boston College, which may be an example of the "Flutie effect" on college admissions, in which a winning sports team raises the profile of the school and thereby increases applications. In more recent years, the percentage of those going on to Catholic colleges has cooled a bit from the 1993–2001 period, with 31 percent going from the class of 2007 and 35 percent from the class of 2009. In regard to Ivy League schools, 16.6 percent of the students from the period 1993–2001 won and accepted admission to these institutions.[101] Another change worth noting is that since 1980, a growing number of graduates have been going on to attend the select group of other highly competitive schools, though not in the Ivy League. For example, again for the period 1993–2001, Regians went on to the following institutions in these numbers: Amherst (17), Duke (6), Johns Hopkins (17), Massachusetts Institute of Technology (8), Stanford (6), University of Chicago (12), and Williams (23). Finally, seven Regians from this period went to one of the four U.S. military academies, or about one per class. Three men from this period entered the priesthood or religious life.[102]

As far as career choices for the men who have graduated since 1980, using the classes of 1980–86 as a representative sampling, a few trends can be detected. The field of law continued to dominate, with 464 out of about 900 alumni from this period working in this field. The number of Regians in business, banking, or auditing was also quite large, with about 378 in these areas. Fifty men from these classes have gone on to become physicians. Relatively few have gone on to fields such as K–12 teaching, with just about a dozen from this era choosing such a path. In 1998, only seven were serving active duty in the U.S. Armed Forces, and today only one is working as a firefighter.[103] Two work in print journalism. The vast majority of Regis graduates since 1980 have gone on to careers that either have required extensive graduate training, are generally well paying, or both.

Conclusion

In late 2007, Lucie Grant, the last member of Regis's founding family, died in her hundredth year. With the final disposition of her will (which was still in process in the fall of 2013), the school was poised to receive another major gift (about $10 million) from the Grant family fortune. But this would be the last of the family's generosity to Regis. The end of the Grants' relationship with Regis coming just a few years before the school's centennial provides the opportunity for reflection on both how much has changed since Julia M. Grant helped found the school as well as some of the challenges Regis will face as it embarks on its next hundred years.[1]

From the time of the school's opening in 1914 through the late 1940s, Regis provided a high-quality Jesuit education to thousands of boys who, for the most part, would not have been able to attend one of the other four Jesuit high schools in New York City, all of which charged substantial tuitions while offering only a few need-based scholarships each year. Providing a free Catholic education to Catholic boys who otherwise could not have afforded it was one of the goals of Mrs. Grant and Father Hearn in founding Regis, and there is little doubt that this goal was achieved during the school's first three decades. Regis certainly did make an enormous impact on the lives of the more than three thousand young men who graduated from the school between 1918 and 1948. This opportunity for a free Jesuit secondary education enabled many of the school's early graduates to move on to college and the professions while also advancing up the socioeconomic ladder into the middle class. More than 12 percent of the graduates during the period 1918–48 entered the legal profession alone. Since Regis was the only free Jesuit high school in the United States at this time, the impact of the school on the lives of Catholic boys in New York City was really a singular contribution in the history of the American Catholic community. In addition, during these early years literally hundreds of the school's graduates entered the priesthood or religious life, which reflected another goal of Mrs. Grant and Father Hearn for the sons of an increasing number of Catholic families. The role played by the alumni of Regis in leadership positions in the American Catholic Church was another singular contribution of Regis to both the Church and the wider society.[2]

An analysis of the student population from 1948 to 1980 reveals a change in the school's influence on the wider Catholic population. Because of growing prosperity of Americans as a whole as well as the expansion of Catholic high school education in the New York City area, the relative impact of Regis, while still significant, was not as singular as it had been during the school's first thirty years. The decade of the 1950s brought unprecedented prosperity to Americans, including to those groups who had often been left behind during earlier periods of economic growth. Thanks to increased wages and relatively low inflation, by 1960 the average American family had 30 percent more purchasing power than it had in 1950.[3] The Catholic population shared in these material blessings, and this had a significant impact on the demographic and socioeconomic makeup of the Regis student body.

While the school continued to draw heavily from the urban parochial schools, this potential pool of students was changing, as was the economic background of the families of these Regis students. While the class of 1928 included forty-three boys from Manhattan, that number had fallen to only fifteen for the class of 1950, with the number of boys from lower-middle-class neighborhoods of Queens (such as Maspeth and Elmhurst) expanding from ten to seventeen. By 1970, the number of boys from these parts of Queens constituted almost one-third of the entire class. In addition, by 1970 one could see the impact of the growth of the suburbs on the school's population, since 62 of the 132 graduates in this class came from Long Island and the northern suburbs (Westchester and Rockland Counties in New York and Fairfield County in Connecticut). Only eight boys in this class were from the Bronx and only five were from Manhattan, which demonstrates that suburbanization of the United States during this period was reflected in the student population of Regis as well. However, it would be a mistake to think that the boys coming from these new areas were all wealthy or upper middle class. Although there is no extant financial data about their families, a fair number of these suburban students came from cities and towns with large lower-middle-class populations, such as Jersey City, Bayonne, Yonkers, Valley Stream, and Floral Park. In fact, in the class of 1978, seven out of the nine students from Westchester County came from Yonkers.

In addition to the growing prosperity and suburbanization of the nation (and Regis) in the 1950s and 1960s, the period after World War II also saw changes in the landscape of Catholic secondary education in the New York metropolitan area, making it both more available and affordable. As a high school degree became increasingly the norm for American teenagers in the postwar era, both the Archdiocese of New York and the Diocese of Brooklyn (which also includes Queens) expanded their existing parish and diocesan high schools and opened several new ones. In the archdiocese alone during the administration of Francis Cardinal Spellman (1939–67), the number of diocesan high schools expanded from one to ten. At one point, Cardinal Hayes High School enrolled close to 4,000 students and Cardinal Spellman High School over 2,300 students.[4] The tuition at these institutions was kept relatively low ($150 per year at many of them in the 1950s), making them far more affordable than Xavier or Fordham Prep, which had tuitions of between $300 and $350 during this same period. Thanks to an expanding middle class and relatively modest tuition at the new diocesan high schools, a Catholic high school education was now possible for a large percentage of the Catholic population of the New York City area. While it is true that enrollment at these new institutions did not carry the same cachet as enrollment at a Jesuit school (let alone the prestige of a Regis education, whose admissions standards remained highly selective), these schools maintained high educational standards. They not only helped to catechize and form another generation of Catholics, but they also propelled many of these young men and women into the middle class and the professions.[5] (Perhaps most impressive, U.S. Supreme Court Justice Sonia Sotomayor was the valedictorian in the 1972 graduation from Cardinal Spellman High School.) Thus, while the opportunities for Regis graduates from the school's first thirty or so graduating classes differed greatly from the other boys from their neighborhoods, this was far less the case during the next three decades.

In addition to analyzing the changing trends of the economic backgrounds of Regians between 1918 and 1980, the question of the race of these students during this period also merits discussion, though finding data is not easy. Not surprisingly, none of the official enrollment material from the school for the first fifty years contains any references to race or ethnicity. A recent attempt by the members of Heritage (Regis's African American student organization) to determine the school's first students of color revealed how little material there is on this topic. Seemingly, William Aloysius Robinson, '30, was the first student of color to graduate from Regis. A native of the British West Indies, William graduated from St. Joseph's Parochial School in Yorkville. However, it was almost another two decades before another black student graduated from the school, Alan Pinado in

1949.[6] There may have been other students of color who were accepted or attended the school before this, but the evidence is strong that Robinson and Pinado were the first two to graduate. For the 1950s, the total number of black students for the entire decade did not rise above the single digits.[7] In addition, even those students with Spanish surnames would not necessarily qualify as minority (Latino), since the city had a population of immigrants from Spain going back to the early twentieth century.[8] By the early 1980s, the school's racial diversity had expanded considerably from thirty years earlier. In that academic year, it was computed that the total minority population (18.8 percent) of the school comprised twenty blacks, forty-four Hispanics, and thirty-one "Orientals."[9] In terms of students who had one or both parents who were immigrants, in the freshman class that arrived in the fall of 1980, 45.6 percent had a father and 42.3 percent had a mother born outside the United States, though of course this number includes white Europeans. Interestingly, the country that produced the largest number of Regis parents for this academic year was Ireland (nineteen fathers and eighteen mothers).[10]

The issue of minority enrollment at Regis is complex for several reasons. First, while the school did not specifically look to increase its enrollment of students from poorer backgrounds until the 1960s, it has never had a stated policy to expand its minority population. However, since people of color are more likely than the whites to be economically disadvantaged, any attempt to increase enrollment of disadvantaged students would indirectly increase overall minority enrollment at the school. Second, another complicating factor is that the New York City area (unlike Baltimore, New Orleans, and Washington, D.C.) has never had a large black Catholic population. This demographic reality has certainly had an impact on the number of black students at the school, since Regis admits only Catholics. (Other area Catholic schools have had much higher percentages of black students than Regis has because they admit non-Catholics.) Not surprisingly, those students of color who have attended Regis over the last three decades have usually been the sons or grandsons of immigrants from the Caribbean or Africa, since the immigration from both these areas have had fairly high percentage of Catholics.[11] (The older, more established black community of New York City, whose numbers greatly increased with the migration of southern blacks to northern cities between the World Wars, was overwhelmingly Protestant.) Over the most recent decade, the minority (nonwhite) population of the school has remained stable at about 30 percent. For the freshman class of 136 boys (which entered in the fall of 2012), the breakdown was as follows: 4 percent

African American, 11 percent Asian American, 13 percent Hispanic American, 3 percent "other" minority, and 69 percent Caucasian.[12] Since the 1980s, the percentage of African American students at Regis has remained at between 3 percent and 8 percent, while the percentage of Hispanic and Asian students has shown steadier growth. Regis's racial breakdown in recent years has been somewhat in keeping with averages for Catholic secondary schools on a national level, whose student population on the whole is 75.4 percent white, 7.6 percent African American, 10.3 percent Hispanic, Asian 3.7 percent, and "other" 3.0 percent, though Regis has higher percentages of Hispanics and Asians than the national average.[13]

The establishment of the REACH program in 2002 has been a strong sign of the commitment to the Board of Trustees' guarantee that Regis continue to enroll Catholic boys from economically disadvantaged families, many of whom would also be from minority backgrounds. Since the first group of REACH students graduated from eighth grade in 2005, eighty of them have gone on to attend Regis, which has helped to assure an economic diversity to the student body. An analysis of the freshman class that arrived in the fall of 2012 reveals that more than 21 percent of them came from families earning less than $80,000 while 34 percent came from families earning more than $220,000.[14] It is a fact that for many decades now, a small percentage of the students have come from a disadvantaged background. Although Regis was founded for Catholic boys who were graduates of parochial schools (which then were almost all free and founded for the poor), even at its start there was never a means test to gain admittance. Thus, there was always some "economic diversity" among the student body, though clearly in recent decades the overall percentage of students coming from upper-middle-class families is far higher than in the school's first few decades. Since the Board of Trustees is committed to maintaining its very high entrance standards, it has decided to fund the REACH program in an effort to help nurture more students from disadvantaged backgrounds. Since these children tend to live in neighborhoods with underfunded and underperforming elementary schools, this of course has affected the quality of their education and thus their ability to succeed on the Regis entrance examination. Although performance on this test is a very important part of the admissions process, it is not the only criterion: a written application and a personal interview are also required. In addition, as the school website states, "In the admissions process, special consideration is given to those who cannot otherwise afford a Catholic education."

In December 2010, an impromptu Regis hockey team took on Xavier's varsity squad at a rink in Bayonne, New Jersey, as part of a fundraiser for the REACH program.

REACH students and their teacher, Mr. Joseph Carroll (who also teaches Latin at Regis), after Sunday Mass at the University of Scranton in July 2012. Each summer, REACH students spend three weeks engaged in academics as well as activities to foster spiritual growth and leadership development.

Only time will tell if the school is able to increase the percentage of the student body from disadvantaged backgrounds. In any case, Regis remains singular among all Jesuit (and all Catholic) high schools in the nation in that all its students are academically gifted and on scholarship.[15] While of course the students come from a variety of economic backgrounds, the fact that they all attend Regis gratis is a great equalizer. This special characteristic of this school has helped it to avoid some of the inherent tension in other private schools between those students on scholarship and those whose parents are able to pay full freight, a controversial topic that was put into the national spotlight by a recent *New York Times* article with the provocative title, "Admitted, but Left Out."[16] For almost a century now, Regis has been able to maintain this egalitarian environment among the student body, which is a remarkable financial feat that no other Catholic high school in the United States has been able to replicate.[17] The preservation of an all-scholarship and highly competitive high school composed of students from a distribution of economic backgrounds may be the most distinctive feature of Regis today, but whether this model will continue to be financially viable in the years ahead is open to question. However, there is no question that Regis remains one of the most popular schools in the New York City area. Over the past two decades, after some initial prescreening, on average more 800 eighth-grade boys have sat for the entrance exam each fall. From this number about 250 are invited back for an interview in early January, and ultimately 135–40 are offered spots in the next freshman class. There was some concern after the September 11, 2001, terrorist attacks on New York City that the number of applicants to the school would decrease. While there was somewhat of a drop in the number taking the entrance exam that next month, by the next year things returned to how they had been before.

Although many observers have often referred to the Regis "endowment," the school's savings have not been treated as an endowment in the strict sense of the term for many decades. Since the school's investments have never been able to generate enough income to finance the entire (or even substantive portion of) annual budget, the school has regularly had to liquidate assets in its investment portfolio to meet operating investments. (Recall that during some financial difficulties in the 1950s, one president proposed charging tuition to at least some students.) Although financial support from the alumni has been strong and growing since the first major appeal in the late 1960s, this revenue stream has not been enough to bridge the gap between gains on the investment and the budget. (For the fiscal year 2011–12, alumni donated more than $3 million.) To

Ms. Kristin Ross, assistant principal, and the members of her senior advisement, 2011–12. These seniors are dressed in "Regis Red" in anticipation of that evening's basketball game against Xavier, which the varsity Raiders won by a score of 49–47.

make up some of this shortfall, the school has had to rely on other sources, most notably parents, both current and those of alumni, and their giving in 2012 totaled slightly more than $1.16 million. Until recently, these requests to parents have been relatively "soft," taking the form of a major spring auction. However, more recently there has been some targeting of wealthier parents for individual gifts, and in response to the economic crisis of 2007–8, for the first time the school asked for $1,000 from the parents of each student for a one-time recession fund (which wound up raising $319,000). Unfortunately, these budgetary challenges will add even more complexity to the challenge of maintaining economic diversity among the student body, let alone expanding it.[18]

A final challenge Regis will face in the years ahead is the preservation of its identity as a Jesuit school. Since the 1970s, Jesuit leaders on the provincial level have recognized that in light of the rapidly declining number of Jesuit priests, brothers, and scholastics, the future of their schools will lie in the hands of the laymen and -women who will lead them. In preparation for this change, the Jesuits on a national level (principally through the

JSEA) have sponsored a series of workshops and symposia to help form educational leaders in both Ignatian spirituality and Jesuit educational philosophy. In addition, as mentioned in Chapter 6, many schools, including Regis, now have faculty chaplains on staff, to offer regular spiritual formation for faculty and staff. With a growing number of Jesuit high schools employing laypeople in the top positions of both president and principal/headmaster (e.g. Xavier), there is tangible evidence that laypeople are able to carry on the tradition of Jesuit education with few or even no Jesuits actively involved in the life of the school. As Regis faces the prospect of one day having no Jesuit on faculty, there has been both ample preparation for this as well as strong hope based on the experience of other Jesuit high schools that the Jesuit identity of Regis will endure. But, again, only time will tell.

The vision of Mrs. Grant and Father Hearn of a selective, all-scholarship Jesuit high school for Catholic boys who otherwise could not afford a Catholic school has clearly changed now that Regis strives to welcome students from a diversity of financial backgrounds. However, Cardinal Newman famously said that "to live is to change, and to be perfect is to have changed often." The challenge for Regis is to preserve the essence of this unique example of American Catholic secondary education while accommodating itself to the changing needs of the local Catholic population. It is a daunting task in a rapidly evolving society. However, Jesuit schools have always faced challenges since the founding of the first one almost five centuries ago. And Jesuits and their lay collaborators have continually found creative solutions to these challenges. If the past is any indication of the future, and it usually is, then Regis can face its future with both hope and confidence.

Notes

Introduction

1. Archives Regis High School, Shelf F4, Box 1, Folder 1, Rector's Diary, September 14 and 15, 1914. For information on Francis X. J. Miller, see his permanent record card in the file cabinets in the Faculty Mailroom.

2. Though an attempt was made at offering a free education to all students by the Jesuits at St. John's College High School in Shreveport, Louisiana, financial constraints eventually forced the school to begin charging tuition in 1933. See Charles T. Taylor, S.J., "A Study of an Endowed Jesuit Secondary School" (M.A. thesis, St. Louis University, 1938), 79. It is unclear if this attempt to offer a free education at St. John's began at the time of its founding in 1908 or sometime later.

3. These four other schools included two in Manhattan—Xavier High School (founded in 1847) on West 16th Street and the Loyola School (1900) on Park Avenue—and two in the outer boroughs—Fordham Prep (1846) in the Bronx and Brooklyn Prep (1908), which was in the Crown Heights section of Brooklyn but closed in 1972. The former buildings of Brooklyn Prep now house Medgar Evers College.

4. Henry Foley, *Records of the English Province of the Society of Jesus*, 7 vols. (London: Burns and Oates, 1877–83), 7:343. While the provincial could have been referring to a college in the sense of an educational institution, he could also have been calling for the establishment of a fictional college that could serve as the center of a group of houses. According to the Society of Jesus's constitutions, only a college could possess revenue or real property. Where none existed, as in seventeenth-century England, Jesuit superiors often created a fictional one to which houses and missions in an area were attached.

5. John O'Malley, *The First Jesuits* (Cambridge: Harvard University Press, 1993), 200.

6. The reasons for the suppression of the Society of Jesus by Pope Clement XIV in 1773 are various and complex, and have much to do with conflicts between the Jesuits and civil rulers who eventually put pressure on the papacy to suppress the order.

7. Olwen Hufton, "Every Tub on Its Own Bottom: Funding a Jesuit College in Early Modern Europe," in John O'Malley et al., eds., *The Jesuits II: Cultures, Sciences, and the Arts, 1540–1773* (Toronto: University of Toronto Press, 2006), 6.

8. William J. McGucken, S.J., *The Jesuits and Education: The Society's Teaching Principles and Practice, Especially in Secondary Education in the United States* (Milwaukee: Bruce Publishing, 1932), 55–56.

9. Thomas J. Shelley, *The Archdiocese of New York: The Bicentennial History, 1808–2008* (Strasbourg: Editions du Signe, 2007), 22–24. While no Catholic priest ever suffered this cruel fate, one unfortunate Anglican clergyman, John Ury, was executed after having been misidentified as a Catholic priest.

10. Francis X. Curran, S.J., *The Return of the Jesuits* (Chicago: Loyola University Press, 1966), 25–28. Historically Jesuit schools generally did not charge tuition but rather relied on the fees paid by the young men who boarded at their institutions to help meet overall expenses.

11. Ibid., 3.

12. McGucken, *Jesuits and Education*, 76–77. Since at this time the location of St. John's College was outside the boundaries of New York and actually in Westchester County, it cannot technically be considered the next attempt by the Jesuits to found a school in New York City after the closing of the New York Literary Institution. It was not until 1874 that the Fordham area was annexed by the city.

13. For a study of the successful alumni of Xavier College, see David. E. Nolan, "The Catholic Club of the City of New York: A Study of Lay Involvement in the Archdiocese of New York, 1888–1960" (M.A. thesis, St. Joseph's Seminary, Dunwoodie, 1995).

14. Anthony Andreassi, "On West Sixteenth Street: Xavier High School," *Company* 16 (Winter 1998–99): 21.

15. The first "plan of studies" as an overall rationale for the type of education to be offered in Jesuit colleges was written by the early Jesuits Jerónimo Nadal and Annibal Coudert in 1548 and 1551, respectively. These early plans were later greatly amended, especially after the Fifth General Congregation of the Society of Jesus (1593–94) called for a major revision of the *Ratio* by consultation and input by members of the whole Society. It was through this process that the *Ratio Studiorum* of 1599 was born, and this remained in place as the blueprint for education in Jesuit colleges until the suppression of the Society in 1773. See McGucken, *Jesuits and Education*, 212.

16. A proud product of the University of Paris, Ignatius did not have much respect for the Italian university system. Thus he appointed many graduates of the University of Paris to the faculty at the Roman College. He especially prized the strict obedience students paid to their teachers at Paris, a trait he expected Jesuits to have toward their religious superiors. See ibid., 25–26.

17. Christa Ressmeyer Klein, "The Jesuits and Catholic Boyhood in Nineteenth-Century New York City: A Study of St. John's College and the College of St. Francis Xavier, 1846–1912" (Ph.D. diss., University of Pennsylvania, 1976), 120–21.

18. Near the end of a student's time at one of these Jesuit colleges, a class or two in philosophy were mandated, and throughout the entire course of studies great emphasis was placed on languages, both classical and modern. In addition, not surprisingly catechism was taught each year. See Philip Gleason, *Contending with Modernity: Catholic Higher Education in the Twentieth Century* (New York: Oxford University Press, 1995), 5–6.

19. Founded in 1820 as a house of studies for scholastics, Gonzaga was first known as the Washington Seminary. However, shortly after its opening the school began taking in lay students, whom many of the scholastics taught while also taking courses themselves. In 1824, the scholastics were withdrawn and sent to study elsewhere, but the school remained opened for lay students. In 1827, under orders from Jesuit superiors in Rome, the school was closed when it was learned that tuition was being charged. (According to the Jesuit constitutions, fees for boarders could be charged but not tuition.) The school was reopened again in 1848 with the name changed to Gonzaga College. As was the case with most of the other Jesuit institutions of this type at the time, Gonzaga had the right to award degrees in the arts and sciences, but by the end of the nineteenth century it was doing this far less often. Though the charter still gives the school the right to college grant degrees (in addition to high school diplomas), today Gonzaga grants them *honoris causa* and does so infrequently. See McGucken, *Jesuits and Education*, 73–74.

20. Klein, "The Jesuits and Catholic Boyhood in Nineteenth-Century New York City," 181.

21. Ibid. At this time most professional schools (e.g., medicine, law) did not necessarily require a bachelor's degree but often accepted one or two years of college studies before admission.

22. Charles W. Eliot, "Recent Changes in Secondary Education," *Atlantic Monthly* 84 (1899): 43, as quoted in Gerald McKevitt, S.J., "Jesuit Schools in the USA, 1814–ca. 1970," in Thomas Worcester, S.J., ed., *The Cambridge Companion to the Jesuits* (New York: Cambridge University Press, 2008), 283.

23. Robert Emmett Curran. *A History of Georgetown University: The Quest for Excellence, 1889–1964*, vol. 2 (Washington, D.C.: Georgetown University Press, 2010), 87–88.

24. Klein, "The Jesuits and Catholic Boyhood in Nineteenth-Century New York City," 181–82.

25. Ibid., 343.

26. The Jesuits had desired for some time to open a school in the Diocese of Brooklyn, but the long-reigning and founding bishop John Loughlin (1853–91) had a general aversion to religious-order priests. As evidence of this, in 1889 a reporter for the *Brooklyn Eagle* remarked that Loughlin had a strong dislike for "two classes of persons—reporters and Jesuits." His successor, Charles E. McDonnell, had attended the College of St. Francis Xavier in Manhattan and thus had a much more favorable attitude toward the Society. In fact, at his episcopal ordination he asked Father Thomas Campbell, the Jesuit provincial, to preach. Thus, when he approached by the Jesuits with the idea of starting a college in his diocese, he was more than happy to give his approval. See Patrick McNamara, "Brooklyn's Jesuit College," http://irishcatholic humanist.blogspot.com/2011/03/brooklyns-jesuit-college-1908-1921.html (accessed March 18, 2011).

27. Klein, "Jesuits and Catholic Boyhood in Nineteenth-Century New York City," 340–43; McGucken, *Jesuits and Education*, 124.

28. Robert F. Meade, *The Centennial History of Loyola School, 1900–2000* (Concord, N.H.: Capital Offset, 2000), 3.

29. O'Malley, *First Jesuits*, 211, 226.

30. McGucken, *Jesuits and Education*, 235.

31. Ibid., 235–36

32. Ibid., 236.

33. Meade, *Centennial History of Loyola School*, 2.

34. Charles Morris, *American Catholic: The Saints and Sinners Who Built America's Most Powerful Church* (New York: Times Books, 1997), 256.

35. Daniel J. Burke, S.J., "Regis High School," *Jesuit Seminary News* (September–October 1937), 23.

36. McGucken, *Jesuits and Education*, 236.

37. Interview, Rev. Francis Principe. November 12, 2012. Father Principe, a New York archdiocesan priest, is a 1945 graduate of Cardinal Hayes High School, the first of a dozen diocesan high schools founded by Cardinal Spellman between 1941 and 1963. Father Principe joined the faculty of Hayes in 1959. See also "School Dedicated as Hayes Symbol: Bronx Institution Hailed as Living Monument to Late 'Cardinal of Charities,'" *New York Times*, September 9, 1941. When Archbishop Stepinac High School was opened in White Plains in 1948, its tuition was set at fifteen dollars per month. See "New Stepinac School Will Open This Week," *New York Times*, September 6, 1948.

38. As late as 1970, there will still fewer than 60,000 black Catholics in the New York archdiocese out of a total Catholic population of over 1.8 million. See Florence D. Cohalan, *A Popular History of the Archdiocese of New York*, 2nd ed. (Yonkers, N.Y.: U.S. Catholic Historical Society, 1999), 342.

39. Morris, *American Catholic*, 264.

40. Diane Ravitch, *The Troubled Crusade: American Education, 1945–1980* (New York: Basic Books, 1983), 149.

41. In 1968, there were 157,435 pupils in parochial schools in the archdiocese. By 1983 that number had declined to 88,753. There was also a comparative decrease in the student population in Catholic schools in the Brooklyn diocese during this period. See Thomas J. Shelley, *The Archdiocese of New York: The Bicentennial History, 1808–2008* (Strasbourg: Editions du Signe, 2007), 588.

42. Thomas J. Shelley, "Empire City Catholicism: Catholic Education in New York," in Thomas C. Hunt and Timothy Walch, eds., *Urban Catholic Education: Tales of Twelve Cities* (South Bend: University of Notre Dame Press, 2010), 85.

1. Mrs. Grant's Gift

1. In addition to his wife and three children, the former mayor's residence was also home to six live-in servants, all of whom were born abroad (three in Ireland, two in Sweden, and one in France). All were female, except for the Swede who served as a footman. See "Thirteenth Census of the United States: 1910." This census was enumerated on April 19, 1910, seven months before Grant's death.

2. Several of the city's major newspapers carried accounts of Grant's death the next day (November 4, 1910), including the *New York Times*, the *Tribune*, the *World*, and the *Sun*. Each had slightly different accounts of Grant's death as well as some discrepancies concerning his biographical data.

3. I am indebted to Mr. James Simmons, Regis class of 2009, for his research in writing "'Teach Me to Be Generous': The Founding Family of Regis High School," a paper he wrote in his senior year at Regis as part of an independent study course. In this excellent paper, in which he used limited extant sources, Simmons compiled biographies of both Hugh and Julia (Murphy) Grant as well as the details surrounding the various gifts Julia gave to the school from the time of its founding in 1914 until her death in 1944. For much of the biographical information on Hugh, Simmons relied on Lawrence V. Cullen, "Hugh J. Grant, Mayor of New York City, 1889–1892: Tammany Hall and the Fulfillment of Civic Responsibility in Elected Office" (M.A. thesis, Fordham University, 1988).

4. Various sources list Grant's year of birth as between 1853 and 1858. However, the Grant family mausoleum in Calvary Cemetery in Queens lists his birthdate as September 10, 1858. An 1878 passport application also lists this year. See Michael Pollak, "Answers to Questions About New York: Young and Younger," *New York Times*, April 17, 2011.

5. Cullen, "Hugh J. Grant, Mayor of New York City," 4.

6. The above-referenced newspaper accounts of Grant's death and the short entry in *First Citizens* are at variance as to when Hugh was orphaned. The *New*

York Times and the other newspapers state that he was "left orphan as a small boy," while Lewis Randolph Hamersly states that his parents took him on a tour of Europe after he graduated from Manhattan College. See *First Citizens of the Republic: An Historical Work Giving Portraits and Sketches of the Most Eminent Citizens of the United States* (New York: L. R. Hamersly & Co., 1906), 165.

7. While several sources mention that Hugh's father bequeathed him a huge sum of money, the figure of $500,000 was given by Mrs. Lucie Grant in an interview with Father Edwin J. Brooks, S.J., on May 19, 1990. She was the widow of Hugh's son, Hugh J. Grant, Jr., who had died in 1981. See Archives Regis High School (hereafter ARHS), Shelf K4, Box 1, Folder 9 (hereafter K4-1-9), "Data from Mrs. Lucie Grant, May 19, 1990."

8. Cullen, "Hugh J. Grant, Mayor of New York City," 4.

9. Daniel Okrent, *Last Call: The Rise and Fall of Prohibition* (New York: Scribner, 2010), 47.

10. Cullen, "Hugh J. Grant, Mayor of New York City," 5–6.

11. Edwin G. Burrows and Mike Wallace, *Gotham: A History of New York to 1898* (New York: Oxford University Press, 1999), 1108.

12. Cullen, "Hugh J. Grant, Mayor of New York City," 6–7.

13. This was the second Croton Aqueduct. The first was completed in 1842.

14. Cullen, "Hugh J. Grant, Mayor of New York City," 10–11.

15. Ibid., 11–14.

16. Ibid., 9–11; and *First Citizens of the Republic*, 166.

17. George J. Lankevich and Howard B. Furer, *A Brief History of New York City* (New York: National University Publications, 1984), 184–87.

18. ARHS, K4-1-9, Edwin J. Brooks, S.J., "A History of the Grant Family," 1–2. After a twenty-three-year close association with Hugh Grant, Jr., his wife, Lucie, and Edna Grant (which included the celebration of daily Mass in the family chapel in their residence on East 72nd Street), in 1990 Father Brooks typed a five-page, double-spaced account of the family's history based on conversations with the three family members listed above. See also *New York Times*, April 30, 1895, which contains the wedding announcement of Julia Murphy and Hugh Grant and corroborates several of the facts put forth by Brooks in this document.

19. Francis S. Barry, *The Scandal of Reform: Grand Failures of New York's Political Crusaders and the Death of Nonpartisanship* (New Brunswick: Rutgers University Press, 2009), 64.

20. Cullen, "Hugh J. Grant, Mayor of New York City," 16.

21. ARHS, K-4-1, "Data from Mrs. Lucie Grant," May 19, 1990. This is a two-page document typed on letterhead of the president of Regis High School,

who at the time was Father James Fischer, S.J. It contains basic biographical information concerning Mrs. Grant's in-laws, Hugh and Julia Grant, as well as how Hugh and Lucie met.

22. ARHS, I6-3-5, "Certificate of Death: Julia M. M. Grant." Julia was born on March 11, 1873.

23. "Senator Murphy, Edward, Jr., (1836–1911)," *Biographical Directory of the United States*, http://bioguide.congress.gov/scripts/biodisplay.pl?index=M001090 (accessed September 22, 2010). For information on Julia Delehanty Murphy, see "Hudson-Mohawk Genealogical and Family Memoirs: Murphy," http://www.schenectadyhistory.org/families/hmgfm/murphy.html (accessed January 4, 2011). The exact year of her birth is not able to be determined.

24. This residence no longer exists.

25. *New York Times*, April 30, 1895.

26. *New York Times*, May 1, 1895. The city of Washington was under the ecclesiastical jurisdiction of the archbishop of Baltimore until 1947, when the Archdiocese of Washington was created.

27. *New York Times*, May 1, 1895.

28. *New York Times*, August 4, 1895.

29. *New York Times*, August 24, 1900. This "In the Real Estate Field" column states that on the previous day, "ex-Mayor Grant" took title to a piece of property adjacent to his residence on the south side of 72nd Street, east of Fifth Avenue.

30. New York City, Department of Buildings, Manhattan, Plans, Permits and Dockets: East 72nd Street, South Side, Nos. 16–20. I am indebted to Mr. Brendan Coburn of CWB Architects for helping me to find this source.

31. *New York Times*, October 15 and 29, 1899. I am indebted to Mr. John Leopoldo Fiorilla for uncovering this information on the history of the residence before the purchase of it by the Grants.

32. Anthony Gronowicz, "Upper East Side," in Kenneth T. Jackson, ed., *Encyclopedia of New York City* (New Haven: Yale University Press, 1995), 1217.

33. John Fink, "Railroads," in *Encyclopedia of New York City*, 977. This process of covering over the tracks was not completed until 1910. On the south side of the center island at Park and East 86th Street, there is a small tablet commemorating Mayor Grant's involvement in covering over the tracks and beautifying Park Avenue.

34. The Harlem River Speedway was a dirt roadway for racing and training horses, which ran for two and half miles along the west bank of the Harlem River north from West 155th Street.

35. *First Citizens of the Republic*, 166.

36. Originally founded as the Xavier Union by alumni of the College of St. Francis Xavier, the Catholic Club was established in 1888 as a private Catholic

men's association with a clubhouse on Central Park South. This was at a time when Catholic professional men often had a hard time joining the elite but almost exclusively Protestant clubs in New York. See David E. Nolan, "The Catholic Club of the City of New York: A Study of Lay Involvement in the Archdiocese of New York, 1888–1960" (M.A. thesis, St. Joseph's Seminary, Dunwoodie, 1995).

37. ARHS, K-2-2, "Pocket Data and Note Book of Hugh J. Grant [Jr.]." This small six-ring binder contains an assortment of personal information and data, including items such as Hugh's Social Security card. A handwritten slip of paper notes his birthday as April 8, 1904.

38. *New York Times*, November 8, 1910.

39. Brooks, "History of the Grant Family," 2.

40. Tertianship is the final component of a Jesuit priest's training process. Until the Second Vatican Council, it came shortly after ordination, and upon completion, a Jesuit made his final vows.

41. "Obituary of Father David W. Hearn," *Woodstock Letters*, vol. 47, 233.

42. Archives of the College of St. Francis Xavier, "Litterae Annuae, 1862," RG 9:1, Box 1, Folder 6. Although their administration of St. Ignatius was supposed to give the Jesuits a closer place for these chaplains to live, for some unknown reason some of these men still continued to live at Xavier well into the twentieth century.

43. *Church of St. Ignatius Loyola and St. Lawrence O'Toole* (New York: Church of St. Ignatius Loyola, 1966), 21–25.

44. *New York Times*, July 21, 1911. In 2013, this would be worth about $200 million.

45. ARHS, L6-2-10, "Notebook of Benefactors to the Church of St. Ignatius Loyola (NYC)." The Regis Archives has a photocopy of a small notebook of 130 pages that Father Hearn began in 1909. On the first page, he wrote, "No record was ever kept of gifts or benefactors. It is known that we have had good friends in the past, but no one seems to know who they were, except a name or two."

46. Archives Maryland Province of the Society of Jesus (hereafter AMPSJ), Box 27, Folder 502 (hereafter 27–502), Hearn to Richards, November 4, 1916. In this letter Hearn writes of Mrs. Grant's reliance on him, "She sent for me in her grief and from that hour I did all in my power to help and comfort her in a simple, quiet way." At the time of this writing these archives were located in Lauinger Library at Georgetown University.

47. "Notebook of Benefactors to the Church of St. Ignatius Loyola," 49.

48. Roman Archives of the Society of Jesus (hereafter RASJ), Maryland Province Series, File 1015, Hearn to Father General, June 21, 1912.

49. Christa Ressmeyer Klein, "The Jesuits and Catholic Boyhood in Nineteenth-Century New York City: A Study of St. John's College and the College

of St. Francis Xavier, 1846–1912" (Ph.D. diss., University of Pennsylvania, 1976), 171–72.

50. ARHS, J5-2, "Records of Regis High School." Hearn to Catholic Parents, May 15, 1907. This letter is pasted in a record book put together by Hearn, which also includes other information concerning the planning and foundation of Regis.

51. Klein, "Jesuits and Catholic Boyhood in Nineteenth-Century New York City," 196–97.

52. "Notebook of Benefactors to the Church of St. Ignatius Loyola," 45, 47.

53. Ibid., 51.

54. ARHS, J5-2, "Records of Regis High School," 6.

55. Archives New York Province of the Society of Jesus, "Regis File," Memo to the Files, February 2, 1962. After the death of the Superior General Wlodimir Ledochowski in 1942, Father Norbert de Boyne, vicar general of the Jesuits, was given charge of governance of the Society until a general congregation could be called, which was in 1946. It was he who at the death of Mrs. Grant publicly mentioned her name in asking all Jesuits to offer "the usual suffrages."

56. This shrine is on the north side rear of the church and contains statues of Saints Aloysius Gonzaga, Stanislaus Kostka, and John Berchmans, Jesuits who all died while still very young.

57. RASJ, Maryland Province Series, File 1015, Hearn to Father General, June 21, 1912.

58. Hearn thought the Jesuits could get $1 million from the sale of Xavier and could purchase land and build a new school for $500,000. With the remaining sum invested, they could expect an annual return of $20,000, which would be enough to support an enrollment of five hundred students.

59. R. Emmett Curran, *Shaping American Catholicism: New York and the Chesapeake, 1805–1915* (Washington, D.C.: Catholic University of America Press, 2012), 282. The Jesuits paid $750,000 for the property, which some Jesuits both in the province and in Rome felt was far too high a price. While a theologate was never built here, a Jesuit novitiate named St. Stanislaus-on-Hudson was conducted on the site from 1917 to 1924. The forty or so novices lived in the old mansion that was on the property. See *Woodstock Letters*, vol. 40, 266; vol. 47, 18; vol. 53, 421.

60. RASJ, File 1016, Folder 2, Hearn to Superior General, September 25, 1915.

61. AMPSJ, 27–502, Hearn to Richards, November 4, 1916, 4.

62. I am indebted to Father Patrick J. Ryan, S.J., '57, for suggesting this theory on the origin of the school's name.

63. ARHS, J5-2, "Records of Regis High School," 7.

64. *Woodstock Letters*, vol. 56, 167.

65. AMPSJ, 27–502, Hearn to Richards, November 4, 1916, 3.

66. "Notebook of Benefactors to the Church of St. Ignatius Loyola," 57.

67. *The Jesuits of Yorkville, 1866–1966* (Hackensack, N.J.: Custombook, 1966), 27.

68. RASJ, Maryland–New York Series, Box 1015, Maas to Superior General, January 4, 1913.

69. ARHS, J5-2, "Records of Regis High School," 7. At this time, the term "embarrassed" also connoted being in a compromised financial condition.

70. Ibid., 8–18. One of the smallest parcels was on the extreme east of the footprint on the 84th Street side. Hearn hoped to get this as a gift from the owner, Mr. James Meehan, since he was a graduate of the College of St. Francis Xavier from the school's earliest years. Despite this connection, the Jesuits paid market price.

71. Ibid., 18.

72. Founded in 1905 in Boston, in its day Maginnis and Walsh had a strong reputation for its innovative design of churches and other church-related buildings. In 1909, it was selected by the Jesuits at Boston College after a competition of fourteen of the nation's leading architectural firms to design the school's new campus in Chestnut Hill after the decision to relocate it from the city's South End. Before his arrival at St. Ignatius, Father Hearn had most recently been prefect of studies at Boston College, where he had come to know of their work. In addition to Regis, Maginnis was also involved in another important New York church-related construction project. In 1930, the firm was hired to design a new high altar at St. Patrick's Cathedral, and the project was eventually completed in 1941. See Katherine Burton, *The Dream Lives Forever: The Story of St. Patrick's Cathedral* (New York: Longmans, 1960), 160.

73. ARHS, I6-3-1, "Book of Minutes of Consultations," December 26, 1912. The Regis archives contain a six-page typewritten transcription of the minutes of consultors meetings of the Jesuit Community attached to St. Ignatius Loyola Parish that specifically pertain to Regis High School.

74. RASJ, Maryland–New York Series, Box 1015, Hearn to Superior General, June 21, 1912.

75. "Notebook of Benefactors to the Church of St. Ignatius Loyola," 57–71, 100–101.

76. ARHS, K4-1-9, "David Hearn to Julia Grant," June 28, 1914.

77. *Real Estate Record and Builders Guide*, November 15, 1913. In the "Plans Filed for Construction" section (p. 926), the estimated cost of the building was listed at $370,000.

78. ARHS, J5-2, "Records of Regis High School," 39.

79. Farley had been named a cardinal in 1911.

80. In his 1929 encyclical "Divini Illius Magistri," Pope Pius XI wrote, "False and also harmful to Christian education is the so-called method of 'co-education.'" See also the entry "Single-Sex Schools" in Thomas C. Hunt et al., eds., *Catholic Schools in the United States: An Encyclopedia*, vol. 2 (Westport, Conn.: Greenwood Press, 2004), 598.

81. ARHS, I6-3-1, "Book of Minutes of Consultations," July 21, 1913.

82. At the end of the nineteenth century, the Jesuits and the De La Salle Christian Brothers had several skirmishes over their schools in the United States, mostly because of Jesuit complaints to Rome that the Brothers were teaching Latin (in violation of their constitutions), and thus their schools were in competition with the Jesuits for the limited number of boys from Catholic families who could afford to pay their not so modest tuitions. The end result was that Brothers were forbidden to teach Latin. Thus it is not surprising that Father Hearn had to perform some careful diplomacy with the Brothers on the School Board so as not to reawaken old wounds. For more on this see, Ronald Eugene Isetti, F.S.C., "The Latin Question: A Conflict in Catholic High Education Between Jesuits and Christian Brothers in Late Nineteenth-Century America," *The Catholic Historical Review* 76, no. 3 (July 1990): 526–48.

83. ARHS, I6-3-1, "Book of Minutes of Consultations," July 21, 1913.

84. ARHS, K-4-1, Wernz to Hearn, February 5, 1913, in Latin. In this letter, in which Wernz gives his permission to build the school, he makes the demand that no classes be held in the area above the chapel ("non posse permitti ut scholae super Sacellum habeantur"). I am indebted to Father Arthur Bender, S.J., Regis class of 1967, for his help with this translation.

85. Curran, *Shaping American Catholicism*, 288.

86. ARHS, K4-1-9, "The Foundations of Regis High School." This is a four-page typed document that is unsigned. Much of the information in it seems to have been drawn from the consultors' minutes from the St. Ignatius Jesuit Community on East 83rd Street. Unfortunately these minutes are no longer extant.

87. ARHS, F4-1-1, Rector's Diary. A final bill from McGinnis and Walsh dated March 3, 1915, taped into the Rector's Diary.

88. John O'Malley, "The Jesuits," in Richard L. DeMolen, ed., *Religious Orders of the Catholic Reformation: In Honor of John C. Olin on His Seventy-Fifth Birthday* (New York: Fordham University Press, 1994), 151.

89. William J. McGucken, S.J., *The Jesuits and Education: The Society's Teaching Principles and Practice, Especially in Secondary Education in the United States* (Milwaukee: Bruce Publishing, 1932), 124. In 1908, the Jesuits opened St. John's College High School in Shreveport, Louisiana, and attempted to operate it

without tuition but were unable to do so for long. While still in existence but now called Loyola Prep, the school is no longer sponsored by the Jesuits. E-mail exchange (September 15, 2010) with Father Raymond Fitzgerald, S.J., socius of the New Orleans Province.

2. Strong Beginnings, 1914–1930

1. Archives Regis High School (hereafter ARHS), Shelf F4, Box 1, Folder 1 (hereafter F4-1-1), Rector's Diary, September 22, October 2, December 23, 1914.

2. Archives New York Province of the Society of Jesus (hereafter ANYPSJ), Regis High School Box, Charles F. Wheelock to David Hearn, July 9, 1913.

3. Daniel Burke, S.J., Feeney Oral History Project. (Father Martin E. Feeney, S.J., performed this project in the late 1970s.) This El ended its service in Manhattan in 1955.

4. ARHS, F4-1-1, Rector's Diary, October 2, 1914

5. In 1935, the owl was moved to the south end of the quad, where it was placed over the center door. See *The Owl*, October 8, 1937.

6. ARHS, F4-1-1, Rector's Diary, September 22 and 28, 1914.

7. Ibid., September 28, 1914.

8. Ibid., October 2 and 16, 1914.

9. Ibid., October 16, 1914. Born in 1878, Nicholas Brady converted to Catholicism when he married his wife, Genevieve Garvan. He inherited a huge fortune after the death of his father and continued to expand his wealth principally by further investment in public utilities. The Bradys were extremely generous toward the Catholic Church, especially the Jesuits, and St. Ignatius parish in particular. For example, they gave $400,000 toward the purchase of property and the building of the St. Ignatius Day Nursery at 240 East 84th Street, which opened in 1915. In the late 1920s they helped build the immense Jesuit novitiate in Wernersville, Pennsylvania, with their gift of $2 million. Although Genevieve remarried after Nicholas's death in 1930, upon her own death in 1938 she was buried alongside him under the main altar at the novitiate. Genevieve also donated their mansion (Inisfada) on Long Island to the Jesuits. See "Nicholas Frederic Brady," in John J. Delaney, *Dictionary of American Catholic Biography* (New York: Doubleday, 1984), 59.

10. Grades were recorded on a student's permanent record card almost monthly: September/October, November, December, January, February, March, April, and May/June.

11. ARHS, F4-1-1, Rector's Diary, October 26, 1914.

12. Charles T. Taylor, S.J., "A Study of an Endowed Jesuit Secondary School" (M.A. thesis, St. Louis University, 1938), 50.

13. Ibid., 14.

14. Ibid., 70–71. For example, in 1927 1.45 million teens started high school in the United States; 47 percent of this number graduated four years later.

15. ARHS, L6-2-5, Martin E. Feeney, S.J., "History of Regis High School" (unpublished paper), Chapter 5, p. 4. In the 1980s, Father Feeney began researching a history of the school and wrote a rough draft running about sixty pages including notes. The pagination is not continuous but starts anew with each chapter.

16. ARHS, F4-1-1, Rector's Diary, September 25, 1916.

17. From a gritty neighborhood on the West Side, Coleman came from a family of six children with a father who was a policeman. Because of the family's financial needs, he did not return for his sophomore year at Regis (though every grade on his freshman report card was over 90 percent) after landing a job as a page boy on Wall Street. It not take him long to make a name for himself, starting an investment house with a partner before turning twenty-seven. His firm soon became enormously successful, and eventually he was elected chairman of the New York Stock Exchange in 1943. In addition to his success in finance, he was also very involved in charitable work and support for the archdiocese, and was considered a confidant of both Patrick Cardinal Hayes and Francis Cardinal Spellman. See Robert J. Cole, "John A. Coleman, Philanthropist, Big Board Chairman, Dies at 75," *New York Times*, February 25, 1977.

18. ARHS, I6-3-1, "Book of Minutes of Consultations," July 21, 1913.

19. ARHS, F4-1-1, Rector's Diary, June 29, 1915.

20. Father Daniel Burke, S.J., class of 1920, Feeney Oral History Project. Burke was from the parish of Our Savior in the Bronx, which did not have a parochial school at this time.

21. ARHS, Rector's Diary, June 18, 1920. It is noted that when hearing the news, the deceased boy's parents "showed real Catholic resignation" and "NO BLAME LODGED" (emphasis original). Regis paid for the funeral expenses. His funeral Mass was celebrated at the former St. Bernard's Church on West Fourteenth Street in Manhattan. The Jesuits used to own this entire island (which is now connected to the mainland by a causeway) but eventually sold it to a utility company, which now operates a power station on the site.

22. Martin J. Feeney, S.J., "Rev. Daniel J. Burke (1902–1981): Two Remembrances," *Regis Alumni News* 47, no. 2 (Winter 1982): 4.

23. ARHS, F4-1-1, Rector's Diary. See separate small-page note inserted near diary entry of May 23, 1920.

24. Philip Gleason, *Contending with Modernity: Catholic Higher Education in the Twentieth Century* (New York: Oxford University Press, 1995), 40.

25. James Hennesey, S.J., *American Catholics: A History of the Roman Catholic Community in the United States* (New York: Oxford University Press, 1981), 182.

See also *Acta et Decreta Concilii Plenarii Baltimorensis Tertii* (Baltimore: John Murphy & Co., 1886), 104.

26. ARHS, J3-4-2, Wlodimir Ledochowski, S.J, to All Reverend Fathers and Brothers in Christ, June 7, 1928. The archives contains an English translation of this seven-page letter, which addresses a series of concerns the general had in regard to the Society's schools. This letter also reiterates the "time-honored traditions of the Society" against admitting women to its schools. The general clearly states, "And therefore our high schools and colleges must continue to close their doors against female students, no matter what pressure may be brought upon them."

27. Although some religious women and men operated schools for wealthier students, this did not mean that these nuns and brothers were not involved in the education of the poor. On the elementary level, often the sisters operated an exclusive academy where tuition collected from wealthier families would be used support a nearby free school where sisters from the same order also taught. For example, by 1864 the Religious of the Sacred Heart were operating two exclusive academies in New York, each charging a tuition of $250 per student. But the sisters used revenue from these schools to support a free school for poor children. See Thomas J. Shelley, *The Archdiocese of New York: The Bicentennial History, 1808–2008* (Strasbourg: Editions du Signe, 2007), 354.

28. Thomas J. Shelley, "Empire City Catholicism: Catholic Education in New York," in Thomas C. Hunt and Timothy Walch, eds., *Urban Catholic Education: Tales of Twelve Cities* (Notre Dame: University of Notre Dame Press, 2010), 80.

29. Harriette A. Maritre, "A History of Catholic Parochial Elementary Education in the Archdiocese of New York" (Ph.D. diss., Fordham University, 1955), 83–87.

30. *Catholic News*, March 13, 1915. This advertisement for Xavier includes information on both the high school and grammar department. The evening classes for these young boys ran until 9:45 P.M. In 1915, the evening school had an enrollment of 220. See *The Official Catholic Directory* (New York: P. J. Kenedy & Sons, 1915), 148.

31. Daniel Burke, S.J., Feeney Oral History Project.

32. *The Official Catholic Directory* (New York: P.J. Kenedy & Sons, 1914), 152–57. Some of these schools were still referred to as academies, especially those for girls. Many of these girls' schools also had elementary grades, and often admitted boys but only in these lower grades. Regis is not listed among the boys' schools in Manhattan, since the directory was published in February of that year.

33. Bureau of the Census, "Statistical Abstract of the United States (2003)," http://www.census.gov/statab/hist/HS-20.pdf (accessed November 4, 2010). It was

not until 1929 that a majority of fourteen- to seventeen-year-olds were enrolled in high school.

34. ARHS, L6-2-15, "Transcript Summary of Kilroy Interview," April 24, 1965. This interview of Father James Kilroy was conducted by Father John McGinty, New York provincial.

35. "Regis High School: A Step Forward," *The Columbian* (May 1915), 14.

36. *New York Evening World*, May 2, 1914. The article quotes Father Hearn: "There are plenty of private Catholic academies, but this is the first free school for Catholic youths of high school rank." It also reiterates this point stating that "the school is open to all Catholic boys . . . and no tuition will be charged."

37. ARHS, I6-3-1, "Book of Minutes of Consultations," July 21, 1913.

38. John O'Malley, *The First Jesuits* (Cambridge: Harvard University Press, 1993), 207. In the Jesuit school in Prague in the sixteenth century, Lutheran and Hussite boys were admitted, and the Jesuits even agreed to exempt them from the recitation of the Litany of the Saints. However, these non-Catholic students were required to attend Mass and sometimes even went to confession.

39. For a recent history of Trinity School see Timothy C. Jacobson, *Charity and Merit: Trinity School at 300* (Lebanon: University Press of New England, 2009).

40. For more on this battle between Bishop John Hughes and civic leaders over state support of parochial schools in the 1840s, see Joseph J. McCadden, "Bishop Hughes Versus the Public School Society of New York," *Catholic Historical Review* 50, no. 2 (July 1964): 188–207.

41. ARHS, F4-1-1, Rector's Diary, February 3, 1918. Since the New York State Board of Regents decided to no longer allow students who entered in February of their freshman year to graduate in June of their senior year, the last February class accepted into Regis was in 1918. Some of the boys who entered in these February classes actually had to return to school in the fall after they should have graduated for one more semester. Rather than do that, a few boys quit Regis and went to a public school, where they could graduate on time. See ARHS, L6-2-5, Feeney, "History of Regis High School," Chapter 5, p. 2.

42. ARHS, L6-2-15, "Transcript of Interviews: George Brooks, Class of 1918," 1.

43. ARHS, "The Regian: The History of the Class of Nineteen-Eighteen, Class of 'F.' " By the time the pioneer class began senior year in 1917, their numbers were so depleted that the various sections were merged, leaving only "A," "B," and "F." For the only time in the history of the school, each class produced its own history. However, the class of 1919 had the distinction of producing Regis's first yearbook, which included all the members of the senior class.

44. Taylor, "Study of an Endowed Jesuit Secondary School," 10.

45. Victor J. Dowling, "Why Latin?" *Regis Monthly* (November 1924), 57–58. This student publication was begun in 1918 and published generally seven issues per year. Unfortunately, issues from first five years are no longer extant.

46. Joseph Hamilton, class of 1919, Feeney Oral History Project.

47. ARHS, F4-1-1, Rector's Diary, October 3, 1914.

48. Ibid., September 20, 1915.

49. Taylor, "Study of an Endowed Jesuit Secondary School," 12; ARHS, A5-1, "Bulletin of Information, 1943–1944."

50. ARHS, J5-2, "Record Book the Regis High School Homeric Academy, 1937–39," 1. There is a clipping from *Jesuit Seminary News* (September–October 1937) pasted on this page with this information.

51. ARHS, F4-1-1, Rector's Diary, June 5, 1923. At the time of its start, it was called the "Iliad Academy." See ARHS, L6-2-8, "Regis High School: 25 Years of Work," 13. This sixteen-page typed document was seemingly written in 1940, since it mentions that the completion of the school's twenty-fifth academic year coincides with the four-hundredth anniversary of the papal approbation of the Jesuit constitutions

52. *The Owl*, December 23, 1936.

53. ARHS, J5-2, "Record Book the Regis High School Homeric Academy, 1937–39," 7–9. Using his strong background in classical languages, after his ordination in 1941 Father Burghardt went on to get earn a doctorate in patristics, which he then put to good use teaching a generation of Jesuit seminarians at the Woodstock seminary in Maryland.

54. ARHS, F4-1-1, Rector's Diary, November 8, 1923.

55. ARHS, L6-2-14, Thomas M. Harvey, S.J. (principal), to Parents of Incoming Freshmen, April 3, 1952. It is also worth noting that in this letter, parents were reminded that it was expected that every graduate of Regis who goes on to college "will make application to a *Catholic* college" (emphasis original).

56. ARHS, A5-2, "Bulletin of Information, 1948–1949," 6–7.

57. Joseph Hamilton, class of 1919, and Frank Cassidy, class of 1919, Feeney Oral History Project.

58. Msgr. Thomas McMahon, class of 1926, Feeney Oral History Project. McMahon wound up taking chemistry in night school after he graduated from Regis.

59. ARHS, L7-1-1, Father Lorenzo K. Reed, S.J., to Father Provincial, January 13, 1958. In this memorandum, Reed presents a history of the curriculum at Regis with the various electives offered over the previous forty-four years.

60. A "specimen" was a public exhibition of a student's proficiency in a Latin or Greek. Sometimes they were conducted as competitions.

61. ARHS, F4-1-1, Rector's Diary, November 22, 1915.

62. Ibid., March 5, 1917.

63. Ibid., December 22, 1915. It seems that to "manage a lantern" meant to take care of the lighting.

64. Ibid., June 19, 1916.

65. *The Regian "F," 1918.* This book is not paginated but this quote comes from the section that recaps this class's freshman year,

66. ARHS, F4-1-1, Rector's Diary, March 1, 1915.

67. Gerald McKevitt, S.J., "Jesuit Schools in the USA, 1814–ca. 1970," in Thomas Worcester, S.J., ed., *The Cambridge Companion to the Jesuits* (Cambridge: Cambridge University Press, 2008), 280.

68. O'Malley, *First Jesuits*, 96, 253.

69. *The Regian"F," 1918.*

70. *Regis Monthly* (October 1924), 35–36.

71. ARHS, F4-1-1, Rector's Diary, December 23, 1914, and December 23, 1915.

72. "Program for King Henry the Fourth, April 29, 1918." This program is pasted into the Rector's Diary.

73. Taylor, "Study of an Endowed Jesuit Secondary School," 51.

74. "Theatre Notes," *New York Times*, February 10, 1931.

75. Feeney, "History of Regis High School," Chapter 5, p. 6; Taylor, "Study of an Endowed Jesuit Secondary School," 34.

76. *The Regian "F," 1918.*

77. ARHS, F4-1-1, Rector's Diary, January 23, 1915. The college department at Brooklyn College was soon dropped and the Jesuit-run school became popularly known as Brooklyn Prep.

78. Ibid., March 18, 1922.

79. *The Regian, 1923*, 52.

80. Rector's Diary, September 29, 1923.

81. Feeney, "History of Regis High School," Chapter on Sports, p. 1. The coach, Mr. Rudolph Boudreau, S.J., had taught French.

82. *The Regian, 1927*, 157; *The Regian, 1928*, 167.

83. *The Regian, 1930*, 187–89.

84. ARHS, F4, "Program Book: September, 1928 to January, 1935." Small index card titled "Regis Cheers" accompanying the 1929 schedule of football games.

85. Daniel Burke, S.J., Feeney Oral History Project.

86. *New York Times*, September 1, 1931. Because of the virulence of this outbreak, the city's health commissioner delayed the opening of public schools by more than a week, with all the Catholic schools following suit. On August 15 alone, 111 new cases of infantile paralysis were reported in the city. In September 1916,

the opening of school had been delayed as well because of an outbreak of this disease. See ARHS, F4-1-1, Rector's Diary, September 21, 1917. In addition, at least one alumnus felt that the economic crisis of the Great Depression was really the cause of the demise of the team, as the school looked to cut its budget. See Thomas Hilbert, '32, Feeney Oral History Project.

87. *The Regian, 1932*, 151.

88. Interview, Msgr. Thomas Leonard, class of 1945, November 4, 2010.

89. *The Regian, 1933*, 129.

90. Feeney, "History of Regis," Chapter on Sports, p. 4.

91. *The Owl*, January 28, 1937.

92. Taylor, "Study of an Endowed Jesuit Secondary School," 52.

93. *The Owl*, October 8, 1937. A page-one story on Taylor's transfer from Regis heaped praise on the departing scholastic, saying that "all the success that has come to the paper" was due to him.

94. Taylor was sent to St. Louis University for his third year of regency, which is the period a Jesuit scholastic spends in active ministry (such as teaching) between his philosophy and theology studies. The entire period of formation from the time a man entered the Society to his taking of his final vows after ordination was carefully laid out by St. Ignatius himself, and for the most part the structure has remained unchanged since its first articulation. Thus, it was a bit unusual for Taylor to spend a year of his regency engaged in full-time study. However, even from the Society's earliest days, segments of the formation could be modified for individual circumstances.

95. Taylor, "Study of an Endowed Jesuit Secondary School," 1, 11.

96. Harry W. Kirwin, "On the Main Stairs," *Regis Monthly* (November 1926), 60–63. The English translation of the motto is "Religion, Guide and Nourisher of Talents, Mother and Teacher of the Sciences." This bas-relief was created by the New York City firm Rochette and Parrini, which specialized in models. This firm also was responsible for the bas-relief in the 85th Street lobby and the plasterwork and modeling in the chapel. Since the late nineteenth century, firms such as this one brought Italian artists to the United States to create bas-reliefs around the country, including some of the mansions of the robber barons in Newport, Rhode Island. Generally, the artist did not sign his creation. Rather, the artwork was identified by the studio that had been hired to make it. I am indebted to Father Philip Judge, S.J., class of 1980 and president of the school since 2005, for finding a photograph of "Religio" with this firm's name on the reverse while searching the papers of Maginnis and Walsh (the architectural firm that designed the school), which are archived in the Boston Public Library.

97. Assistant Head Master Mr. John Tricamo relaxed the rule on the use of this staircase, allowing all students to use it without restriction.

98. Taylor, "Study of an Endowed Jesuit Secondary School," 2–3, 9–11, 16.

99. Ibid., 19–20. The first provincial exams were administered at Regis in 1921.

100. *The Owl*, October 8, 1937.

101. Taylor, "Study of an Endowed Jesuit Secondary School," 23. The first New York State Regents exams were administered in 1866 but only for students on the primary (elementary) level. In 1878, the system was expanded and for the first time included secondary-level subjects.

102. Taylor seems to assume that the vast majority of those who left before graduation did so for academic reasons, though the Rector's Diary in the early years of the school note that at least some boys left because their families needed them to begin working.

103. Ibid., 70–74.

104. ARHS, A7-1-2, *Regis Alumni*, vol. 3, no. 1.

105. ARHS, A7-1-2, *Regis Alumni*, vol. 3, no. 4.

106. Daniel J. Burke, S.J., "Regis High School," *Jesuit Seminary News* (September–October 1937), 23.

107. ARHS, A7-1-2, *Regis Alumni*, vol. 3, no. 3.

108. A total of fifty-three young men were ordained this year. See Thomas J. Shelley, *Dunwoodie: The History of St. Joseph's Seminary, Yonkers, New York* (Westminster, Md.: Christian Classics, 1993), 287.

109. ARHS, Permanent Record Card of John J. Maguire.

110. Peter Steinfels, "Archbishop John J. Maguire, 84, Longtime Spellman Aide, Is Dead," *New York Times*, July 9, 1989.

111. ARHS, Permanent Record Card of George A. Brooks.

112. "G.M. Legal Official to Retire," *New York Times*, May 29, 1965.

113. ARHS, Permanent Record Card of John V. Connorton.

114. Sheila Rule, "Dr. John Connorton Served as Deputy Mayor in 1960s," *New York Times*, August 13, 1981.

115. ARHS, I5, "Regis Alumni Association Directory, June 1958."

116. ARHS, L6-2-10, "Notebook of Benefactors to the Church of St. Ignatius Loyola (NYC)," 67, 69, 100–101.

117. ARHS, K4-1-9, Edwin J. Brooks, "A History of the Grant Family," 3.

118. *Woodstock Letters*, vol. 46, 232–34.

119. ARHS, K4-1-9, J. Richard Havens, S.J., to Anthony Maas, S.J., September 24, 1916. A few short pieces appeared in two editions of *America* magazine (September 23, 1916, and December 2, 1916) that made veiled attack against Hearn. Havens, who succeeded Hearn, wrote to the provincial, complaining of the magazine's inappropriate criticism of Hearn, though he admits that the disagreements were "common property" in being well-known to many Jesuits.

120. Archives Maryland Province of the Society of Jesus (hereafter AMPSJ), Box 27, Folder 502 (hereafter 27–502), Hearn to Richards, November 4, 1916, 3. This typewritten document is described as "extracts from Letter of Fr. Hearn to Fr. Richards." Also noted on top of the first page is that this document was originally part of the "Rector's File 84th St.," though it is no longer extant in this location.

121. A. J. Elder Mullan was a native of Baltimore who entered the Society of Jesus in 1882. After ordination, he was sent to teach at the novitiate at Frederick, Maryland, but soon was soon transferred to Oxford to earn a degree in literature. Upon his return to the United States, he taught at both Georgetown and the Jesuit seminary at Woodstock, but in 1906 he was sent to work at the Jesuit Curia in Rome, where he became assistant secretary for the English-speaking provinces. He remained in Rome until 1915, when he returned to the United States. He died in 1926. See his obituary in *Woodstock Letters*, vol. 60, 98–99.

122. AMPSJ, 27–502, Hearn to Richards, November 4, 1916, 3.

123. Ibid., 1916, 3–4.

124. Ibid., 4. Since none of the letters between Mrs. Grant and Father Mullan is extant, it is necessary to rely only on Mrs. Grant's reporting of the contents of their correspondence.

125. Ibid., 5.

126. Ibid., 7; *Woodstock Letters*, vol. 60, 99.

127. ARHS, F4-1-1, Rector's Diary, February 25 and March 6, 1916.

128. Ibid., November 26, 1916.

129. ANYPSJ, "Regis File," J. Havens Richards to Anthony Maas, December 6, 1916.

130. Ibid.

131. ANYPSJ, "Regis File," Agreement Between Foundress and Provincial and Rector, December 6, 1916.

132. ANYPSJ, "Grant File," Julia Grant to James Kilroy, May 7, 1919. These brownstones were razed, and in 1954 the current residence was constructed.

133. ANYPSJ, "Grant File," Memo to the Files, February 2, 1962.

134. ANYPSJ, "Grant File," Julia M. Grant to John J. McMahon (provincial), December 7, 1951. In this letter, Miss Julia Grant expresses her puzzlement at a recent article in *The Catholic News*. The piece mentioned a Jesuit who had recently referred to the need for money to build a chapel at the new seminary at Shrub Oak. Julia wondered how he could have said this when they had given $500,000 for this in 1947. However, Julia graciously suggested that if another donor had also put money for the chapel, then "just think no more of it and put the donation in the general fund." Julia passed away in 1962, and this seminary closed in 1973.

135. ANYPSJ, "Grant File," John McGinty (provincial) to Julia, Edna, and Hugh Grant, December 25, 1960. To deal more effectively with the unprecedented growth in vocations the New York province had experienced since the end of World War II, in 1960 upstate and western New York was carved out to create the Buffalo Province. However, because of the lack of a strong donor base as well as the dramatic drop-off in vocations and the defection of a large number that came in the late 1960s, in 1969 this province was suppressed, with the territory reincorporated into the New York Province.

136. *Jesuit Seminary News*, November 15, 1930. In terms of enrollment, Regis was surpassed by Xavier High School (1,054), Boston College High School (1,027), and Brooklyn Prep (854). The Loyola School had the smallest student body of the high schools in the New England and the Maryland–New York provinces with only 40 boys.

137. ARHS, F4-1-1, Rector's Diary, May 19, 1921.

138. *The Regian, 1926*, 16.

139. ARHS, L6-2-4, Lawrence J. Kelley, S.J., to Rector, February 2, 1924. This letter mentions the provincial's directive of June 1923 to appoint spiritual directors in all the province's colleges and high schools.

140. ARHS, F4-1-1, Rector's Diary, December 18, 1916.

141. Ibid., June 14, 1924.

142. ARHS, F4, "Program Book: September, 1928 to January, 1935," "Syllabus of Entrance Requirements." This booklet was put together in preparation for the June 1930 entrance exam.

143. ARHS, Permanent Record Card of Emile Xavier Huerstel. This boy must have been sick for several weeks because the April marks for all of his subjects are recorded as 50 percent. Before that, he had received no grade below 80 percent. While Emile was technically the first Regian to die while still at the school, an incoming freshman sadly drowned to his death in Connecticut in August 1916 before the actual start of his time at Regis. See ARHS, F4-1-1, Rector's Diary, September 21, 1916.

144. ARHS, F4-1-1, Rector's Diary, November 2–6.

145. Daniel Burke, S.J., '20, Feeney Oral History Project.

3. "See You in North Africa!": Regis Through the Depression and World War II

1. Regis has never had an endowment in the strict sense of the term, only spending the growth on its capital. Since the late 1970s, the school has almost always spent down the principal to meet budget.

2. See http://research.stlouisfed.org/fred2/series/M1329AUSM193NNBR (accessed October 13, 2012).

3. In this year, Regis had the highest freshman class enrollment of the twelve high schools in the Maryland–New York Province. See *The Jesuit Seminary News*, November 15, 1930, 1.

4. Thomas Hilbert, '32, Feeney Oral History Project.

5. Diane Ravitch, *The Great School Wars, New York City, 1805–1973: A History of the Public Schools as Battlefield for Social Change* (New York: Basic Books, 1974), 236. While more young people were staying in school because of the lack of jobs, this only put more strain on the public schools, which were now dealing with budgetary cuts because of the Depression.

6. Archives Regis High School (hereafter ARHS), Shelf E5, Box 1 (hereafter E5-1), Prefect's Diary, September 10, 1934.

7. Father Daniel J. Burke, S.J., '20, Feeney Oral History Project. By way of comparison, today with a school population of 530, the school has a cleaning staff of four full-time and one part-time employee.

8. Father Jerome Guszczyk, S.J., '33, Feeney Oral History Project.

9. Joseph Flaherty, '35, Feeney Oral History Project.

10. Brendan Meagher, '34, Feeney Oral History Project.

11. Christopher Lehmann-Haupt, "Robert Giroux, Publisher, Dies at 94," *New York Times*, September 5, 2008. According to Giroux's permanent record card, on December 20, 1930, he transferred from Regis to Dickinson High School in Jersey City, with no mention of employment as the reason for his departure. While at Regis, Giroux maintained decent grades, earning only a few below 80 percent.

12. ARHS, L7-3-4, Herman H. Schutte to Father James Carney, S.J. '43 (alumni director), February 24, 1998.

13. ARHS, A7-1-4, *Regis Alumni*, November 1939.

14. *The Owl*, October 16, 1942.

15. *Regis Alumni*, June 1945, 6.

16. ARHS, K7-1-10, "List of Regis Alumni Chaplains." The Alumni Association sent small checks (mostly for twenty-five dollars) to the family members (parents or siblings) of these seven Jesuits and eight diocesan priests serving as chaplains.

17. *The Owl*, December 3, 1943.

18. *The Regis, 1942*, v.

19. *The Regis, 1943*, iv–v.

20. ARHS, I6-2-7, "Recollections of the Class of 1946 on the Occasion of Their 50th Anniversary." Roman Chapelsky recalled that both he and his classmate Willie Clarke went to summer school in case they were called up before graduation.

21. Interview, Msgr. Thomas Leonard, class of 1945, November 4, 2010.

22. Born in Calabria in 1891, Father Gabriel Zema and his family settled on the Lower East Side and worshipped at Our Lady of Loreto, which had been

founded by an Italian American Jesuit. He and his other siblings all attended the Loreto parochial school before going on to the College of St Francis Xavier, where he was given a scholarship. By the time of his junior year of high school, he had already discerned a call to the priesthood, but wound up delaying his entrance to the Jesuits for several years after graduation because of his father's opposition to another son entering the ministry (his older brother Demetrio had already become a Jesuit). His father eventually relented, and he entered the Society and was ordained in 1929. After leaving Regis, he went to spend time as a chaplain in the various hospitals and asylums on Welfare Island, a ministry the Jesuits had begun in the mid-nineteenth century. He died in 1959. See Anthony De Maria, S.J., "Obituary: Gabriel A. Zema," *Woodstock Letters*, vol. 92, 377–88.

23. ARHS, I6-2-7, "Recollections of the Class of 1946 on the Occasion of Their 50th Anniversary." J. Kenneth Hickman recalled Father Zema getting him a summer job earning sixteen dollars per week at a wholesale jewelry firmed owned by a man from the class of 1919.

24. The archives do not contain any correspondence between Zema and Regians who survived military service in World War II.

25. ARHS, K7-1-8, Bedder to Zema, March 23, 1943; June 28, 1943.

26. Ibid., October 3, 1943.

27. ARHS, K7-1-8, Mrs. Christian Becht to Zema, March 15, 1945; newspaper clipping of Becht's obituary, n.d.

28. ARHS, A7-1-9, *Regis Alumni*, May 1944, 5.

29. ARHS, K7-1-8, Helene Wohlrab to Zema, March 20, 1945; *The Regis, 1940*, 71.

30. ARHS, A7-1-9, *Regis Alumni*, May 1944, 3. Shortly before this card party, Father Burke had returned from Salerno, Italy, and was able to "greet the assemblage and give a short talk that will be long remembered."

31. ARHS, K7-1-10, Rev. Charles Brady to Edmund Chambers, chairman of the Alumni Association, May 25, 1944.

32. ARHS, K7-1-8, Gerald J. Doyle, class to 1924, to Members of Alumni Association, July 25, 1945; "Special Notice to Returning Veterans," Regis Alumni Veterans' Committee, postcard.

33. ARHS, J6-4-6, John E Grattan, S.J., to John J. McMahon, S.J., July 19, 1948. The estimated cost of the overall project was $4,128. In his letter to the provincial, Grattan, who was rector, said that he would ask the alumni if they could come up with more funds to make up the difference. However, he wrote that "fortunately this year Regis High School has a very fine balance," presumably meaning that if necessary the school could make up the difference.

34. ARHS, K7-1-8, Helen Krall to Zema, n.d.

35. Charles Finch, '18, Feeney Oral History Project.

36. Taylor blamed the high turnover of lay faculty on low salaries. See Charles T. Taylor, S.J., "A Study of an Endowed Jesuit Secondary School" (M.A. thesis, St. Louis University, 1938), 67–69.

37. In 1937, the name of the yearbook was changed from *The Regian* to *The Regis.* A small note opposite the frontispiece explains this change: "Because of its incorporation with 'The Regis' Quarterly, the Yearbook is now called 'The Regis' instead of by its former title, 'The Regian.'" This name change lasted until 1946, when the yearbook was again titled *The Regian.*

38. *The Regis, 1939,* 10, 19–21.

39. ARHS, A7-1-9, *Regis Alumni,* February 1944.

40. ARHS, K4-4-6, Informational Pamphlet for Pilgrimage to the Shrine of the North American Martyrs, September 26, 1937. The Jesuit Mothers' Guilds of the Maryland–New York Province cosponsored the event.

41. *The Owl,* October 18, 1940, 1.

42. Taylor, "Study of an Endowed Jesuit Secondary School," 7, 58. The quote from Pope Pius IX was taken from his 1929 encyclical on Catholic education titled *Divini Illius Magistri.*

43. *Regis Monthly* 7, no. 1 (October 1924): 25.

44. ARHS, F4-1-1, Rector's Diary, November 5, 1915.

45. Taylor, "Study of an Endowed Jesuit Secondary School," 53–54

46. ARHS, F4-1-1, Rector's Diary, December 22, 1921.

47. Charles Finch, '18, George Gilligan, '18, Daniel Burke, S.J., '20, Feeney Oral Interview Project.

48. ARHS, F4-1-1, Rector's Diary, February 5, 1915.

49. Up until 1957, Catholics were required to fast from midnight from all food and drink (including water) if they intended to receive Communion that day. Catholics took this discipline very seriously, which meant that many who went to Mass (Sunday or weekday) often did not receive Communion because of the demands of such a fast. When Pope Pius XII relaxed the fast to three hours in this year, now food or alcohol could be consumed up to three hours before the reception of Communion. For nonalcoholic beverages, the fast was one hour, and there was no prohibition on water. In the late 1960s, the fast was again relaxed and now stands at one hour for all food and drink except water, which is always allowed. See Kay Toy Fenner, *American Catholic Etiquette* (Westminster, Md.: Newman Press, 1961), 24–35.

50. Alfred Blake, '32, Feeney Oral History Project.

51. Thomas Hilbert, '32, Feeney Oral History Project.

52. ARHS, F4-1-1, Rector's Diary, 1940–41.

53. Ibid., January 23, 1920.

54. At this time, Catholics commonly referred to this as "Passion Week."

55. ARHS, F4-1-1, Rectory's Diary, March 25–27, 1915.

56. *The Owl*, November 8, 1940, 1.

57. *The Owl*, November 25, 1936.

58. *The Owl*, April 30, 1937, 2.

59. John O'Malley, *The First Jesuits* (Cambridge: Harvard University Press, 1993), 197–99.

60. ARHS, F4-1-1, Rectory's Diary, December 8, 1914; November 9 and 15, 1915; May 15 and June 1, 1916.

61. ARHS, K4-4-6, "Eighth Annual Field Day of the Regis Athletic Association: June 6, 1924."

62. *The Regian "F," 1918.*

63. *The Regis, 1942*; ARHS, K7-1-8,, "Alumni Deaths in Service: 16 February 1946."

64. *The Owl*, November 22, 1938, 3. This mission was led by Father Horace McKenna, S.J., who over the years became widely known for both his love for the poor and his personal holiness. After working in southern Maryland, he later spent many years working with African Americans in Washington, D.C., while assigned to St. Aloysius Gonzaga parish.

65. *The Owl*, November 15, 1937, 1, 3.

66. ARHS, A7-1-1, *The Regis Alumnus* 2, no. 1 (June 1935): 3.

67. *The Regis, 1944*. See the section titled "Blessed Virgin Sodality."

68. In the original formulation of the Guard, there were three degrees of membership based on frequency of the reception of Communion: weekly, at least twice weekly, or almost daily. Recall that at this time, in 1917, the required Eucharistic fast was still from midnight, so promising to receive Communion on a regular basis required a good deal of self-discipline. Because of the reforms initiated by Pius X, as time went on the regular reception of Holy Communion was becoming more common for Catholics, so the Guard updated its rules to reflect this. See Taylor, "Study of an Endowed Jesuit Secondary School," 62. Taylor also refers to a "Guard of Honor Diary" that he had access to when writing his thesis. Unfortunately, this source is no longer extant.

69. *The Owl*, April 30, 1937, 2.

70. ARHS, F4-1-1, Rectory's Diary, 1944–45, "Memo to Freshmen Students, August 21, 1944."

71. Ibid., "Taylor to Freshman Parents," September 11, 1944.

4. A Winning Team, Father Gannon, and Anniversary Celebrations

1. Archives Regis High School (hereafter ARHS), Shelf K4, Box 1, Folder 9 (hereafter K4-1-9), "Data From Mrs. Lucie Grant, May 19, 1990," 1.

2. Archives New York Province of the Society of Jesus (hereafter ANYPSJ), Grant Family Box, "List of Mrs. Grants' Gifts." A total of twenty-nine burses were given, mostly in the amount of $8,000 each.

3. ARHS, M4-2, "Souvenir of the Chapel of the Holy Spirit." The three chaplains were Jesuit Fathers William Fox (1914–29), Patrick Quinnan (1929–57), and Edwin Brooks (1957–81). The chapel was designed by Maginnis and Walsh, the same architects Father Hearn had hired for Regis.

4. Interview, Mrs. Patsy Miller, May 25, 2011. Mrs. Miller's late husband, Lindley, was the son of Mrs. Grant's youngest sister.

5. ARHS, K4-1-9, "Data From Mrs. Lucie Grant, May 19, 1990," 1–2.

6. ARHS, K2-2, Bede Jarrett, O.P. to Hugh J. Grant, Jr., September 17, 1929. In this handwritten note, the Dominican congratulates Hugh for beginning studies at Columbia Law School and promises to pray for him daily. He also speaks of some other topics, including the recent signing of the Lateran Treaties between Benito Mussolini and Pope Pius XI. He praises the Roman pontiff for being "so dignified in refusing to be a king. He has refused territory & subjects. He has only his sovereign freedom." On a visit to New York in 1926 shortly after his trip in Europe with Hugh, Jr., Father Jarrett celebrated Mass in the family chapel.

7. ARHS, K2-2, "Military Record and Report of Separation: Major Hugh J. Grant."

8. Interview, Mrs. Patsy Miller, May 25, 2011.

9. ARHS, I6-3-5, "Certificate of Death: Julie M. M. Grant."

10. ANYPSJ, Grant File, "Memo to Files: February 2, 1962." Signed by the socius of the province, this memo records the announcement of Julia (Julie) Grant in 1962 and recalls de Boyne's disclosure of her mother's name at the time of the latter's death in 1944. The letter from de Boyne is unfortunately not available, since the Roman Archives of the Society of Jesus are not available for documents dated after 1938. Since the war had prevented the calling of a General Congregation to elect a new superior general with death of Father Wlodimir Ledóchowski in 1942, de Noyes served as vicar general until the election of Father Jean-Baptiste Janssens in 1946.

11. ARHS, I6-3-11, James Sweeney, S.J., to Major Hugh Grant, May 25, 1944. De Boyne was vicar general of the Society, not superior general.

12. ARHS, J3-5-4, "St. Regis High School Financial Report: June 30, 1952." Prepared by the firm of Edmund F. Bowen & Co. of 11 Park Place, the report looks at the previous three fiscal years. This is the first audited financial report of Regis in the Regis archives. All other financial documents were prepared in-house.

13. ARHS, K4-1-9, "Notes from Conversation with Fr. Brooks about the Founding Family," September 1990. These notes were taken down by Father James

Fischer, S.J., who was president of Regis from 1980 to 1992, in an interview he conducted with Father Edwin Brooks. After teaching at Regis from 1952 to 1960, Father Brooks remained in residence at the Jesuit residence on 83rd Street until 1999 while engaged in other apostolic works, such as with the Jesuit Seminary and Mission Bureau. For much of this time, Brooks also served as a chaplain to the Grant family (when members were still living in the house on East 72nd Street until the early 1970s) as well as acting as an intermediary between them and the school. Since the family was very intent on protecting their anonymity, the use of a go-between seemed appropriate.

14. ANYPSJ, Grant Family Box, Julia M. Grant to Kilroy, S.J., February 19, 1921.

15. ANYPSJ, St. Ignatius Loyola Box, McMahon to Gannon, June 7, 1954. Attached to this letter is a Photostat of the Regis Account Book with entries from September 1919 and April 1920 listing the bonds (Liberty and Victory) for "New Building for Teachers."

16. ANYPSJ, Regis Files, Thomas E. Henneberry, S.J. (provincial), to Robert I. Gannon, S.J., October 4, 1955; Gannon to Henneberry, October 7, 1955; Henneberry to Gannon, October 10, 1955.

17. ARHS, J3-5-3, "Annual Financial Statements of Jesuit Residence, 1958–61." For example, in the 1960–61 fiscal year, Regis and Loyola (which are listed together) paid close to $69,000 for room and board for their Jesuit faculty.

18. ANYPSJ, St. Ignatius File, "Memorandum: Regis Problems," 1

19. The Jesuit Educational Association had its offices at Regis for many years before its dissolution in 1970.

20. This was not the first time New York's archbishop had set his sights on underutilized space at Regis. In a letter to the superior general in 1932, house consultor Father Charles Kleinmeyer, S.J., voiced his concern that a larger number of students were admitted to the school "in order to frustrate the wishes of the Bishop to allow the Christian Brothers the use of the top floor of the building." In doing this, according to Kleinmeyer, the school had taken in boys who were "without proper qualifications" and thus were doing very poorly. Despite this, the prefect of studies, Father Archdeacon, refused to dismiss these boys since he was told that he must first see the rector, Father Edward Sweeney, S.J., but Archdeacon "would seemingly rather wreck the school than see Father Rector about a boy's dismissal." See Roman Archives of the Society of Jesus, Maryland-New York Series, Box 1031, Kleinmeyer to Superior General, January 16, 1932.

21. ANYPSJ, St. Ignatius File, Memorandum: Regis Problems, 1–2.

22. Robert I. Gannon, *Up to the Present: The Story of Fordham* (New York: Doubleday, 1967), 231.

23. ANYPSJ, St. Ignatius File, Gannon to Henneberry, July 10, 1956. A four-page memorandum is attached to the letter. Gannon was clearly right on at least one point. Nuns in the elementary schools were coaching their brighter eighth grade boys. Father Joseph T. Lienhard, S.J., class of 1958, recalls his eighth-grade nun meeting with him and a few other boys in the evenings to practice for the exam. Interview, December 17, 2010.

24. ANYPSJ, St. Ignatius File, Gannon to Henneberry, July 10, 1956.

25. Ibid.

26. ANYPSJ, St. Ignatius File, Wood to Henneberry, July 1, 1956. Before ending this letter, Wood mentioned his fear that his disagreement with Gannon could weaken the latter's support for the Jesuit Seminary and Mission Bureau, of which Wood was the head. Gannon was a popular and sought-after speaker in the Catholic fund-raising world, and Wood did not want this disagreement to affect Gannon's relationship with the Bureau. Clearly, Gannon was a man of power and strong influence, and one did not disagree with him without considering the possible implications.

27. ANYPSJ, St. Ignatius File, Henneberry to Gannon, July 8, 1956.

28. ANYPSJ, St. Ignatius File, Thomas Harvey, S.J., "Comments in Father Rector's REGIS PROBLEMS MEMORANDUM" (emphasis original), May 24, 1956.

29. See ANYPSJ, St. Ignatius File, Tuite to Father Rector, May 27, 1956, and notes summarizing Daly's and Burke's positions.

30. Peter McDonough, *Men Astutely Trained: A History of the Jesuits in the American Century* (New York: Free Press, 1992), 418.

31. ANYPSJ, St. Ignatius File, Lorenzo K. Reed, "Special Confidential Report to Very Reverend Father Provincial on Regis," March 22, 1957, 1.

32. Ibid., 1–2.

33. Ibid., 2.

34. "Regis High to Expand," *New York Times*, March 11, 1957.

35. ANYPSJ, St. Ignatius File, Lorenzo K. Reed, "Special Confidential Report to Very Reverend Father Provincial on Regis," March 22, 1957, 2.

36. Patrick Kelly, S.J., *Catholic Perspectives on Sports: From Medieval to Modern Times* (New York: Paulist Press, 2012), 40–45.

37. Francois de Dainville, *L'Education de Jésuites: XVI–XVIII siècles* (Paris: Editions de Minuit, 1962), 519, as cited in Kelly, *Catholic Perspectives on Sports*, 49.

38. ARHS, L3-4-3, "Transcript of interview with Don Kennedy," 1982.

39. Ibid. The New York College of Dentistry merged with New York University in 1925.

40. Ibid. Kennedy claimed that an unnamed basketball coach at the University of Notre Dame popularized his invention.

41. Started in 1870 by two German immigrants, the Rubsam & Horrmann Brewery remained in business until the early 1960s. It even stayed open during Prohibition producing "near beer."

42. Trauggy Lawler, "Mr. Kennedy Leaves Regis," *The Owl*, June 3, 1953.

43. *The Regian, 1948*, 119–22.

44. Tom McCoy, "Big '5' Honored at Victory Dance," *The Owl*, March 4, 1948.

45. *The Regian, 1941*, n.p. I am indebted to Mr. Thomas J. Hickey, class of 1953, for providing the information on Kelly in his post-Regis years.

46. Lawler, "Mr. Kennedy Leaves Regis."

47. After Regis, Kennedy went on to coach St. Peter's for twenty-two years while helping to turn the team into a national contender several times. In addition to his career in basketball, Kennedy also was married for many years to Gertrude Smith, with whom he had a large family. In 2004, Don Kennedy died at the age of ninety-seven. See Frank Litsky, "Don Kennedy, 97, Who Turned St. Peter's Team into Contender, Dies at 97," *New York Times*, November 4, 2004.

48. "New Regis Gym Blessed by Father Rector," *The Owl*, March 10, 1958.

49. ANYPSJ, St. Ignatius Loyola Box, Harvey to Henneberry, April 2, 1957.

50. *Regis Alumni News* 63, no. 2 (Winter 2004): 10.

51. ARHS, A7-1-1, "Records Reveal First Alumni Reunion, 1919," *Regian Alumnus* 2, no. 1 (June 1935): 1, 4.

52. ARHS, J7-1-9, J. Frank Morris to Fellow Regian, May 31, 1956.

53. ARHS, J7-1-9, Thomas Henry to Cyril Egan, June 23, 1956.

54. ARHS, J1-4-1, "Notes to the File: Mr. Cy Egan," n.d. The provenance of this document is unclear, but it may have been written by the rector or the socius. It contains information about Egan's retirement plan, in which Regis guaranteed an annual income of about $1,400.

55. James Carney, S.J., "Remembrances of Father Stephen V. Duffy, S.J.," *Regis Alumni News* 70 no. 3 (Spring 2005): 10. Father Duffy came to Regis in 1945.

56. ARHS, B3-4, "Interview of Cyril Egan," 1979, Audio Cassette 1. This interview was conducted by Michael Della Rocca, class of 1980. Father Gannon had a well-deserved reputation among his fellow Jesuits as someone who was always looking to save a buck. For example, in the 1950s, while on the committee overseeing the construction of the new seminary at Shrub Oak, Gannon, who had been appointed because of his skills in fund-raising, came to practically every meeting with an idea on how they might save a bit more money by cutting something here or snipping something there. Soon his penchant for frugality began to exasperate the other members of the committee, including the usually irenic and unflappable provincial, Father John McMahon, S.J., class of 1921. When on one occasion Gannon said they could save $1 million if they simply cut a foot

off every bedroom, McMahon barked that they could save several million more if they didn't build the new seminary at all. After this exchange, no more mention was made of cutting the square footage. This anecdote was told to me by Dr. John Tricamo, who was told it by Father Henneberry, socius at the time and thus present at all these meetings.

57. Ibid.

58. Martin E. Feeney, S.J., "Cyril B. Egan," *Regis Alumni News* 49 no. 2 (Winter 1984): 4.

59. Cyril B. Egan, "Subway Stations of the Cross," *America*, March 21, 1964, 367–69.

60. Martin E. Feeney, S.J., "Cyril B. Egan," *Regis Alumni News* 49 no. 2 (Winter 1984): 4.

61. ARHS, Permanent Record Card of Joseph T. Quintavalle.

62. James R. Carney, S.J., class of 1943, "An Appreciation of Joseph T. Quintavalle, '30," and Joseph A. Dorgan, S.J, "Farewell to Joseph T. Quintavalle, '30," *Regis Alumni News* 63, no. 1 (Fall 1997): 4–5, 13–14.

63. Interview, Dr. John Tricamo, May 9, 2011. In 1974, Tricamo was Regis's assistant headmaster, a title that had only a brief life at the school.

64. I am indebted to Mr. Jeff Weinlandt, class of 1964, for contacting several members of his class, who offered these memories of Quintavalle.

65. *The Regian, 1962*, 11.

66. Joseph Quintavalle died on September 30, 1997, at the age of eighty-four.

67. ANYPSJ, St. Ignatius Loyola Box, "Confidential Report of the Province Prefect for High Schools: 1955," 4.

68. In the 1959–60 school year, there were nine Jesuit priests and eight scholastics in a total faculty of thirty. This number does not include the four Jesuits who served as rector, principal, vice principal, and student counselor. See ANYPSJ, St. Ignatius Loyola Box, "Confidential Report of the Province Prefect for High Schools: 1960," 2.

69. ARHS, E-4, Rector's Diaries: 1955–59, n.p.

70. ARHS, J3-2-2, "Some Suggestions for Conducting the Home Room Interview," n.d., but probably from the 1950s. I am indebted to Mr. John Connelly, Regis faculty member and member of the class of 1956, for providing a copy of this.

71. Father Reed thought it was a poor decision to make Greek mandatory. For the first few years of the 1950s, about half the sophomore class had elected to study Greek, which demonstrated that a "fine attitude toward Greek" had been built up in the school. He also thought that the provincial should have been consulted on this change. See ANYPSJ, St. Ignatius Loyola Box, "Confidential Report of the Province Prefect for High Schools: 1955," 6–7.

72. ARHS, A5-2, "Bulletins of Information: 1946–1957." These publications could basically be described as the course catalog in addition to including the academic regulations.

73. ARHS, J3-2-2, "Report of the Committee Visiting the School [Regis High School]: November 14 thru 17, 1955." While all the members of this committee were not from other Catholic schools, they were all male. This was not true for the 1966 Middle States visiting team, which included women.

74. *The Regian, 1964,* 185, 192, 215.

75. ANYPSJ, St. Ignatius Loyola Box, "Confidential Report of the Province Prefect for High Schools: 1960," 4.

76. Interview, Father Joseph O'Hare, S.J., class of 1948, May 5, 2011. Father O'Hare served as interim president of Regis from 2004 to 2005.

77. ANYPSJ, St. Ignatius Loyola Box, "Confidential Report of the Province Prefect for High Schools: 1955," 5.

78. ANYPSJ, St. Ignatius Loyola Box, "Confidential Report of the Province Prefect for High Schools: 1950," 4.

79. Edward Wakin, "Regis: Spectacular High School," *The Sign* (September 1962), 29.

80. ANYPSJ, St. Ignatius Loyola Box, "Student Enrollment at Regis High: 1923–1956." These figures were complied by Father Reed.

81. ANYPSJ, St. Ignatius Loyola Box, "Confidential Report of the Province Prefect for High Schools: 1950 and 1960." Both reports were compiled by Father Reed.

82. I am indebted to Mr. Brian Varian, class of 2007, for his research in writing "The Pioneer Class: A Prosprographical Study of the Regis High School Class of 1918," unpublished paper, 25.

83. ARHS, E4, Rector's Diaries: 1961–64, n.p.

84. ARHS, K6-1-6, "1964 Scholarship Data." Twenty-five of the 188 who were originally admitted chose not to enroll. A further eight were admitted after this, yielding an incoming class of about 171 in the fall of 1964.

85. ARHS, K6-3-6, "New York Regents Statistics for Class of 1964."

86. I am indebted to Mr. Timothy Pelletier, class of 2013, for helping me compile these statistics on the class of 1961.

87. I am indebted to Mr. Michael Chiappone and Mr. Ryan Masserano, both class of 2011, for compiling these statistics on the graduating classes in the 1950s.

88. Archives Maryland Province of the Society of Jesus, Box 27, Folder 502, Harvey to Edward Bunn, S.J., December 10, 1952.

89. John LaBonte, "Second Semester Starts with Ignatian Year Mass," *The Owl*, February 10, 1956.

90. ARHS, I4-1-4, "A Commemorative History of Regis High School: 1914–1964."

91. ARHS, I6-2-5, "Regis Golden Jubilee Dinner Seating List."

92. ARHS, I6-2-5, "Tentative Program of Speakers."

93. Robert I. Gannon, S.J., *After Black Coffee: After-Dinner Speeches of Fr. Gannon, President of Fordham* (New York: Declan X. Mullen, 1947).

94. ARHS, I4-1-4, Rt. Rev. Msgr. Edwin B. Broderick, class of 1934, "A Sermon Preached on the Occasion of the Golden Jubilee." The sermon was published in pamphlet form and widely distributed among the alumni. The entirety of the text was also reprinted in *The Regian, 1964*. In 1967, Broderick was ordained a bishop by Spellman.

95. ARHS, I6-2-7, "Regis Alumni Association: Committee Report—Financial Support for Regis High School," n.d. This report can be dated to early 1969.

96. James L. Killgallen, "50 Years of Scholarship: 'Outstanding' Is Well-Earned by Regis H.S. Students," *New York Journal–American*, February 8, 1964.

97. Wakin, "Regis: Spectacular High School," 26.

98. ARHS, E4, Diaries: 1964–1967, Horgan to Parents, October 2, 1964.

5. Neat and Clean with Socks and Covered Shoes: A Revised Dress Code, a New Curriculum, and Other Changes, 1964–1980

1. Archives New York Province of the Society of Jesus (hereafter ANYPSJ), Grant File, Julia Grant to John McMahon, S.J., December 7, 1951. The Grants provided $1.8 million for the building of Loyola Seminary in Shrub Oak (in northern Westchester County).

2. Archives Regis High School (hereafter ARHS), Shelf K4, Box 1, Folder 10 (hereafter K4-1-10), James Fischer, S.J., "Conversation with Fr. Ed Brooks, S.J., February 25, 1992."

3. ANYPSJ, Grant File, McGinty to Julia, Edna and Hugh Grant, December 25, 1960. McGinty actually wrote two letters to the family dated December 25. One was more formal and typewritten and the second was more personal and handwritten. In the latter, he both explained why he decided not to give them a fancy parchment declaring their naming as founders, as well as his own promise for continued prayers and offering of Masses. By way of example of the family's reluctance to accept public honors, though invited several times, Hugh never accepted the invitation to join the Knights of Malta, the premier association of Catholic laymen

4. ANYPSJ, Grant File, "Memo to Files: February 3, 1962." While Julia may have been honored to have the cardinal officiate at her funeral, her brother Hugh was not equally as fond of the great churchman. In fact, according to Father Brooks, who knew the family very well, Spellman came to the Grant home once each year on Palm Sunday bringing the blessed palm, but Hugh would remain

upstairs during his visit, leaving it to his sisters to receive him. See ARHS, K4-1-10, "Memo of Conversation with Fr. Ed Brooks and Fr. Jim Fischer," February 25, 1992.

5. ARHS, K4-1-10, James Fischer, S.J., "Conversation with Fr. Ed Brooks, S.J.: February 25, 1992."

6. ANYPSJ, Grant File, Eugene Quigley, S.J., to Father Provincial, December 30, 1971. In this memo, Quigley suggests that a thank-you letter be sent to Hugh "for the generosity of the family, especially since Hugh is not feeling too friendly to us." It is not clear why relations between Hugh and the Jesuits had soured.

7. ARHS, J3-5-5, "Regis High School: Audited Financial Statement by Hurdman and Cranstoun, Penney & Co., Year Ended June 30, 1971," 5. These gifts, which on June 30, 1971, were valued at $1.79 million, were "to be used primarily to help defray the increasing costs of teachers' salaries and fringe benefits." By 1976, the value of this investment had fallen to $1.4 million. See ARHS, J3-5-6, "Regis High School: Financial Statements, June 30, 1976," 2.

8. ARHS, K4-1-10, Hugh Grant to John McGinty, S.J, December 14, 1965. Hugh noted that he and Julia would like to make the gift in that calendar year to "avail ourselves of certain tax advantages."

9. ARHS, K4-1-10, Joseph T. Browne, S.J., to William Wood, S.J., January 21, 1966.

10. ARHS, K4-1-10, James Fischer, S.J., "Conversation with Fr. Ed Brooks, S.J.: February 25, 1992."

11. Interview, Mrs. Patsy Miller, May 25, 2011.

12. Archives St. Ignatius Church (Sacramental Records). I am indebted to Ms. Patricia Schneider for her help accessing these materials.

13. ARHS, L6, "Auction Catalogue for Estate of Mrs. Hugh Grant: May 6, 2009," Doyle New York, Auctioneers and Appraisers, 11. Though they had no children, the couple maintained an active social life, entertaining a large circle of friends at both their New York City and Hamptons homes. However, after her husband's untimely death in 1959, Lucie began studies at the New York School of Interior Design, after which she embarked on a career in decorating, opening her own firm with a friend.

14. ARHS K-4-1, "Data from Mrs. Lucie Grant," May 19, 1990.

15. Interview, Mrs. Patsy Miller, May 25, 2011. Sometime after the ceremony, Patsy Miller and her husband, Lindley, a cousin of Hugh's, hosted a reception for the newlyweds at Patsy's father's apartment on Park Avenue at 64th Street

16. Ibid.

17. While the public areas of the house, such as the formal living rooms, libraries, and chapel, were commodious, there were only three bedrooms, and the top-floor servants' quarters lacked running water.

18. ANYPSJ, Grant File, Joseph Novak, S.J., "Memo to the Files: Phone Conversation with Father Ed Brooks, January 31, 1975." According to Novak, the property transfer took place on this day, with the new occupants expected to move in by June of that year.

19. ARHS, K4-1-9, Edwin J. Brooks, S.J., "A History of the Grant Family," 4–5.

20. See, for example, http://www.metmuseum.org/toah/works-of-art/1974.214.26a%2Cb (accessed July 6, 2011). Some of the more notable of these donations included a Tiffany lamp; a 1901 sterling silver ewer and plateau engraved with the monograms of Hugh's parents; and a painting by an artist of the Hudson River School. According the Metropolitan Museum of Art's website, the museum may no longer be in possession of all the objects Lucie and Hugh had given in the 1970s. At the time of the donation, the Tiffany lamp was valued at $30,000.

21. ARHS, K4-1-9, Edwin J. Brooks, "A History of the Grant Family," 4.

22. Kevin Murray, "Frs. Bowes, Neville to Leave Posts; Fr. Newton Named New Principal," *The Owl*, May 15, 1972, 1.

23. Diane Ravitch, *The Troubled Crusade: American Education, 1945–1980* (New York: Basic Books, 1983), 235.

24. Ibid., 236.

25. William J. O'Malley, S.J., "Staying Alive in High School," *Jesuit Educational Quarterly* (June 1967), 46–47.

26. Ibid., 42.

27. Robert R. Newton, S.J., "Self-Renewal in Jesuit High Schools," *Woodstock Letters*, vol. 95, 84.

28. Ibid., 87–88.

29. Ibid., 89. In calling for a renewal in Jesuit education, Newton also called for the renewal and updating of individual Jesuits. Citing Erich Fromm and his work on psychology in totalitarian regimes, Newton suggested that far too often Jesuit teachers in the order's high schools had surrendered their autonomy to superiors, thus sapping the schools (and themselves) of the energy that comes when people offer their own insights into problems. Now Jesuits should be taught to think for themselves and use creativity when looking at solutions to problems.

30. Ibid., 95.

31. "*Bay-Belle* Sails May 20" and "Homeric Academy Plans Greek Night," *The Owl*, May 9, 1967.

32. ARHS, J4-6-3, "Evaluation Report: Regis High School, March 30–April 1, 1966," 3.

33. ARHS, J4-6-1, Edward Horgan, S.J., to Commission on Secondary Schools, July 13, 1966.

34. Ibid.

35. "The New Look," editorial, *The Owl*, June 2, 1967.

36. ARHS, J4-6-1, Horgan to Commission on Secondary Schools, July 13, 1966.

37. Interview, Mr. John Connelly, class of 1956, October 13, 2011.

38. Interview, Father Philip G. Judge, S.J., '80, November 8, 2011.

39. Jay Salvest, "Ferguson Reveals Rank Removal," *The Owl*, November 14, 1972.

40. ARHS, H4-1-13, "College Choices: 1973."

41. At this time, the number of students who were given awards was much smaller than in later years. For example, only three students were awarded general excellence in each class and were given gold, silver, or bronze medals. In more recent years, 10 percent of the entire class (ten to thirteen boys) has been given this award.

42. "Laus Tibi Regis," *The Owl*, November 18, 1966.

43. "Student–Faculty Talks Begin," *The Owl*, February 28, 1968.

44. "Move Starts to Reform Marks System," *The Owl*, April 2, 1969, 1. De Luca had previously taught as a scholastic at Regis in the early 1960s. Mr. Kenneth Gavin, S.J., '62, who was now a scholastic teaching on the faculty, "dismissed as impractical" DeLuca's suggestion, given the huge cost that would come with such a large expansion of the faculty.

45. Steve Berdel, "McGovern Choice of Regis Voters," *The Owl*, May 15, 1972.

46. "Student Opinion Poll," *The Owl*, June 3, 1966.

47. "Jesuits Kick the Habit," *The Owl*, February 17, 1970.

48. "Senior Lunch Privileges Start Today; Clothing Suspension to Begin Monday," *The Owl*, April 27, 1970. In addition to relaxing the dress code, the administration also permitted seniors to go out every day for lunch and juniors could exercise this right on Fridays.

49. "Let It Be," *The Owl*, October 9, 1970.

50. John Donvan, "The Polls Are Clothed," *The Owl*, October 30, 1970.

51. Interview, Dr. John Tricamo, October 17, 2011. Originally hired as assistant principal, Tricamo's title was soon changed to assistant headmaster (and Newton's to headmaster) to be more in keeping with the other Upper East Side private (non-Catholic) prep schools. The title was changed back to principal in 1998. It was his task as assistant headmaster to tighten up the dress code a bit while not causing unrest among the student body at a time when many young people seemed to be perpetually looking for a cause to fight for (or against).

52. James T. Patterson, *Grand Expectations: The United States, 1945–1974* (New York: Oxford University Press, 1996), 686–87.

53. Raymond A. Schroth, S.J., *Fordham: A History and Memoir* (Chicago: Jesuit Way, 2002), 282–83.

54. John Donvan, "Trimester Adopted," *The Owl*, September 28, 1971.

55. "Manual for Jesuit High-School Administrators," Jesuit Educational Association, March 1952, 2–3. This document contains the constitutions of the JEA, which stated, "The only policy-making body of the JEA as a national organization is the Board of Governors. . . . [However,] each Provincial determines how the policies established by the Board of Governors will be carried out in his province."

56. John Donvan, "Jesuits Reevaluate Educational Goals," *The Owl*, November 8, 1971.

57. James F. Clarity, "Brooklyn Prep to Close After 64 Years," *New York Times*, May 30, 1971. Some of Brooklyn Prep's more famous alumni include Joe Paterno, class of 1945, and Joseph Califano, Jr., class of 1948. The building was eventually sold to the City University of New York and now houses Medgar Evers College.

58. John DiPinto, "Work Begins on Five Year Plan," *The Owl*, December 10, 1971.

59. Kevin Murray, "Committees Work on 5 Yr. Plan," *The Owl*, February 7, 1972.

60. John Rasiej, "To the Editor," *The Owl*, February 7, 1972.

61. ARHS, K6-7-1, "Regis High School: 5 Year Plan," 5-6. When the Province Planning Council reviewed this plan in June 1972, the Jesuits on this body stated that the "question of admissions was not covered in enough depth," and wondered about the exact definition of poor, asking whether this was meant to refer to members of "minority groups." See ARHS, J5-5-1, "Report of the Province Planning Council on the Regis Five Year Plan (Gonzaga Retreat House, May 31 to June 2, 1972)," 3.

62. ARHS, K6-7-1, "Regis High School: 5 Year Plan," 18.

63. Schroth, *Fordham*, 279.

64. ARHS, K6-7-1, "Regis High School: 5 Year Plan," 22.

65. Ibid., 31, 36.

66. "Goodbye . . . to Fr. Bowes and Fr. Neville," *The Owl*, May 15, 1972.

67. ARHS, K6-7-1, Newton to Faculty Member, August 1973.

68. Rich Slattery, "Structural Renovations for Regis," *The Owl*, April 3, 1973. To purchase the land and build the school in current dollars, Strother estimated the cost to be about $22 million. Interview, Dr. John Tricamo, November 21, 2011.

69. Rich Devane, "Plans Fixed for New Academic System," *The Owl*, May 16, 1973.

70. ARHS, K6-7-1, "Individualization, Regis Plan (1973)," 4.

71. Ibid., 11.

72. "Teachers Only Teach," *The Owl*, February 11, 1975.

73. Rich Slattery, "Regis Goes Mod," *The Owl*, October 2, 1973.

74. ARHS, J4-5-3, Memo: Newton to Theology Department, May 6, 1974.

75. ARHS, K6-7-1, Newton to Faculty Member, August 1973, Appendix D: Regis Floor Plan, 1973–74.

76. Alex Gray, "Fires of Change Sweep Regis," *The Owl*, October 2, 1973.

77. ARHS, K6-7-1, Newton to Faculty Members, August 1973, Appendix B: Report on Unstructured Time.

78. ARHS, K6-7-1, "Individualization, Regis Plan (1973)," 9.

79. "Regis Community Evaluates System," *The Owl*, December 13, 1973.

80. Mark Garcia, "Guidance Gets Its Head Together," *The Owl*, October 24, 1973.

81. ARHS, L3-5-6, Newton to Anthony Padovano, March 2, 1973.

82. ARHS, J4-5-3, Memo: Newton to All Faculty and Students, Re: Additions to "X" Day, February 8, 1974.

83. Angelo Grima, "X-periment Day," *The Owl*, March 5, 1974.

84. Edward Wakin, "Regis: Spectacular High School," *The Sign* (September 1962), 28.

85. "Guard of Honor Presents New Liturgical Services," *The Owl*, December 18, 1958.

86. See *Gaudium et Spes*, no. 4

87. Raymond A. Schroth, S.J., *The American Jesuits: A History* (New York: New York University Press, 2007), 200; Garry Wills, *Bare Ruined Choirs: Doubt, Prophecy, and Radical Religion* (Garden City, N.Y.: Doubleday, 1972), 202. By 2010, the number of American Jesuits was well below 3,000, with their median age close to seventy.

88. Mary Ann Hinsdale, "Jesuit Theological Discourse Since Vatican II," in Thomas Worcester, S.J., ed., *The Cambridge Companion to the Jesuits* (New York: Cambridge University Press, 2008), 299.

89. Schroth, *American Jesuits*, 238.

90. Although it was claimed that moving to the Upper West Side would give these young Jesuits the ability to live among the poor, on a visit to one of their new residences, Garry Wills found their new digs to be far from humble and described the West 98th Street community (one of four in the area) as designed with a "clubby vision and posh tastes." These thirty-one apartments housing about sixty men (two to three to a unit) were in a building "largely inhabited by Jewish and Puerto Rican families able to pay a hefty rent." See Wills, *Bare Ruined Choirs*, 198.

91. When Woodstock announced is closing in January 1973, there were at that time eight Jesuits studying here while also teaching part-time at Regis. See Mark MacLaren, "Woodstock Closing Ends N.Y. Experiment," *The Owl*, January 29, 1973.

92. Neil Grealy, "Senior Choice: Yoga or Sex," *The Owl,* October 22, 1974.

93. "Tony Meyer and the Holy Ghost Reception Committee #9," *The Sign* (September 1968), 22.

94. Ibid.

95. Lou Jerome, "New Lenten Choices," *The Owl,* March 6, 1975.

96. *The Regian, 1972,* 122.

97. *The Regian, 1968.* The "Religious" section of this yearbook runs from page 154 to 170.

98. *The Regian, 1955,* 78; *The Regian, 1965,* 116.

99. "CAP Concentrates on Its Fourth Year," *The Owl,* October 7, 1966.

100. "New Feather in Regis CAP," *The Owl,* November 10, 1967; "CAP Extends Itself to Appalachia", *The Owl,* September 29, 1967

101. "Forums Widen Christian Experience," *The Owl,* March 22, 1967.

102. Kit Konolige, "Forum Report," *The Owl,* May 24, 1968.

103. *The Regian, 1970,* 130.

104. Shane Ulbrich, "Changes to the Religious Life of Regis, 1950–1975," unpublished paper, 28.

105. "God for Me, God for Us," *The Owl,* March 4, 1976.

106. ARHS, J4-3-1, "Middle States Report, 1976: Section 12," 2, 7.

107. ARHS, L4-5-4, "Impressions of Regis High School Based on the Visit of the Province Committee, February 7–11, 1972," 3–4.

108. "Senior Halos Polished in 3 Day Closed Retreat," *The Owl,* March 3, 1954.

109. "Louder Than Words," *The Owl,* Nov 10, 1967.

110. Tom Dudar, "Sophs Search Souls," *The Owl,* May 7, 1974.

111. ARHS, J4-3-1, "Middle States Report, 1976: Section 12," 2.

112. ARHS, E4, "Diaries: 1964–1967," 1964 Graduates Colleges. Of the remaining nine, five went to Columbia and one each to Dartmouth, Princeton, New York University, and Brooklyn College. This "1964 Graduates Colleges" is a document glued into a large diary-type book with other items for the period 1964–1967.

113. ARHS, H4-1-13, "College Choices: 1973."

114. ARHS, H4-1-13, "Colleges to Be Attended by the Class of 1977." Two students of this graduating class of 109 deferred going on to college.

115. In the class of 1922, one graduate attended Yale and another went to New York University, in addition to a few others who went on to engineering schools or to pre-med programs. See *Woodstock Letters,* vol. 51, 155. In reviewing the college choices of this class, it was noted that: "All the boys were desirous of going to a Jesuit college or university, but as they had to depend on some help, they accepted free scholarships in the various secular institutions . . . Some graduates are working for a year to save for college . . ." However, the school was not always willing to help its students matriculate at a secular college. Father Lienhard of the class of 1958 recalls that Regis would not forward the transcript

of his classmate Walter Corey who had applied to Princeton. Interview, Joseph T. Lienhard, December 17, 2010.

116. Will Herbert, *Protestant, Catholic, Jew* (Garden City, N.Y.: Doubleday, 1960), 153–54.

117. James D. Davidson, "The Catholic Church in the United States: 1950 to Present," in Leslie Woodcock Tentler, ed., *The Church Confronts Modernity: Catholicism Since 1950 in the United States, Ireland, and Quebec* (Washington, D.C.: Catholic University of America Press, 2007), 187.

118. ARHS, H4-1-13, "Colleges Attended: 1964–1974."

119. National Center for Education Statistics, "Tuition Costs: 1980–2011," http://nces.ed.gov/fastfacts/display.asp?id=76 (accessed July 11, 2013).

120. ARHS, H4-1-13, "Class of 1979 Stat Sheet." There were 120 students in this class.

121. *Regis High School Alumni Directory, Fall 1998*, 94–97.

122. Since 1998, Edward J. McGovern, '73, one other graduate from this era, has gone on to religious life, becoming a Maryknoll priest.

123. Charles J. Beirne, S.J., "Death and Resurrection at a Jesuit High School: Steven Zwickert (1963–1980)," *The Jesuit* (Autumn 1980), 3; Barbara Basler, "Honor Student, 16, Slain on Way Home from Prom," *New York Times*, May 16, 1980.

124. Peter Kihss, "Youth, 16, Surrenders in Murder While 900 Mourn Queens Victim," *New York Times*, May 23, 1980.

6. The Return of the Missing Owl

1. Interview, Dr. John Tricamo, February 14, 2011.

2. Greg Larsen, "Regis Challenged: Swords Requests Changes," *The Owl*, October 12, 1976.

3. In a letter to Hugh J. Grant, Jr., Father Swords mentioned that he had been given two assignments in his appointment as president of Regis: "to help ascertain whether the school was operating on an efficient and financially sound basis and, if the answer was in the negative, to suggest where expenditures might be reduced"; and "to investigate the possibility of raising sufficient funds to meet the annual operating deficit." See Archives Regis High School (hereafter ARHS), Shelf K4, Box 1, Folder 7 (hereafter K4-1-7), Swords to Grant, August 26, 1977.

4. ARHS, L4-1-1, "Regis High School: Comparison of Operating Expenditures: 1969 to 1974," 2.

5. ARHS, I6-2-8, "Regis High School Faculty Salary Scale: 1963–1973."

6. In 1981 the school recognized the Lay Faculty Council as the collective bargaining agent for the faculty, and since then this executive committee of this council has bargained collectively with the school for salary and fringe benefits. Although the 1979 U.S. Supreme Court decision NLRB vs. Catholic Bishop of Chicago ruled that schools operated by a church are not within the jurisdiction

granted by the National Labors Relations Act, the board of trustees nevertheless decided to recognize this group. See ARHS, K8-3-4, Executive Committee of Regis Lay Faculty Council to Father Charles J. Beirne, S.J., October 14, 1982.

7. ARHS, I6-4-2, Minutes of Executive Council of Regis Alumni Association: May 14, 1969.

8. ARHS, J3-5-5, "Financial Statements: 1971 and 1973."

9. ARHS, J3-5-5, "Financial Statement: 1975."

10. By 1970, Regis had three accounts directly under its control and on deposit with Chase Manhattan Bank: Account 14 or the "Foundation," which was "subject to the restriction of canon law, that is, only income may be spent and capital may not be touched for any reason"; Account 24 or the "Reserve Fund"; and Account 27 or the "Loyalty Fund." Account 14 was under the supervision of the province. Because of Father Gannon's controversial tinkering with the endowment during his tenure as rector, the founding family had decreed that the gifts they made in the 1960s toward faculty salaries be placed in account be under control of the provincial, not under the rector–president of Regis. See ARHS, K1-4-18, Joseph T. Browne, S.J., to Charles T. Taylor, S.J., April 28, 1970.

11. ARHS, K4-1-2, George B. Fargis to Gerald T. Shevlin, December 22, 1970. Shevlin represented Regis in the settlement of Edna's estate. The New York Province of the Jesuits was also a beneficiary of Edna's will, receiving $466,000 in cash and over $320,000 in stocks. The archdiocese and Corpus Christi Monastery in the Bronx were the other two beneficiaries.

12. ARHS, K4-1-2, Joseph W. Walsh to John C. Connelly, S.J., January 3, 1972.

13. ARHS, K4-1-2, George B. Fargis to John C. Connelly, S.J., February 7, 1973. Presumably, income generated from Edna's assets continued to flow to Regis for the rest of the decade, but because the financial statements from 1975 are vague as to the sources of some income, the yearly amounts are unclear.

14. ARHS, J3-5-6, "Financial Statement: 1976"; ARHS, K2-2, Hugh J. Grant: Day Book. In addition to his gift to Regis, Hugh was planning to donate to the following other organizations: Archbishopric [of New York], $100,000; Catholic Medical Missions, $10,000; Calvary Hospital, $50,000; Corpus Christi Monastery, $1,000.

15. ARHS, K4-1-10, Edwin J. Brooks, S.J., to Eamon Taylor, S.J., December 18, 1977.

16. ARHS, K4-1-10, Vincent M. Cooke, S.J., to Mr. and Mrs. Hugh Grant, December 23, 1980.

17. Lawrence Cagney, "School Debt Deepens," *The Owl*, November 22, 1971. According to figures compiled by the Alumni Association (and which were republished in *The Owl*), for the 1959–60 academic year, the school ran a deficit of $27,117, which was up from $21,981 for the year 1949–50.

18. ARHS, I6-2-8, "Alumni Annual Fund Contributions According to Figures Published in Annual Fund Brochures," and "Growth in Annual Fund Participation and Contributions, 1970–1979."

19. ARHS, I6-4-2, Carney to Taylor, December 30, 1966.

20. ARHS, K1-4-18, Joseph T. Browne, S.J., to Charles T. Taylor, S.J., April 28, 1970.

21. ARHS, K1-4-18, Murray, Page, Powers, and Sullivan to Taylor, September 29, 1971.

22. In 1972, Barry Sullivan was appointed senior vice president at Chase Manhattan, the youngest person to ever hold this position. In 1980, he moved to First National Bank of Chicago, where he went on to become both CEO and chairman of the board.

23. The audited financial statement for the year ending June 20, 1972, claimed the endowment was worth over $9.2 million, but this figure included the value of the school's real estate and the building itself, which was listed at $2.4 million. See ARHS, J3-5-5, "Audited Financial Statement for Year Ending June 30, 1972," 4.

24. ARHS, K1-4-18, Sullivan to Murphy, September 20, 1972.

25. ARHS, I6-4-2, "Notes from Alumni Finance Committee, 1975," 3.

26. ARHS, J3-3-10, "Total Yearly Enrollment: 1914 to 1981."

27. Greg Tino and Jim Connolly, "Million Dollar Gift Marks First Step to Stability," *The Owl*, January 20, 1978.

28. "Walkathon Wednesday, First Ever, Nets $5,000," *The Owl*, May 26, 1977.

29. Mark Young, "Walkathon Nets 24 Grand in Pledges," *The Owl*, October 30, 1981. The walkathon continued as an annual fall event for the students through 2010, when it brought in over $110,000. The administration decided to discontinue it in 2011, citing the immense amount of work that went into its preparation and execution, and the relatively stagnant amount it was generating. For example, in 2010, the event raised about $100,000, which then represented less than 1 percent of the school's annual budget. To replace it, the school has begun experimenting with asking the students to sell a few high-priced ($100) raffle tickets. See ARHS, K3-5-7, e-mail from Judge to All Faculty, September 13, 2011.

30. ARHS, K1-6-3, "Summer Repairs: 1977."

31. ARHS, K1-6-2, Thomas P. Murphy, S.J., to Richard J. Powers, November 8, 1975. According to Murphy, "For sixty years this board met only once a year unless an emergency occurred. . . . In the past, all five board members have been Jesuits from the 84th Street complex."

32. Schroth, *Fordham*, 383.

33. Charles M. Whelan, S.J., "The Legal Status of Jesuit High Schools: Relationships with the Provincial and the Province Corporation," JSEA, 1975.

34. After graduating from Regis, Cusack went on to earn undergraduate and law degrees from Fordham University. A highly successful attorney, Cusack was a founding partner of Cusack and Stiles, a firm specializing in taxation and estate and trust planning. A leading Catholic, he also offered legal representation to the archdiocese, served on boards of various nonprofits, and was president of the Friendly Sons of St. Patrick.

35. ARHS, K1-6-3, Cusack to Swords, October 27, 1977.

36. ARHS, K1-6-3, Swords to Cusack, March 23, 1977.

37. ARHS, K4-1-7, Grant to Murphy, November 9, 1975.

38. ARHS, K4-1-3, "Surrogate's Court: Petition for a Will Construction," 5. The gifts were made according to the following schedule: 1977, $1 million; 1978, $500,000; 1979, $500,000; and 1980, $100,000.

39. ARHS, I6-4-2, "A Special Report: The Regis Capital Campaign," 2, 6–7.

40. Interview, Mr. Frank Walsh, June 12, 2011.

41. "Hugh J. Grant, Lawyer and Philanthropist, 76," *New York Times*, March 25, 1981.

42. ARHS, K4-1-3, "Regis Board of Trustees: Report of the Finance Committee, April 30, 1981."

43. The trust set up by Hugh after his death occasioned some unhappy relations between Regis and the archdiocese. It was a condition of Hugh's trust that Regis would receive the net income of the trust as long as the school met certain conditions, including that it be "rated as superior" by the Middle States accrediting association. In the event that Regis failed to meet this, the income of the trust was to be paid to the archbishopric of New York.

44. ARHS, J3-3-10, "Admissions," 4.

45. I am indebted to Mr. James Elliott, class of 2012, for his research assistance on the changes to the Regis admissions policy and procedures in the period of the 1970s and 1980s.

46. "Entrance Policy Modified," *The Owl*, October 4, 1968.

47. At the time of this meeting, this building on Demong Drive was the provincial of the Buffalo Province. In 1960, the Buffalo Province of the Society of Jesus had been carved out from the New York Province but soon reincorporated in 1969.

48. In an effort to "concentrate resources," the Demong Drive Decisions called for the province to hold on to only five schools and spin off McQaund, the Loyola School, and Brooklyn Prep. As it turned out, however, this did not happen strictly as planned, and Brooklyn Prep was closed in 1972 as part of the plan. See ARHS, K9-3-8, "Demong Drive Plan: Part II," 15.

49. "Jesuits Will Add to School Staffs: More in Order to Be Made Available for Teaching," *New York Times*, September 21, 1968. With the huge number of men

who left the Society during this period, this goal of expanding the Jesuit presence at secular colleges never had much of a real effect.

50. ARHS, K9-3-8, "Demong Drive Plan: Part II," 13, 16.

51. "Admissions Policy," *The Owl*, October 4, 1968.

52. "New Policy Admits Success for '74 Class," *The Owl*, October 9, 1970.

53. Darren Fortunato, "School Changes Interview Policy," *The Owl*, December 1, 1981.

54. Interview, Mr. Frank Walsh, February 29, 2012. Frank came onto the faculty of Regis in the fall of 1974 and continued working at the school in various capacities, including administration, until his retirement in 2011. During the 1970s, he served several times on the Admissions Committee.

55. Interview, Mr. Frank Walsh, February 29, 2012.

56. ARHS, F1-2-7b, "Admissions at Regis: January 1976," 1–2. This document is marked "Confidential—not for distribution or communication outside of Regis."

57. ARHS, F1-2-7b, "Admissions at Regis: January 1976," 2.

58. ARHS, F1-2-7b, Memo: From Headmaster to Financial Review Committee, January 1975.

59. Interview, Mr. Frank Walsh, February 29, 2012.

60. ARHS, F1-2-7b, Memo: Newton to Regis Scholarship Committee, December 1977.

61. ARHS, F1-2-7b, "Admissions at Regis: January 1976," 3.

62. Interview, Mr. Eric DiMichele, March 5, 2012.

63. ARHS, F1-2-3a, "Regis Student Population: 1991–1992" and "Class of 2016: Overview."

64. *The Owl*, March 6, 1939.

65. Greg Larsen, "Regis Challenged: Swords Requests Changes," *The Owl*, October 12, 1976.

66. ARHS, K9-3-8, "Regis Ethnic Distribution: 1980–81" and "Minority Enrollment: 1993–1994."

67. ARHS, F1-2-3s, "Class of 2016: Overview."

68. ARHS, F1-3-12, Minutes: Student Services Committee Meeting, November 25, 1993.

69. ARHS, F1-3-12, "Proposed Statements of Objectives [for the Excelsior Program]."

70. Kenley Chew, "Insignis Launches Program," *The Owl*, February 8, 1980. Photos of the students involved in Insignis appear in only the 1980 and 1981 *Regian*.

71. ARHS, F1-3-12, Memo: Frank Walsh to Members of the Student Support Services Committee, April 26, 1994.

72. ARHS, K9-1-13, Biagi to FitzGerald, e-mails, March 11 and 17, 2000.

73. ARHS, F1-3-12, Brian FitzGerald, "Outreach Notes."

74. *REACH: 10 Year Anniversary Magazine* (Fall 2011), 11.

75. ARHS, F1-3-12, Brian FitzGerald, "Outreach Notes."

76. *REACH: 10 Year Anniversary Magazine* (Fall 2011), 12, 19.

77. Marty Barry, "John Paul II's Visit Puts Infosino on *Prime Time*," *The Owl*, October 18, 1979.

78. Tony DiNovi, "Religious Survey Results: Seniors Well Informed, but Critical," *The Owl*, October 18, 1979.

79. I am indebted to Dr. Nofi for sharing a copy of his report, "Selected Results from the Student Profile Surveys: July 29, 2003."

80. ARHS, K9-1-13, Minutes of the First Meeting of the Regis Jesuits: September 8, 1982.

81. *The Regian, 1978*, 76.

82. ARHS, K9-1-13, Minutes of the First Meeting of the Regis Jesuits: September 8, 1982.

83. See http://www.jsea.org/programs/symposium and http://www.jsea.org/colloquium-ignatian-education (accessed July 23, 2013).

84. ARHS, K3-5-7, e-mails: Gary Tocchet to All Faculty, April 30, 2012, and Judge to All Faculty, May 4, 2012.

85. It is also worth noting that over the recent decades, these self-evaluations prepared for Middle States have been growing in size by leaps and bounds. For example, while the 1986 self-evaluation, which was done on a typewriter, ran to 249 pages, the 2006 version, which was done entirely electronically, topped out at over 700 pages.

86. ARHS, J4-3-1, "Middle States Evaluation: 1986," 159–60.

87. The 1996 visitation by Middle States marked the first time that all the self-evaluations were prepared on a computer—or more precisely, the documents that were originally done in either longhand or by typewriter were then keyed into a computer by Mrs. Patricia Peelen, who has worked in the principal's office since 1980, to produce a final report that also existed in electronic form.

88. ARHS, J4-4-18, "Middle States Evaluation: 1996," 4.13.3–5. I am grateful to Dr. Ralph Nofi for sharing with me materials from the three most recent Middle States reports and self-evaluations.

89. Prior to this, because of the quirks of scheduling, juniors who elected to begin a second language did not take physics that year. Instead, they took the class in their senior year but only for two, not three, trimesters.

90. Michael King, "History in the Making: Sophs Take American Studies," *The Owl*, January 15, 1988.

91. Interview, Mr. James Phillips, May 17, 2012. Upon her retirement in 2010, Mrs. Diane Walsh was the longest-serving full-time female teacher at Regis, having been originally hired in 1972.

92. Kevin Delaney, "Mr. Phillips' New Toys: New Apples in the Computer Room," *The Owl*, December 25, 1987.

93. Interview, Mr. Jose Machuca, '92, May 16, 2012.

94. David Barbrack, "New Marking System Makes the Grade: Non-numerical Grades Still Meet with Mixed Reviews," *The Owl*, December 9, 1983.

95. Victor Lavella, "Making the Grade Regis Style: Evolution of the Grading System," *The Owl*, January 1, 1989.

96. Father Arrupe made this statement as part of his address on July 31, 1973, Feast of St. Ignatius Loyola, to the Tenth International Congress of Jesuit Alumni in Europe, which was held in Valencia, Spain.

97. Bill Bowling, "Christian Service Channels Seniors' Varied Talents," *The Owl*, March 24, 1983.

98. "Christian Service, an Alternative," editorial, *The Owl*, February 1987.

99. After the repeated entreaties of Luke Gatta, class of 2008, Mrs. Mary Henninger began teaching culinary arts and nutrition in the spring of 2008, which has remained a favorite choice of seniors in their third trimester ever since.

100. The class on *Mad Men*, which has been team-taught by Dr. Ralph Nofi, Ms. Kristin Ross, and Father Anthony Andreassi, has proved to be one of the most popular third-trimester senior electives since it was first offered in 2011, with the 2012 class attracting more than twenty-five students.

101. "Colleges Attending: 1993 to 2001." I am indebted to Ms. Kristin Ross, Regis's assistant principal, for sharing with me all this data from her own files dealing with college selection since the mid-1990s.

102. Those who entered and have remained in the priesthood or religious life from this period are Anthony Acevedo, C.F.X., '94, Daniel O'Reilly, '93, and Anthony Soo-Hoo, S.J., '93.

103. Statistics on careers for alumni are from either the 1998 Alumni Directory or the school's electronic alumni database.

Conclusion

1. Mrs. Lucie Grant died on December 18, 2007. In the obituary that appeared in the *New York Times*, she was recognized as a "benefactor and supporter of Regis High School," though no mention was made that she has married into the family that had founded the school and offered it enormous financial support for almost a century. Lucie's funeral Mass was celebrated at St. Ignatius Church by Father Judge, who was also the homilist. In addition, Archbishop Celestino Migliore, permanent observer of the Holy See to the United Nations, who lived in the former Grant house on East 72nd Street, attended. See *New York Times*, December 21, 2007.

2. The period of the 1920s and 1930s actually saw a greater increase in the rate of vocations than did the postwar era, which is still considered by some to

be the "golden age" for vocations. In fact, the decade of the 1920s saw the overall Catholic population grow by 14 percent, but the increase in the number of priests was actually double this. In the 1930s, the increase in the Catholic population slowed to 6 percent while the rate of increase in the number of priests was calculated at 26 percent. See Dennis Castillo, "The Origin of the Priest Shortage," *America* (October 24, 1992), 303.

3. James T. Patterson, *Grand Expectations: The United States, 1945–1974* (New York: Oxford University Press, 1996), 312.

4. Thomas J. Shelley, "Empire City Catholicism: Catholic Education in New York," in Thomas C. Hunt and Timothy Walch, eds., *Urban Catholic Education: Tales of Twelve Cities* (Notre Dame: University of Notre Dame Press, 2010), 83.

5. With regard to the caliber of the faculty at some of these new diocesan high schools, at the opening of Cardinal Hayes High School in 1941 Archbishop Spellman mandated that all the diocesan priests teaching there (which numbered over forty at one point) should either have master's degrees in the field they were teaching or be working toward the degree. Some of Hayes's more notable graduates include the filmmaker Martin Scorsese, the writer Don DeLillo, and John Sweeney, former president of AFL-CIO. Interview, Rev. Francis Principe, November 12, 2012.

6. ARHS, L7-5-4, "Mystery Solved: Regis' First African American Student."

7. ARHS, J3-3-21, Memo to the Files by Father Robert Newton, S.J, November 2, 1977. At Jug Night (an alumni reunion), Father Newton had a discussion with Mr. Pinado about minority recruitment at Regis, and Newton explained the challenges the school had faced with this effort.

8. In 1920, there were more than ten thousand residents of New York City born in Spain, and in 1940 this figure had risen to more than fourteen thousand. These numbers, of course, do not include the children or grandchildren of Spanish immigrants to the city. See "Immigration," in Kenneth T. Jackson, ed., *The Encyclopedia of New York City* (New Haven: Yale University Press, 1995), 584.

9. ARHS, J3-3-21, "Minority Students at Regis: October 10, 1981."

10. ARHS, J3-3-21, "1980 Minority Students at Regis."

11. Interview, Mr. Eric DiMichele, October 22, 2012. Mr. DiMichele has been director of admissions at Regis since 1993 and has studied enrollment patterns both during his time in this position as well as before.

12. ARHS, J3-3-21, "Summary of Freshman Parent Survey: 2012 (Class of 2016)."

13. James M. Frabutt, "Integration in Catholic Schools," in Thomas C. Hunt et al., eds., *Catholic Schools in the United States: An Encyclopedia*, vol. 1 (Westport, Conn.: Greenwood Press, 2004), 368. These figures are from 2002.

14. ARHS, J3-3-21, "Summary of Freshman Parent Survey: 2012 (Class of 2016)."

15. The Red Cloud Indian School on the Pine Ridge Reservation in South Dakota, founded by the Jesuits in 1888, is also free, but it receives some government money because of its Native American connections.

16. Jenny Anderson, "Admitted, but Left Out," *New York Times*, October 19, 2012.

17. The Cristo Rey network of schools, which charges a relatively modest tuition ($3,000 or less), comes close to the Regis model, but this new model of secondary education also includes a day of work each week, and students do not have to prove outstanding academic talent to gain admission.

18. I am indebted to Mr. Don Allison, vice president for finance, and Mr. Jim Buggy, vice president for development, for providing me with this financial data.

Index